HOW COURTS GOVERN AMERICA

HOW COURTS GOVERN AMERICA

RICHARD NEELY

New Haven and London   Yale University Press

Designed by Nancy Ovedovitz and set in VIP Times Roman type.
Printed in the United States of America by Vail-Ballou Press, Binghamton, N.Y.

Library of Congress Cataloging in Publication Data

Neely, Richard, 1941–
How courts govern America.

Includes index.

1. Judicial power—United States. 2. Political questions and judicial power—United States. 3. Judgemade law—United States. I. Title.

KF5130.N43 347.73′1 81-1048
ISBN 0–300–02589–0 347.3071 AACR2
0–300–02980–2 (pbk.)

10 9 8 7 6 5 4 3

Dedication

To my mother and father, whose love, affection, enthusiastic support, and continued sacrifices over the years on my behalf have made my career and this book possible

The science of Politics bears in one respect a close analogy to the science of Mechanics. The mathematician can easily demonstrate that a certain power, applied by means of a certain lever or of a certain system of pulleys, will suffice to raise a certain weight. But his demonstration proceeds on the supposition that the machinery is such as no load will bend or break. If the engineer, who has to lift a great mass of real granite by the instrumentality of real timber and real hemp, should absolutely rely on the propositions which he finds in treatises on Dynamics, and should make no allowance for the imperfection of his materials, his whole apparatus of beams, wheels, and ropes would soon come down in ruin, and, with all his geometrical skill, he would be found a far inferior builder to those painted barbarians who, though they never heard of the parallelogram of forces, managed to pile up Stonehenge. What the engineer is to the mathematician, the active statesman is to the contemplative statesman. It is indeed most important that legislators and administrators should be versed in the philosophy of government, as it is most important that the architect, who has to fix an obelisk on its pedestal, or to hang a tubular bridge over an estuary, should be versed in the philosophy of equilibrium and motion. But, as he who has actually to build must bear in mind many things never noticed by D'Alembert and Euler, so must he who has actually to govern be perpetually guided by considerations to which no allusion can be found in the writings of Adam Smith or Jeremy Bentham. The perfect lawgiver is a just temper between the mere man of theory, who can see nothing but general principles, and the mere man of business, who can see nothing but particular circumstances.

Thomas B. Macaulay
The History of England

CONTENTS

Preface xi

Acknowledgments xv

1. The Power of Courts 1

2. Inertia, Money, and Incumbency in Politics 23

3. The Legislature 47

4. Bureaucracy and the Executive Branch 79

5. The Political Machine 115

6. Courts and the Institutional Dialogue
Part I: Criminal Law Reform 145

7. Courts and the Institutional Dialogue
Part II: The School Finance Cases 170

8. The Courts as an Institution 190

9. Next to the Last Chapter 218

Index 227

PREFACE

There are only approximately as many federal and state senior appellate judges as there are congressmen and senators, yet the courts are everywhere, and no one is untouched by one or another court intrusion into everyday life. Oddly enough, most people are aware of only a few court decisions which concern their geographical area, social class, or industry; if everyone were aware of the extent to which the courts turn other people's lives upside down every day, the level of concern would be substantially higher. In the past twenty-five years there has been no appeal to politically accountable, elected officials from court legislation, because the decisions of life-tenured, anonymous judges are for all practical purposes beyond the reach of the democratic process.

The principal thesis of this book is that American courts, both state and federal, are the central institution in the United States which makes American democracy work, contrary to the assertion that courts are a uniquely undemocratic institution in an otherwise completely democratic society. After years of observing all three branches of government and serving in two of them, I have concluded that the legislative branch and the executive branch are not nearly as democratic as they are alleged to be and that the courts are not nearly as undemocratic.

I have always been dissatisfied with the way the functions of the courts were explained in academic texts, because it appeared to me that academicians were struggling to create an elaborate theoretical structure to explain a fairly simple phenomenon which the man in the street understood perfectly well. When the man in the street is asked why courts legislate, he answers that courts must do what the other branches of government seem incapable of doing. Furthermore, unless a local court has recently done something which he finds personally threatening, the man in the street is usually not at all concerned about the problem and considers the courts an entirely benign governmental institution.

Most commentators on courts find the view of the man in the street unsatisfactory, because it is completely at odds with one of our democratic society's basic premises: electoral control of the lawmaking process. Consequently, there is little practical discussion of the institutional infirmities of the elected branches of government, because any analysis which disparages the sovereignty of one-man, one-vote democracy is dangerous elitism. Yet, it is neither dangerous nor elitist at this stage in America's development to point out that America has evolved a total process for government, of which one-man, one-vote is but one necessary part. Unless the paradoxes of elected politics and the structural infirmities of the legislative and executive branches are fully understood, it will be impossible to explain the complex function which courts perform in a balanced system. Part of any understanding of the strengths and weaknesses of the elective process consists of a knowledge of the danger of bureaucracies and political machines which, if left to themselves, can subvert the entire elective process.

The young law clerks who work with me occasionally characterize my writings as exercises in cheerful cynicism, at least until they come to know me well. My efforts at humor in an attempt to liven up this book should be taken neither as evidence of cynicism nor as evidence of a cavalier disregard for the fact that many areas of government do not work very well. Fifteen years ago as an instructor of undergraduates I learned that it is usually the funny, absurd, or ironic example which sustains the interest of people studying complicated and technical material. Consequently, as I believe that there is a great deal at stake, not only at home but also in our politics abroad, which depends upon whether we understand the evolution of our American court structure and the implications of that development for the science of government as a whole, I would prefer to be read rather than admired. The shelves of libraries are full of heavy, unread, and unreadable tomes, which, although the authors are much admired for erudition, like Gray's flower, were born to blush unseen.

The accusation of cheerful cynicism also misunderstands an important part of my point of view—that human beings and human institutions are capable of only so much perfection. I frequently find myself laughing at the outcome of particular governmental processes because the only other choice is to choose another profession. A sense of humor is usually evidence of a sense of proportion. I have probably had more bills killed, more programs scuttled, and more agendas torpedoed by the political process than almost anyone reading this book, yet I know that in the United States there will always be another day and another reach for the brass ring—something almost no other society on earth can boast. Also, it is true that I find the bumbling, leaderless, lethargic, and generally benign legislative and executive process preferable to a process which has at its helm a group of energetic, ideological, purposeful puritans determined to cut down my Maypole at Merrymont. At this stage in my life I have a reasonable tolerance for inactivity if the alternative is wrong activity. Somehow I hope that is not a sign of cynicism, but of maturity.

This is a book about institutions and how they relate to one another. Preeminently, it is a book about how one institution, the courts, has evolved over nine hundred years into an engine for alleviating the more dangerous structural deficiencies of the other institutions of democratic government—the legislative branch, executive branch, nonpolitical bureaucracies, and political machines. While it may appear cynical to point out with equanimity the shortcomings of other democratic institutions, I think it enormous optimism to demonstrate how society has compensated for these shortcomings by molding our unique court structure. I am not an expert in reengineering other governmental institutions, so I leave extreme moral outrage with respect to them to their own members. Explanation of shortcomings devoid of moral outrage is not cynicism, but merely economy of effort. I reserve my moral outrage for my own institution, the courts, though not necessarily in their political capacity.

Courts serve political functions, but more importantly for most people, they serve a conflict resolution function among private litigants. Furthermore, they are the final arbiters in the enforcement of the criminal law. This book focuses exclusively on the political functions of courts—a function which I believe that they perform at least as well as other political institutions. However, my positive evaluation of courts in this regard should not be taken as an endorsement of the current way of doing business in routine litigation. When it comes to private law suits and criminal prosecutions, courts do not work. While it is true that their quality improves somewhat in the higher-level state and federal courts, the courts which most people see are local magistrate, justice of the peace, or district courts (depending on the name in any given locale), and at that level justice is often for sale, incompetently administered, or so late as to be useless. The civil and criminal courts of this country are successful primarily because of the cases they do *not* decide rather than the cases which they *do* decide; it is voluntary compliance with the criminal and civil law based on the threat of court proceedings, along with voluntary settlements (plea bargains in the criminal courts) when violations occur, which make the court system effective. Once anyone actually sets foot in a court, any court, he is a loser—even if he comes out of the litigation a technical winner.

In order to place many of the issues of this book in proper perspective, I have had to make some very broad historical generalizations. As this is a book about modern courts and not a book about history, I have been content to draw a few oversimplified conclusions, fully recognizing that scholars who devote their entire lives to the study of the evolution of the British and American legal systems are often in disagreement about what went on in the dim, distant past from which we have so few written records. After spending many years in the amateur study of legal history, I have the feeling that the outline I give is more or less correct for the purposes of this book; however, history is always multicausal, and diverse institutions in society never operate at any moment according to neat principles. I hope that the professional historian will not find that I have taken excessive license with the material available.

Finally, I have not attempted to make this appear a scholarly work, since in a way it is a primary source, that is, my own analysis of what I do as an appellate judge. Since a skillful legal writer can find a footnote to support almost any proposition, I have foreborn tedious documentation, which would be useless and boring to the lay reader and entirely redundant to the professional reader. I am content to sketch the broad outline of a theory in a way which I hope will sustain the attention of busy and overworked readers, fully realizing that in the social sciences no theory is completely explanative of all phenomena. I leave it to critics and scholars to test the theory against the facts which they observe.

Fairmont, West Virginia
August 2, 1980

ACKNOWLEDGMENTS

The ideas advanced in this book have been stirring in my mind at least since I became a member of the West Virginia Supreme Court of Appeals. But it is one thing to formulate a concept in general terms and quite another to develop its precise articulation. That latter process was enormously advanced when I had the opportunity in July 1976 to test out my ideas with some of the best legal minds in the nation. The occasion was a seminar at the Aspen Institute on The Role of the Judiciary in a Public Law System. The seminar was conducted by Professor Abram Chayes of the Harvard Law School and was financed out of a grant to Professor Chayes from the National Science Foundation to support his research on this subject. It was held under the aegis of the Aspen Institute's Justice Program. Participants included Chief Justice Warren E. Burger, Federal Judges John P. Fullam, A. Leon Higginbotham, Shirley M. Hufstedler (subsequently Secretary of Education), William Wayne Justice, the late Harold Leventhal, and Wade H. McCree, Jr. (subsequently Solicitor General of the United States); William H. Erickson of the Colorado Supreme Court; Professor Maurice Rosenberg of Columbia University; Antonia Handler Chayes (subsequently Assistant Secretary of the Air Force for Manpower and Installations); and Robert B. McKay, Director of the Justice Program at Aspen.

It would not be fair to say that my distinguished colleagues for this stimulating seminar unanimously endorsed my views then—or would now. But the occasion gave me an unparalleled opportunity for the refinement of views still being formed. Manifestly, nothing I say in this somewhat heretical volume should be blamed on my illustrious friends or that seminar. I can say only that I was greatly benefited by the exchange at that meeting, and I am grateful.

My preeminent thanks for a direct contribution to the manuscript must go to my faithful administrative assistant, Pauline H. Jenkins, who agonized with me over draft after draft of this volume. Since I am a much better editor than writer, Pauline suffered while I rewrote, reorganized, and rethought all of this material for over two years. Furthermore, she corrected my ever-so-sloppy spelling and made sure that what I was saying could be understood by the interested layman as well as the professional reader. Many nights she worked late to meet deadlines and worked as hard on the book as I did.

This book would never have been completed without the help of my former law clerk, James M. Hingeley, and his wife, Rosalind, who closeted themselves with me for a month in a dilapidated farmhouse and reduced my notes and outlines to a book. Jim graduated from the University of Virginia Law School and is one of the most naturally talented lawyers I have ever met; it was he who eliminated many of my extraneous ideas and digressions. Rosalind not only typed the entire manuscript four times, but also did a substantial amount of the editing and reorganization; of the three of us, she carried far more than her share of the load.

Many of the analyses in this book come from extended conversations with my two closest friends, Larrie Bailey, the State Treasurer of West Virginia, and my former high-school roommate and traveling companion, R. Witter Hallan. Larrie's brilliant sociological mind and incisive analytical ability during thousands of hours of conversation in the last ten years helped me to understand the inner workings of many of the political structures discussed in the book, and Witter's wide reading and keen faculties for accurate observation have helped me to understand during our trips overseas some of the forces at work in the Third World, particularly the democracy/wealth correlation which is discussed at length in the book.

Much of the material in this book, by academic standards, is somewhat heretical; more importantly, I have attempted to present heretical material in such a way that it is accessible to everyone. Frequently university presses operate on principles similar to those upon which the pre-Reformation, medieval Church operated, namely, that an author may say anything heretical as long as he says it in Latin. Were it not for the insight and encouragement of Marian Neal Ash, Yale University Press's senior editor, this book might not have been published. Marian guided it through academe's Byzantine bureaucracy and actively encouraged both its style and voice during weekly telephone conversations over a period of a year. Her enthusiasm and sense of humor were contagious.

As this book progressed, three of my law clerks, Barbara Jean Groves, Stephen Moorhead, and Dan Hardway, made substantial contributions in terms of both research and editing. All three of them spent their own time writing lengthy memoranda on weighty subjects which I frequently distilled into two sentences or a short footnote. It was their research which gave me security for some of my more sweeping generalizations.

Finally, I must thank my friend Susan Bolotin, who supplied invaluable advice while I was struggling to find an acceptable voice in which to present this material. It was she who found what I think is the happy medium between the overdocumentation endemic to legal writing and the popular writer's tendency to assert propositions without proving them.

1
THE POWER OF COURTS

The people who make their living writing about or teaching government are not the people who run government. Most of the people who run government are not intellectuals, do not have a compulsion to write, and do not wish to take the time to explain what they are doing. Like Molière's M. Jourdain, they speak prose most of their lives without being particularly conscious of it, and if they occasionally become fascinated with the discrepancies between what they do and what they were taught that people like them ought to do, they have already become sufficiently sophisticated to realize that it is dangerous to disturb established myths. Government officials who are tempted to write usually conclude that even if they explained how things actually work, nobody would believe them, and in all likelihood they would be punished for being messengers who bring bad, or at least unexpected, news.

Coming to the courts as a very young man who was never deeply involved in academic theories of law, I became fascinated by the implications of the American court structure. I never expected to be a judge; in fact, I became a state supreme court justice only because my grandfather, who had been a United States senator from West Virginia and governor, had many friends. In 1970, at age twenty-nine, back from Vietnam, I was elected to the state legislature, a political base from which I aspired to run for the United States Senate in 1972. I did enter the 1972 Senate primary, but halfway through what would have been a protracted campaign, I realized that the incumbent senator was about to beat me like a drum. Since being beaten like a drum is not my favorite pastime, I decided to withdraw from the Senate race and use my political visibility to secure a seat on the state Supreme Court to wait for a more auspicious occasion to launch a Senate campaign.

With six months of vigorous campaigning under my belt in my ill-starred race for the Senate, I quite handily won both the Democrat primary and the general election for Supreme Court. It was no great achievement, because winning judgeships, though hard for lawyers, is easy for politicians. The only people who are much interested in judicial elections are lawyers, and they rarely influence the outcome because they are so afraid of being outspokenly on the losing side.

My elevation to the appellate judiciary still reminds me of the old joke about the O.C.S. Army officer who, upon receiving his gold bars, said, "Gee, six months ago I couldn't spell 'lieutenant' and now I are one!" I knew less about the judging business than did the inanimate portraits of my distinguished predecessors hanging in the chambers. However, for the purpose of this book, the advantage which I brought to the observation of the judicial scene was that I had the perspective of both an economist and a politician rather than of a lawyer. At Dartmouth College I had done more than just major in economics, because at that time, in the 1960s, my home state of West Virginia was suffering from severe unemployment, which I aspired to remedy in a future political career. This background led to further experience in economics in the army where, during my tour in Vietnam, I served as staff economist for the Military Advisory Command.

I had always considered law a way of making a living while I pursued my real interests—politics, economics, and literature. I was never a scholarly law student. All I wanted to learn from my professors were the "hammer and saw" techniques of law which would equip me to write wills and deeds, plead cases in the trial courts, and do a respectable job representing individuals in the law practice which had engaged my ancestors for generations in a rural state. The intellectual, theoretical courses at Yale Law School seemed nonsense to me—all form and no function. Foremost among such courses was my perennial nemesis, constitutional law, or the study of how courts tell legislatures and presidents how to do their jobs. Even from an historical perspective I could never understand how those magic words in the Fifth or Fourteenth Amendments to the Constitution of the United States, "due process of law," and some equally vague language in something known as the "commerce clause" of the Constitution, invited the Supreme Court to regulate everything from steamboats on the Hudson River to taxation of small corporations shipping shoes out of state. It is a sad fact that I earned a "C−" from the great Alexander Bickel in constitutional law, because I could never understand what was going on in his course.

Bickel had been the law clerk of Supreme Court Justice Felix Frankfurter, from whom he had learned a theory about judicial restraint. According to this theory, it was all right for courts to intervene in the political process through imaginative interpretations of the Constitution in defense of human or civil rights, but not to preserve the status quo in the economic system. Of course, during the nineteenth century, courts had always intervened in the economic system to protect free enterprise, but not for civil rights, while after Frankfurter and the advent of the New Deal, the Supreme Court intervened for civil rights, but not for free enterprise. After 1937 the market economy was left to fend for itself in the legislature, a complete upending of all prior case law. When I asked why this result was mandated by "law" or the "Constitution," why Frankfurter's approach was so much better than the approach of earlier jurists, I was told that I did not understand the delicate nature of the constitutional process or the concept of judicial restraint, and that one day it would all become clear to me. I scratched my head and noted that if back in West Virginia we applied the same sort of logic to mining coal, not much coal would get mined, but I was advised not to worry about it because the law review types[1] would take care of doing the big-time reasoning. That was refreshing and reassuring—all I wanted was a "B−" for trying, and the law review types could have it all.

I had the feeling even then that the part of law school devoted to constitutional law was much like the Department of Demonology at Harvard in the latter part of the seventeenth century. I imagine that Harvard's curriculum was extensive and rigorous: the catalogue offered Exorcism 104, Potions 101 (with optional lab), and Sorcery 201 (prerequisite to Sorcery 202). The only trouble with the Department of Demonology at Harvard was that there were no demons. Otherwise the science of demonology presented a perfectly consistent body of knowledge; much like mathematical economics today, it was all remarkably logical if you could once establish its basic premise. It occurred to me as I fantasized about the Demonology Department and our Cambridge colleagues of an earlier era that an enormous body of theory attempting to explain a certain phenomenon does not necessarily prove the accuracy of that body of theory, nor does it even prove that the phenomenon to which the theory is devoted actually exists.

I intuited in my student days that the body of knowledge known as "constitutional law" could not explain the courts' extensive participation in the political process in terms of any legal principles which were in-

1. Those students who have shown superior ability through high grades or legal writing competitions are asked to edit the professional journals published by most law schools, known as "law reviews."

telligible to me.[2] What I ultimately realized, after I became a judge and had decided numerous constitutional issues, was that in terms of legal reasoning, such as we would apply in contract or property law, constitutional law could hardly be considered law at all. Constitutional law, it appeared to me as I was grasping for a theory to explain what I did, could not be understood by reference to "legal" principles, but only by reference to some comprehensive theory of economics, politics, and sociology (right or wrong) which I shall attempt to explain in this book.

In order for any of my explanation concerning why and how courts govern America to make any sense to readers who are not lawyers, it is necessary to proceed to the survey course in constitutional law, which this chapter will attempt to make as unsoporific as possible. There are four broad categories of law in America: criminal law, civil law, administrative law, and constitutional law. As everyone knows, criminal law deals

2. A real-life example of why I was confused in law school was the U.S. Supreme Court decision of *Baker v. Carr,* 369 U.S. 186 (1962), which I was required to study in my constitutional law course. This case contains the "definitive" statement of the political question doctrine, an important constitutional law doctrine which supposedly restrains courts from intervening in the political process whenever a case before the Court falls within any of the categories indicating that the case presents primarily "political," rather than "legal," questions. Justice Brennan, writing for the majority of the Court, gave the following statement of the doctrine:

> Prominent on the surface of any case held to involve a political question is found a textually demonstrable constitutional commitment of the issue to a coordinate political department; or a lack of judicially discoverable and manageable standards for resolving it; or the impossibility of deciding without an initial policy determination of a kind clearly for nonjudicial discretion; or the impossibility of a court's undertaking independent resolution without expressing lack of the respect due coordinate branches of government; or an unusual need for unquestioning adherence to a political decision already made; or the potentiality of embarrassment from multifarious pronouncements by various departments on one question. 369 U.S. at 217.

Throughout this chapter, I shall make reference to the proposition that constitutional law is not "law" in any sense which is intelligible to me. Real law involves rules which are immediately intelligible to anyone trained in the profession of law and which can be applied consistently to any set of facts by most people so trained. Consequently, my test for whether there is a clear legal principle is whether if ten lawyers were put in a room, given a legal principle and a set of facts to which that principle could be applied in order to reach a legal resolution of a dispute, nine out of ten would arrive at the same answer. I leave room for the tenth because in such a group one lawyer will inevitably be either stupid or eccentric. The Supreme Court's definition of when an issue presents a "political question" (quoted above) and therefore is not fit for definitive resolution by that Court would give no clear guidance to any lawyer or litigant concerning when a court will intervene in any given political area. Using a rule like this, a court can first determine what it wants to do and then apply the rule selectively to the facts to justify the conclusion it has already reached based on economic, social, or political considerations. *Baker v. Carr* illustrates the infinite flexibility of constitutional rules, since the Supreme Court had consistently used the "political question" doctrine as a basis for declining invitations to intervene in the political process to reapportion state legislatures, while in *Baker v. Carr* it alleged the doctrine did not apply.

with the determination of guilt and punishment of persons committing specifically proscribed antisocial acts such as arson, robbery, and murder. Civil law deals with the resolution of private disputes, such as breach of contract, in which society as a whole is only indirectly involved, if at all. Administrative law is concerned with the actions of government agencies supervising certain broad areas of life thought to be of governmental concern. Certain authority is given to these agencies, such as the Federal Power Commission, the Federal Trade Commission, or a state public service commission, and it is the job of the courts to assure that the agencies act according to the directions they have been given by Congress or the state legislatures in the statutes under which these regulatory agencies operate. Constitutional law, the principal subject of this book, concerns the ordering of this country's economy, social structure, and political process according to the mandates of written state or federal constitutions which limit the power of government. It is by interpreting the federal and state constitutions that courts may fairly be said to govern America.

Constitutional law is the primary vehicle for this governing function, because all law except constitutional law can be changed at any time by the legislative branch of government; consequently, all the rules concerning contracts, providing remedies for negligently inflicted injuries, and defining crimes and their punishments, along with almost every other question which a court ever decides, are open to legislative change at will. Courts spend much time administering this routine type of law, and while they are frequently criticized in individual cases for being wrong, stupid, or for deliberately interpreting a piece of legislation in a perverse manner, their actions in routine matters are seldom considered illegitimate, illegal, or usurpatory because the state legislature or Congress can immediately rectify any mistake by changing the law.

However, when we come to constitutional law, the actions of courts are almost entirely outside the control of the legislative branch. The courts' rulings in constitutional matters cannot be changed except by amending the federal or state constitutions, which, as history demonstrates, is extremely difficult to do. Consequently, when the United States Supreme Court says that segregation is unconstitutional, or mandates the reapportionment of state legislatures to give the previously underrepresented citizen in urban areas one-man, one-vote for both houses of the state legislature, or rules that states cannot interfere with doctor–patient decisions concerning abortions during the first trimester of pregnancy, there is absolutely no recourse from its decision except constitutional amendment or impeachment of the court and appointment of a new court which will overrule the offending decision.

The foundation of the American system of government is the tight restriction by state constitutions and the federal constitution of the exercise of power by the state and federal governments, respectively. When either a state government or the federal government acts in a manner inconsistent with either the limitations state constitutions impose on state governments or in excess of the authority granted to the federal government by the U.S. Constitution, the courts may step in and strike down the legislative, executive, or administrative actions which contravene any part of the constitutions. While some state constitutions look like the New York Telephone Directory touching every aspect of life in detail, the U.S. Constitution is very short, and all its clauses are potentially open to almost any interpretation a judge would like to make. Since all of these clauses have been interpreted before, however, radically new interpretations would violate certain well-established judicial traditions of interpretation. While a disposition to adhere to prior interpretations *usually* produces consistent decisions over a long period, that disposition alone does not always stop a court from radical departure from prior interpretations in those rare cases where it believes such a departure is necessary.

The power of the federal courts to interpret the U.S. Constitution and through that vehicle effect dramatic social, economic, and political changes comes from the utter vagueness of certain broad clauses, primarily the Fifth Amendment, the first section of the Fourteenth Amendment, and the commerce clause. The key language from these sections is:

> *Amendment V:* No person shall . . . be deprived of life, liberty, or property, without due process of law; nor shall private property be taken for public use, without just compensation.
>
> *Amendment XIV:* [N]o State shall make or enforce any law which shall abridge the privileges or immunities of citizens of the United States, nor shall any State deprive any person of life, liberty, or property, without due process of law; nor deny to any person within its jurisdiction the equal protection of the laws.
>
> *Commerce Clause:* The Congress shall have power to regulate Commerce with foreign Nations, and among the several States, and with the Indian Tribes.

Obviously the power to give to vague clauses certain detailed meanings in the context of specific cases is the power to make supreme law—law which cannot be changed by the routine proceedings of the legislative process, although the extraordinary proceeding of constitutional amendment is available. Furthermore, since there is hardly any question which cannot be framed in such a way as to assume "constitutional" dimensions, for all intents and purposes every conceivable question of public policy is up for review by the courts. Vested with this power to determine what is and what is not within the purview of their authority, courts can at will substitute their judgment for that of all the other agencies of government. Consequently, it would at first appear that the ultimate lawgivers in this society are not the elected officials who are answerable to the voters for their actions, but the judges who for the most part are not elected and have lifetime tenure.

The frightening difference between court action and political action is that courts frequently give no warning. A person who works for a railroad and hopes to become a conductor may find out in mid-career that the railroad must place minority employees, who had been the victims of past discrimination, ahead of him on the seniority list.[3] Furthermore, the decision may not arise in his own geographical area or even involve the railroad; the decision may stem from the problems of longshoremen working half a continent away. What begins as a lawsuit between a black longshoreman and a union hiring hall can suddenly become law which affects our would-be conductor and his railroad. However, the conductor never had any notice, nor did he have an opportunity to participate in the decision-making process in any way—an opportunity which would have been available to him if either Congress or his state legislature had instigated a similar, grandiose restructuring of society. The same type of problem occurs when a federal court rules that an unduly horrid school board in rural Idaho cannot suspend students from school without notice and a hearing. Immediately school administrators in downtown Los Angeles find themselves involved in expensive, time-consuming, and counterproductive procedures before they can discipline a violent and hostile student body, yet no one in California was invited to point out to the court in Idaho the differences between cities and ranching country.

3. A word on sex. Since almost 40 percent of the policymaking positions on my court at the time this book was written were held by women, I am acutely aware of the importance of women in law practice, the courts, and government. I hope that at least half the readers of this book will be women. Nonetheless, despite my efforts to make nouns and pronouns neutral, there are contexts in which the words "person," "someone," or the impersonal "they" are simply more awkward than "men," "man," or for that matter, "women." Consequently, whenever the word "man" appears in this book it should be taken to mean "woman" as well, and whenever the word "men" appears it should be taken to mean "women" as well. Similarly, "he" and "him" should be read to include "she" and "her."

Although the previous two examples are composite, hypothetical cases, they are typical of what is going on in the United States. The elimination of segregation, the legitimation of abortion, and the practical abolition of capital punishment are well enough known to all readers. However, what about these? Private discrimination in the sale and rental of property is prohibited; private possession of obscene materials is a protected personal freedom; a period of residency cannot be made a condition of voting; a labor organization has a constitutional right to picket on *privately* owned shopping center parking lots; and a legislature *must* impose a personal income tax to support the public education system.

These decisions will not outrage everyone; in fact, many people will wholeheartedly approve of my two hypothetical situations involving the railroad conductor and the suspended schoolchildren. Generally, though, American society breaks down into two camps—those who are for the courts because they like what the courts do and those who are against the courts because they do not like what the courts do. Even those who are favorably disposed to the courts, however, harbor a nagging fear about what would happen if the courts turned against them. What if the courts said that paying welfare benefits to persons able to work was unconstitutional? What if state progressive income taxes were held unconstitutional as a denial of equal protection? The same legal reasoning process which has brought liberal decisions can as well bring us conservative ones.

Although Congress, the state legislatures, the president, and governors are generally held in low esteem, those branches of government are, nonetheless, generally regarded as legitimate, because every new election brings an opportunity for change. Courts, however, do not fit into the theory of a democratic society: they are not usually elected; they cannot be changed; and they do not even talk to the press. Some effort is made to integrate them into the standard theory of democracy by saying that they are interpreting a written constitution which itself is the result of the democratic process, but that hardly makes much sense to anyone who has ever recognized that the Constitution, according to the courts, meant something completely different in 1894, 1936, and 1975.

Almost everyone has been an unsuccessful litigant in court or been the victim of some outrageous rip-off using the legal process. It is important, however, to separate dissatisfaction with court performance in individual cases from the proper role of courts in general. This is not a book about stupid judges, corrupt courts, clogged dockets, or even unjust laws; it is a book about whether courts should make law in the broadest, grandest, political sense. The reason that this book must be written is that courts do, in fact, make law in what often appears a lawless process—one moment people are secure in their jobs, property, or expectations regarding their children's education and the next moment everything has changed, almost without warning.

No consistent philosophy governs the courts from era to era—a look at recent history proves the point. For a century preceding Franklin Roosevelt's first term, the Supreme Court had intervened in economic matters in defense of what could loosely be called the liberal economic model of free contracts, labor mobility, no government competition with private enterprise, and no unions. Then the Court suddenly decided from a combination of New Deal political pressure and appointment of New Deal judges that its intervention in these matters was illegitimate. Known as the "doctrine of judicial restraint," this self-imposed restraint was limited to economic matters. In terms of theory, this course of conduct cannot be explained by "restraint," but only in terms of courts upholding results they like and changing results they do not like. Even law professors who are in the business of making sense out of what courts do and are responsible for showing why courts act according to "legal principles," and not according to what the judges had for breakfast, have to twist themselves out of shape to reconcile these constant ideological shifts with any notion of a written constitution which is being "interpreted." In fact, almost every theory defending or defaming courts has developed backward from the result sought by the commentator to some rule which dictates that result. This is not reasoning from principles, however, but mere apologizing for or criticizing the exercise of raw power.

Any reader who believes that there are issues having no constitutional dimension should consider the following illustration. Many states have passed traffic laws permitting motorists to turn right at a red light after coming to a full stop. Let us assume that a motorist wishes to turn left on a red light. He looks to see that no cars are coming, and then turns left directly in front of a parked police cruiser. The police officer, considering "left turn on red" to be illegal, gives him a ticket, and he appears in court to contest the prosecution. The motorist can argue that prosecuting him for turning left on red is unconstitutional, because the "right turn on red" provision deprives him of "equal protection of the laws" by discriminating invidiously against an entire class of people who wish to turn left on a red light. Absurd? Obviously, but the question has been phrased in constitutional terms, and if judges wanted to eliminate "right turn on red" or, through interpretation, mandate "left turn on red" they could write an opinion which would look very much like logical law.

To take a more reasonable example, why have the courts not struck down the entire scheme of progressive income taxation as a violation of equal protection of the laws? A taxpayer making $10,000 a year may pay but $1,000 in federal income tax, or 10 percent of his income, while a taxpayer making $100,000 a year may pay as much as $40,000 or 40 percent of his income in federal income tax—four times the effective rate. Why is this not a denial of equal protection? Is it fair that one hardworking taxpayer must pay only 10 percent of his income while another must pay 40 percent of his income merely because the latter is able to earn more? The courts would say that it is not a denial of equal protection, because the relevant class for equal protection purposes is not "all taxpayers," but "all taxpayers making $10,000 a year" or "all taxpayers making $100,000 a year." According to this reasoning, which is founded on the mystical definition of the appropriate class, as long as all taxpayers making $10,000 a year are treated equally and all taxpayers making $100,000 a year are treated equally, there is no equal protection violation. Thus, by defining the class, we arrive at the result. However, the real reason that courts do not strike down progressive income taxation is that they agree with the principle and see progressive taxation as beneficial rather than threatening to the proper ordering of a democratic society. Furthermore, courts know that the day they strike down progressive taxation, either a constitutional amendment will be passed and ratified within six months or the judges of the U.S. Supreme Court will be impeached. The Supreme Court can be the supreme lawgiver only as long as everyone is generally satisfied with the laws it gives.

Since every conceivable issue known to government can be phrased in constitutional terms, and since a craftsmanlike judge can write in proper legal form an opinion justifying almost any result which he wishes to achieve, what the Founding Fathers intended in 1789 when the Constitution was ratified is not what constitutional law is now about. Constitutional law is neither about a "constitution," nor about "law"; rather, constitutional law is about *institutions* and the way they interact with other institutions. Most of the time, however, courts do not speak in terms of institutions, but rather in terms of individual cases and the litigants before them, such as Joe Smith, Corporation X, or the First Baptist Church Sunday School—in short, in specifics. Furthermore, courts usually do not rest their decisions on a detailed discussion of the institutional shortcomings they are trying to remedy. Instead, they employ casuistic legal reasoning similar to our hypothetical taxation example, in which they first define the class in an artificial manner ("all taxpayers making $100,000 a year") and then proceed to show why that definition leads ineluctably to the conclusion that there is no violation of the equal protection clause. They do not talk about whether high taxation will have an adverse effect upon the economy or whether there is a social reason for reducing large aggregations of private wealth, but as we shall see later, these considerations play a large role in their decision making.

When courts are not doing medieval scholastic gymnastics with vague language to make distinctions without differences, they frequently resort to an historical method of reasoning to justify their public-policymaking function: the courts assume the power of the Oracle at Delphi and tell us the intention of the gods—in this case, the drafters of the U.S. Constitution or the respective state constitutions. What the courts are really saying when they engage in this pseudohistory is that if the Founding Fathers had grown up in the twentieth century, had had all of our experiences, and perceived the problems from our vantage point, they would decide the case the way the court writing the opinion is deciding it. That is an interesting, but hardly reassuring, approach to applying the mandates of a *written* constitutional document.

At this point in our political development American courts are like the Zeus of the Prometheus legend; they are young, immature gods with limitless and inadequately understood power. Lawyers who are elevated to the appellate bench do not understand what they are supposed to do as makers of political policy; more often than not they have absolutely no criteria for evaluating their own actions. Those who are timid sedulously follow precedent; those who are bold cavalierly disregard precedent. Consequently, law is frequently more a function of the attitudes of the judges than of a set of principles which are understood, although I believe that, by a complex psychological process, law is frequently a function of a set of principles which are *not* understood.

If I am correct, then law is principled, but those principles seldom rise to a conscious level. To the extent of my ability, I intend in this book to raise these principles to a conscious level and expose the imperatives which force judges unwillingly to become politicians. These imperatives do not originate in legal principles, but rather in structural and operational defects in all the great institutions of society. Part of what makes the real principles unconscious is that practical politicians are generally not intellectuals. Even on those occasions when theoreticians become politicians, they immediately become reluctant to talk about what they are doing in a critical way because of fear of *lèse majesté*.

There are certain things which the executive and legislative branches *cannot* do, but woe unto active government leaders who say ''cannot'' instead of ''do not,'' because they have confessed how powerless they are. The intellectually honest politician becomes immediately vulnerable to the rhetoric of his opponents whenever he confesses that it is impossible to improve certain types of government performance. Any practicing politician knows that the average citizen has no voice in routine governmental operation, but to admit that fact publicly as an unalterable element of national government is to invite popular outrage. The catch phrase ''let's return the power to the people'' always works during a campaign speech; however, it is unwise to go into very much detail concerning how this is to be done because, unless you lie, it soon becomes obvious that the phrase is metaphorical at best.

I once had a young neighbor who was vice president of a large bank. One evening I tried to explain to him and his wife the mechanics of an election campaign, and they quite clearly indicated that it was morally reprehensible even to *know* how things really work, much less to take advantage of that knowledge. I quickly saw that emotion was overwhelming any intellectual curiosity about the mechanics of elective politics, so I cleaned up my act and concluded with an altar call.

This experience points out the critical fact that in any society there are two systems of government—the myth system and the operational system.[4] My young banker friend preferred to operate exclusively within the myth system. Theory, idealism, and a fear of certain vicious tendencies in human nature dictate the myth system, while the operational system is how things really work. The myth system affects the operational system in a constructive way, because it provides a standard by which the operational system can be judged and it arouses guilt in those in the operational system when they misbehave. The myth system and the operational system cannot be the same for two important reasons: first, people want to take bribes, help their friends, further their own economic interests, gratify their vanity, and not work very hard; second, there are always design defects in the myth system which make it *impossible* to construct a real edifice on the plan given by the myth. The myth system is

4. I am indebted to Professor W. Michael Reisman of the Yale Law School for having introduced me to the myth system/operational system analysis. He has exhaustively explored the phenomenon in the context of a general theory of jurisprudence in his book *Folded Lies* (New York: Free Press, 1979).

like religion; it has a real effect on the operational system, and any threat to it is punished like heresy in the Middle Ages.

The duty which we have unconsciously thrust upon the courts is to get the results which the myth system promises but which the operational system does not deliver; however, courts are absolutely forbidden to call attention to the difference in the two systems or in any way to threaten the myth system. There are forces other than the courts at work to bring the operational system into alignment with the myth system; campaigns against bribery and corruption are the most noticeable, but in addition there are efforts to recruit good people to government service, reorganizations to get greater efficiency, and election reform. These improvements go to the correction of the first category of causes for disparity, namely, the self-seeking nature of man; however, it is difficult to do anything about the architectural causes of the disparity, because that implies not only a reordering of the operational system, but a reordering of the myth system as well. Since our own myth system for all its imperfections has produced a wondrous society, there is a natural hesitancy to tamper with it. Society's generally cold reception to any suggestion of a constitutional convention is a good example of our reluctance to confront architectural flaws in the myth system directly. Nonetheless, participatory democracy was not able to provide integration for blacks, one-man, one-vote in state legislatures, or reform of the abortion laws in spite of evidence from the Gallup polls that a majority of Americans favored what the Supreme Court did in all of these areas.

Judges never address the myth/operational disparity and their resulting political role in their public utterances or legal opinions. We are so solicitous of the integrity of the myth system that judges seldom discuss this role even among themselves. When, however, men are applying principles which tact and diplomacy require that they never articulate, there is not a great deal of serious scrutiny of the principles or of whether they are being intelligently applied. It is in this regard that almost every American who is not a judge is perplexed and disturbed about courts. Our perplexity increases when we take seriously what judges and lawyers have said they were doing instead of looking primarily at what they actually do. The fact that a court says that it is mandating that a certain thing be done in society because the Constitution commands it does not necessarily mean that this is so, in the same way that when mother says to a four-year-old that it is time to go because "mother has to get home," it does not necessarily mean that mother has to get home; it merely means that mother is bored and wishes to express herself in a tactful way.

All branches of government lie, and so do judges. A government which promises simultaneously to expand energy production, deliver adequate medical services to everyone, provide a comfortable living to the aged and infirm, control pollution, revamp the national transportation network, provide free and limitless schooling, develop the Third World, allocate 5 percent of gross national product to new housing, protect all of the stupid and lazy from themselves, maintain parity in all weapons systems, and increase net disposable income—all without increasing taxes—is obviously lying, yet this is typical campaign rhetoric. When presidential, senatorial, or congressional candidates promise these impossible feats, the press is quick to point out the element of fraud and deceit. Almost every active politician is accused of being a liar on a daily basis. However, when Earl Warren wrote that the U.S. Constitution *required* certain changes in the criminal law during the 1960s, he was accused of being wrong but never of being a liar. Judges are easily believed because, with the black robes, they basically resemble priests.

So far we have been talking rather abstractly about the structural deficiencies of the great institutions of society, but in order for the reader to visualize the problem properly, it is necessary to focus on a few specific cases. *Baker v. Carr,* the 1962 Supreme Court case which required reapportionment of both houses of state legislatures on a one-man, one-vote basis, meets all the conditions for a perfect case for judicial activism. The perfect case for court intervention into the political process is when the operational system breaks down so completely as to become a travesty of the myth system. The politics which gave rise to *Baker v. Carr* involved the state senates which, many decades ago, had been apportioned by geography, rather than population, so that in states with rapidly growing cities the rural counties completely frustrated progress for the urban population. In order to pass a bill to redistrict the state legislatures, it was necessary to receive approval of the state senates—the political equivalent of asking a person to commit suicide. In the absence of action by Congress, there was no agency other than the courts to render relief. Congress was unwilling to act, because the rural interests had sufficient power to stall reform at the national level. If the legitimacy or desirability of judicial activism could be measured on a ten-point scale, where the strongest cases get ten points and the weakest cases get one or fewer, *Baker v. Carr* would get all ten points, because the disparity between the myth system and the operational system was total. Both majority rule and effective participatory democracy were denied by a self-serving structure which had little or no rational justification.

Of course, whenever courts are working with the "perfect case" their results will be almost universally applauded, so that in order to see the broad problem of the potentially "imperial" judiciary, it is necessary to move down my scale to a few specific cases which are far less "perfect." Let me take a case which my court decided, because I can get into the court's head by virtue of having written the opinion. In 1977 the public interest lawyers brought a suit in West Virginia to strike down all the juvenile laws, because the law permitted status offenders, that is, children who had committed no act which would be criminal if committed by an adult, to be placed in reform schools with murderers, robbers, and rapists. The legislature had passed statutes many years ago making truancy, sexual promiscuity in females, and habitual absence from home grounds for juvenile court jurisdiction, with authority for the court to send kids doing these things to reform school. Any adult, however, could do any one with impunity. The West Virginia Supreme Court struck the laws down as unconstitutional under the state constitution because of lack of a rational relationship between a legitimate state interest, namely, protection of children, and the means sought to achieve that end, namely, sending children to reform school where they would come out worse than when they went in. This is called "substantive due process," and I discuss it again later. What I reasoned about the case myself and what I wrote in the court's opinion were two entirely different things. Basically I inferred that the legislature was not particularly interested in truant, disturbed, or promiscuous children—they were interested in other things like dog racing, schools, and branch banking, where the political pressure was sufficiently intense to attract their attention. Many legislators had a concern for juveniles, but there was not enough interest among enough members to appropriate the money necessary to treat different types of juveniles more appropriately. The force of inertia was so great that without court intervention the legislature would pursue agendas made compelling by organized constitutencies and pay no attention to the problems of poor, often retarded, children. When my court held the existing structure of juvenile control unconstitutional, the whole issue was suddenly up for grabs again, and the legislature was forced to rethink the problem. In a case like that, it was argued by the court's detractors, the legislature had *intentionally* declined to act, because it did not think juveniles were a priority for new appropriations; furthermore, many critics argued that the old laws actually served a valid purpose in social control, because they permitted a court or other authorities to threaten children into obedience. Did the inertia of the legislative process create a disparity between myth and operational systems, or did the court merely substitute its judgment for that of politically elected representatives? It is a close case.

Certainly there are cases where courts have been outrageously activist, although there was no disparity between myth and operation—all that had occurred to invite judicial intrusion was that the operational system had failed to give a certain group what they wanted, so they went to court seeking another *operational* system to give them a more favorable result. If the reader thinks that it would be hard to separate the appropriate cases for judicial activism from the inappropriate ones, he or she is not alone, because all the thoughtful judges I know have the same difficulty. Most cases have elements of a myth/operational disparity *and* of judges substituting their judgment for political authorities.

Now let us go one step further down the scale to an even less "perfect" case. Here is an example of judges substituting their judgment for that of the political process: it is found in a West Virginia school finance case called *Pauley v. Kelly,* which, on the basis of the state constitutional mandate of a "thorough and efficient" system of state education, demanded that the courts reorganize the tax system which supports education. It was argued in that case that using property taxes to support a large part of the schools' budgets caused extremely poor schools in property-tax-poor counties and that these schools were inherently less than "thorough and efficient." What gives this case a low score on my hypothethical scale is that all the forces of the operational system were working in that case exactly as the myth system dictates: the legislature had full-time committees staffed by the more intelligent members of that body working diligently to improve education; the teachers had a professional association which constantly lobbied for more money for schools; the parents participated politically to get better schools; and finally, the state Board of Education was staffed with a huge bureaucracy dedicated to research and development in education.

Efforts to get more money for education, which, unlike juvenile detention homes, is no insubstantial part of a state's budget, ran amuck because of competition for the same dollar with roads, the elderly, and the taxpayer's pocket. There was one aspect of the school case, however, namely, that it arose from a property-tax-poor county, which gave even this case one or two elements of myth/operational disparity. Where schools are financed by property taxes, it is exclusively a question of geography whether a child gets a good or bad education. If a county happens to have valuable land and industrial improvements, the schools have more money than they can spend; where, however, a county happens to be rural and there is no revenue the schools suffer. In the *Pauley* case, the plantiffs came from Lincoln County, where the tax base had always been poor; therefore, in spite of some state aid, that school system always had to play catch-up because their plants were so squalid to start with.

If we were to evaluate the three cases I have discussed on my hypothetical ten-point scale, one-man, one-vote gets a ten, reform of juvenile laws a six, and school finance gets a three, although I am the first to admit there is no magic in my numbers. If this scale, or at least the concept it implies, has any validity, a discussion of the courts must start with the inherent limitations of political institutions and proceed to analyze the politics of courts in terms of whether those politics are superior to available alternatives.

The whole body of legal rules and precedents which we call constitutional law can make sense only if we recognize the impossibility of separating a constitution from the agency entrusted to enforce it and conceive of a constitution not only as a document but as a set of remembered experiences occurring, in the case of this country, from the Norman conquest until today. Although men will not interpret any document entrusted to them for very long in a *neutral* way, this is not to say that they will necessarily go one step further and interpret it in an *unprincipled* way. The principles may arise from considerations of the highest order and be inspired by consummate idealism. Furthermore, principles develop from experience, and this experience is at the heart of any workable constitutional structure. When certain clauses such as the Eighth Amendment protection against cruel and unusual punishment were written, the framers had specific historical experiences in mind, such as the merciless flogging of Titus Oates from one London jail to another in 1678 upon conviction for a misdemeanor. Much of our Bill of Rights was taken from the English Bill of Rights of 1689. Since our Constitution was written, we have had new and different experiences which have given rise to new and different principles.

Students of constitutional law are usually confounded by certain obvious historical absurdities in the legal opinions of judges, because it is unreasonable to say with a straight face that the founders of this nation—many of whom owned slaves—really intended the words in the Fifth Amendment to the Constitution to include blacks or that the drafters of the Fourteenth Amendment—almost none of whom would have had a negro as a social guest—actually intended the words "due process" and "equal protection of the laws" to mandate complete economic and social equality for all races. Furthermore, given that the first one hundred and twenty-five years of our history were dedicated in part to the extermination of the Indians, it is even more ludicrous to believe that the Constitution was intended to protect native Americans. Had Earl Warren sat in Washington, George Custer's career would have ended somewhere other than Little Bighorn! Lawyers, certainly, who take seriously recent U.S. Supreme Court historical scholarship as applied to the Constitution also probably believe in the Tooth Fairy and the Easter Bunny. The truth of the matter is that judges do not say these things with a straight face; they are talking in code which most of the bar understands.

When I first became a judge, I used to pride myself on my ability to trace constitutional tradition to medieval law, and I did elaborate manipulations of history in order to arrive at what I thought were just results. At first I thought that I was the only judge around doing it—then I discovered that every judge with an ounce of smarts did it. The pseudohistory of the formal constitutional opinion has many of the endearing qualities of the social lie, to wit, "your hat is really lovely." History *is* important in the development of a constitution, but it is total history—much history before 1789 and all history after 1789. Focusing on the purported intention of the geniuses in 1789 is like looking at one frame in the middle of a motion picture film.

One of the central themes of conservatives is that a written constitution must be interpreted in a neutral way and that a constitution must be separated from the institution to which it is entrusted for enforcement. It would appear from history that such a separation has never occurred in any operational system. No rule determines its own application; only individual men and women can do that, and historically those entrusted to enforce the laws always avail themselves of the power to change which is implicit in the power to interpret. When, for example, the Magna Carta, that alleged cornerstone of English liberties, was written in 1215, it was effective only because the armed men who had extorted it from King John remained armed and threatened to do an instant replay of the "Give us liberty or we'll give you death" routine which they had acted out during several years of revolution. As soon as the civil disturbance culminating in Magna Carta had subsided, its provisions were generally ignored.

None of the priests and barons who dictated the Magna Carta would, in his wildest dreams, have conceived of it as a general protection for individual rights against organized, feudal authority. At its heart was protection of aristocratic and church rights against royal authority. Although there were suits during the Middle Ages grounded on the Magna Carta, they involved its specific provisions having to do with such things as fishing weirs, feudal rents, debts of widows and minors, intestate succession, lands of felons, and foreign merchants. Originally Magna Carta was a guarantee of feudal rights of a specific nature; ultimately, however, exclusively through creative interpretation, the charter was used to vindicate *general* liberty in opposition to a lingering feudal structure.

Since the Magna Carta is often considered the starting point in our constitutional tradition, it is instructive to dwell on it a little more, because it proves something about all constitutions. Magna Carta lay dormant for four hundred years until it was revived in the early seventeenth century to serve as the foundation of a natural law edifice which would support English subjects' demands for greater participation in government and for improved guarantees of their civil and economic rights. A romantic enshrinement of the Magna Carta was used to vindicate certain evolving concepts concerning citizen participation in the government of a civilization four hundred years after Magna Carta was signed. The antiquity of the document alone made it useful for propaganda purposes, and those seeking dramatic change in the order of society were able to allege that "this has always been the law." In fact, hardly one clause of the Magna Carta has ever been observed simply because it was in the Magna Carta, although occasionally a clause may have been observed because it suited the prevailing power to do so.

In spite of my estimation that most of what appears in legal opinions on constitutional law cannot be given or received with a straight face, an enormous volume of discussion of constitutional decisions still revolves around whether this or that was "intended" by the framers of the constitutions. This type of analysis does nothing to make the proper role of courts in the political process more understandable or more "lawful." When the center of focus is either history or intent of the framers, all arguments must be drafted in code, but the code has an insufficient vocabulary to embrace the concepts necessary for a discussion of complex principles involving the nature of the great institutions of society—legislative branch, executive branch, bureaucracy, organized capital, organized labor, and unorganized consumers. The code system of constitutional law does not force a court to decide the crucial threshold issue of "justiciability," that is, whether it is appropriate for a court, as opposed to other institutions, to be doing a particular thing.

If we return for a moment to the West Virginia school finance case, where irate citizens attempted to enlist the courts in their efforts to get more money for the schools, the center of the argument was a "code" contention about what the drafters of the state constitution intended by the words "thorough and efficient system of free schools." The way the issue was framed was absurd and forced the lawyers to dwell exclusively on what a group of bright chaps intended when they discussed schools a hundred years ago—nothing but a mystical undertaking. The real question was whether the other branches of government were capable of addressing the school finance problem in an adequate manner or whether for institutional reasons this issue could best be handled by the courts.

Implicitly it has been recognized that there are many areas where the courts' decisions *are* indeed preferable to those of any other institution. Foremost of these is the area of economics, where historically the courts have made the most important decisions and exercised the most pervasive veto power over the decisions of the other branches. Except for the furor caused by the Supreme Court's resistance to the New Deal in the first five years of Franklin Roosevelt's administration in the 1930s, there has rarely been extensive criticism of either the sagacity or legitimacy of court-initiated economic policy. While courts may not reach the explosive political issues of inflation and unemployment directly, they do determine many nuts-and-bolts economic questions, such as the extent to which government can compete with private enterprise, the types of taxes which can be imposed on interstate commerce, and the permissible degree to which government can regulate entry into certain callings. The Supreme Court decision which required states to permit lawyers to advertise, for example, although grounded in the First Amendment right to free speech, was in reality a decision about the degree to which a professional association can restrict competition in order to raise prices. Again, for my money, the court was talking in code. The economic cases escape public notice almost completely, while the social cases generate a whirlwind; the reason is that the maintenance of a prosperous economy is a governmental goal which is not furthered in the long term by complete, short-term, democratic control.

The economy presents the most easily proven instance of the limitations of politics, because in economics there are right and wrong answers, and in order to know the difference a type of skill not generally available among the electorate is required.[5] The organized political institutions of

5. While at first the notion that there are right and wrong answers in economics might appear laughable, it is important to recognize that intelligent economic debate proceeds within a fairly narrow range. The reason is that all of the totally stupid economic theories have been refuted to the satisfaction of most reasonable men. Thus, no one with the least training in econmics seriously argues a return to utterly unrestrained laissez faire, and the respectable Left does not seriously argue for total state control of all sectors of the economy, since experience elsewhere with that method of organization has been so dismal.

society are very greedy, and their ability to make objective decisions about the right and wrong answers is often clouded by their natural avarice. Government employees, for example, are empire builders, because their salaries, prestige, and emoluments are dependent on the number of operations they control. Government, left unchecked, would swallow all private enterprise through tax-financed capital, low-interest, tax-free bonds, and a host of other "unfair" techniques if there were no restraint. Leaving such restraint to the officials who have everything to gain from the government sucking up private industry would be like sending goats to guard cabbages.

One economic question which has always been relegated to the courts is the permissible level of redistribution of the wealth. To take a recent case, the City of New York sought to keep Grand Central Station as an historic landmark by preventing the Penn Central Railroad from constructing a fifty-story office building which would have earned Penn Central three million dollars a year. Penn Central said that if the city wanted to keep the building for public, historic preservation purposes, it should be forced to condemn and pay damages. The Supreme Court ruled that New York could regulate an historic landmark for public purposes without need to pay condemnation damages as Penn Central was still earning a fair return on its *original* investment, which was for a railroad passenger terminal. There are thousands of cases involving government action adverse to private interests every year, and at their hearts is the central question of redistribution of wealth, government competition with private enterprise, or discriminatory or rapacious schemes of taxation. Someone must decide objectively the appropriate trade-off between regulation and free enterprise. Nowhere in the Constitution is there any elaborate discussion of this function of courts except the vague phrase from the Fifth Amendment, "nor [shall any person] be deprived of life, liberty, or property without due process of law; nor shall private property be taken for public use, without just compensation." The courts probably fell heir to deciding wealth redistribution issues because their neutrality made them superior to other institutions.

The next four chapters dwell at length on the institutional infirmities of elected politics, the legislative branch, the executive branch, and political organizations, sometimes known as machines. All these institutions work well most of the time—otherwise they would not have survived hundreds of years of political evolution. Nonetheless, certain natural outgrowths of their good qualities would, if left unchecked, destroy participatory democracy. It is the job of the courts to protect society from these potential threats. To show why a court structure must perform political functions, we will need to dwell on the dangers of other institutions rather than their strengths. This should not be taken as cynicism; the strengths are adequately handled in eighth-grade civics books.

This book differs significantly from other books on constitutional theory in that constitutional scholars usually consider the defects of the other branches of government as "constitutional flaws" which must be corrected by the "political process" and for that reason outside their legitimate concern in developing constitutional theory. In the well-ingrained tradition of academic specialization, experts in legal theory prefer to consider constitutional law as a part of a self-contained, specialized body of learning known as "law." In fact, constitutional law is no more theoretical than plumbing; it was generated by practical men in response to practical problems. From my own experience, most of the judges who make constitutional law every day on courts below the U.S. Supreme Court would no more understand the meanderings of academic lawyers than they would a treatise on quantum physics. Constitutional law is *only* about correcting flaws in the other branches; it is basically about balance.

2

INERTIA, MONEY, AND INCUMBENCY IN POLITICS

The mechanics of elected politics are at the heart of the myth/operational disparity. Most people are no more interested in the mechanics of government or politics than I am in putting miniature ships in bottles. If a good friend of mine were driven by a desire to place increasingly complicated and delicate ships in progressively smaller and more convoluted bottles, I would watch him for a while with patient but feigned interest. Indulging one's friends is one of the obligations of friendship. Nonetheless, putting ships in bottles bores me to tears. Government in general is even less interesting—and about as tedious—to all but those who make their living from it.

Government is a technical undertaking, like the building of rocketships or the organizing of railroad yards. Except possibly on the local level, the issues which attract public notice usually involve raising money (taxes), spending money (public works), foreign wars (preventing them or arguing for fighting easy ones), education, public morals, crime in the streets, and, most important of all, the economy. When times are bad, or there is a nationwide strike or disaster, interest in the economy becomes all-consuming. However, the daily toiling of countless millions of civil servants in areas such as occupational health and safety, motor vehicle regulation, or control of navigable waterways escapes public notice almost completely.

Furthermore, even with regard to high-visibility issues, significant communication between the electorate and public officials is extremely circumscribed. Most serious political communication is limited to forty-five seconds on the network evening news. In days gone by, when the only entertainment in town on a Wednesday night was to go to the county courthouse to listen to a prominent politician give a theatrical tirade against Herbert Hoover (who may not have been president for twenty years), an eloquent speaker could pack the courthouse and have five thousand people lined up to the railroad tracks listening to the booming loudspeakers. It is unfortunate, in a way, that political communication of that character has been all but foreclosed by the presence of Robert Redford free on the TV in living color in one's own home.

Political communication, much like music, finds its content dictated by form. In the same way that Mozart's symphonies, timed to give German aristocrats as much music as they could stand after stuffing themselves at the table, have been replaced by popular rock groups on 45-rpm records, timed to give the average teenager as little music as he will accept for his two bucks, the political orator of yesteryear has been replaced by a flickering image on the tube unlocking the secrets of the government universe in forty-five-second licks. Gone forever are Lincoln–Douglas-type debates on courthouse steps. Newspapers take up the slack a little, but very little. As anyone who has ever been in politics will attest, newspapers as compared with television are a weak mode of communication. Most of what one says to a local newspaper (maybe not the *New York Times*) gets filtered through the mind of an inexperienced twenty-three-year-old journalism school graduate. Try sometime to explain the intricacies of a program budget, which basically involves solving a grand equation composed of numerous simultaneous differential functions, to a reporter whose journalism school curriculum did not include advanced algebra, to say nothing of calculus.[1]

Because the intricacies of very technical work are lost on professional communicators, they are not transmitted in any attractive way to the electorate. But the electorate is as interested in the whys and wherefores of most technical, nonemotional political issues as I am in putting ships in bottles: they do not particularly care. Process and personalities, the way decisions are made and by whom, the level of perquisites, extramarital sexual relations, and, in high offices, personal gossip dominate the public mind, while interest in the substance of technical decisions is minimal. Reporters focus on what sells papers or gets a high Nielsen rating; neither newspapers nor television stations intend to lose their primary value as entertainment. Since the populace at large is more than willing to delegate evaluation of the technical aspects of government to somebody else, it inevitably follows that voting is a negative exercise, not a positive one.

1. A brief look at the 1979 circulation figures for *Commentary* (50,000), *Foreign Affairs* (75,000), *The New Republic* (85,000), *The Nation* (25,000), *The New York Review of Books* (95,000), and all academic journals demonstrates the limited interest in detailed evaluation of technical problems. Furthermore, the circulation figures just mentioned are actually overly optimistic, since the people who subscribe to one of these publications usually subscribe as well to at least one more.

Angry voters turn the rascals out and, in the triumph of hope over experience, let new rascals in. What voters are unable to do—because they themselves do not understand the technical questions—is tell the rascals how to do their jobs better.

Serious coverage of goings-on in government is deterred by the fact that government is so technical that even career civil servants cannot explain what is happening. In 1978 I attended a seminar on federal estate and gift tax sponsored by the American Law Institute, where the Internal Revenue Service lawyers responsible for this area frankly confessed that they did not understand the Tax Reform Act of 1976. They were, indeed, so confused that there was hardly one question asked by the audience which they satisfactorily answered. Not only did they allow that *they* did not understand the law, they opined that the Congress which wrote it did not understand it and that the courts would seem to understand it only because the courts would make it up as they went along and *pretend* to understand it. Intricate technical issues such as taxation, arms control, and nuclear power are difficult to understand for professionals, to say nothing of the most diligent layman.

That anything gets done by a political body at all is to be applauded as a miracle rather than accepted as a matter of course. When we recognize that in the federal government, with its millions of employees, there are but five hundred and thirty-seven elected officials, put in office to carry out the "will" of a people who for the most part know little and care less about the technical functioning of their government, the absurdity of the notion of rapid democratic responsiveness becomes clear. The widely held tenet of democratic faith that elected officials, as opposed to bureaucrats or the judiciary, are popularly selected and democratically responsive is largely a myth which gives a useful legitimacy to a system that works relatively well in a society which has come to raise the ideal of democracy to the level of a religious creed. In fact, however, far from democratic control, the two most important forces in political life are indifference and its direct byproduct, inertia. This is not irrational, because people want first and foremost for the government to leave them the hell alone, and this sentiment is pervasive among such disparate groups as captains of industry, the solid middle class, and the majority of welfare clients.

Success in politics depends upon money and its equivalent, incumbency, not ideology. It is true that a candidate can destroy himself with ideology (Barry Goldwater and George McGovern spring to mind), but successful politicians are usually colorless, odorless, and tasteless.

Issue-oriented politics is still found on the local level, where it is possible to run for office without a large budget, but on the state and national levels the competition is not for the voters' passionate dedication but rather for a general acceptance which would be jeopardized by positions on hot, emotional issues. In the 1976 presidential race, the campaign was focused on the character of Jimmy Carter, and his startling campaign promise was that he would not lie.

In the 1978 mid-term elections in the United States, barely 35 percent of the American population eighteen years old or older and eligible to vote went to the polls. This minority split in turn into two factions, typically 55 percent to 45 percent, and it was upon this narrow difference (3.8 percent of the total population) that United States senators, governors, congressmen, and a host of powerful state and local officials either won or lost offices. Furthermore, these figures are widely representative of mid-term elections over the past thirty years, improving only about 15 percent for presidential elections. Political participation is relatively low because it is ineffective unless there is a discrete, definable grievance which is widely shared. In secular societies, economic issues are the ones which most frequently generate a broad enough interest to precipitate effective political action. Intense religious belief can also generate political action, as demonstrated by the pope's visit to Poland in 1979, when he attracted voluntary crowds exceeding half a million. Religious activism, however, has not been common in America until recently, except occasionally on the local level. In this society my own conclusion is that the most compelling force in politics is inertia, as demonstrated by the historically low voter turnouts, and that when inertia is overcome, it is almost always economics which does it.[2]

2. The strength of economics versus other issues in the United States can be shown by a comparison of politics during eight depression years with a similar period during the Vietnam war. Between 1928 and 1936 the Republican party was decimated and most of its officeholders lost their jobs, while from 1960 to 1968 there was neither a strengthening of the Republican opposition party nor a significant change in elected personnel. During the depression, from 1928 to 1936, 170 Republicans lost their jobs in the U.S. House of Representatives; during the war period 1960–68 the Democrats lost only 20 seats. The composition of the United States Senate illustrates the difference even better; in 1928, 38 Democrats and 56 Republicans sat in the upper house, while in 1936 there were only 17 Republicans—70 percent of Republicans had been replaced. From 1960 to 1968, notwithstanding street riots over Vietnam, there was only an insignificant 9 percent shift in the U.S. Senate in favor of the Republican opposition. Apparently political action is only effective when there is broad agreement about the nature of the problem and the nature of the solution. These conditions were met during the depression but were not met during the Vietnam war. The Republicans were unable to take advantage of general dissatisfaction in the 1960s, because there was no consensus among them about a new policy.

Everyone, of course, would like to have more of the good things of life supplied by the government at the expense of other groups: industry would like fewer regulations, the middle class would like lower taxes, and welfare clients would like more benefits. At the local level everyone wants better schools and nicer places of public resort, but the nationwide experience with popular votes for special bond issues to improve schools demonstrates that our desire for more government benefits seldom overcomes our unwillingness to pay for them. Most citizens of the United States are now, and always have been, preeminently concerned with their own private life-styles, and while they accept the need for a flourishing community and are often very civic minded at the local level, individualism, which is a pervasive feature of this civilization, implies first a private concern and only secondarily a public one.

As a result of watching politics at close range, I have begun to understand why the average person is somewhat suspicious of politicians and political activism. The inertia which is so vehemently decried by commentators is probably no more than what Franklin Roosevelt once called "the common sense of the common man." Northern Ireland, Lebanon, and Iran offer grand examples of societies torn apart by political activism; on a smaller scale, political factionalism will destroy the government of a state, city, or county. Of West Virginia's fifty-five counties, about forty-five have one predominant party, either Democrat or Republican, and for all practical purposes in these counties there is no effective opposition party. A nominal opposition ticket is usually fielded, but unless there is corruption on the part of the majority party, the contest is not serious. The paradox is that these counties are much better run than the ten counties where there is continuous partisan controversy. Partisan controversy sets the county clerk against the prosecuting attorney, the circuit judge at odds with the circuit clerk, the county commission against the local sheriff and assessor, all in the interest of showing what a bunch of rascals the opposition party is. The result is total lack of cooperation, confusion, and deliberate torpedoing of major economic projects, urban renewal, and any other program which might reflect credit on the opposition.

Apparently my own conclusions based on a lifetime of living in the woods is shared by others from more sophisticated backgrounds. Peter Jay, former economics editor of the London *Times,* and British ambassador to Washington from 1977 to 1979, once commented to me at a dinner party that politics had made Britain a "nation of highwaymen." He explained that British politics centered on the redistribution of wealth; therefore, Britain's economic problems, which consist of paralyzing labor disputes, very low growth rates, low levels of labor productivity, and lack of aggressive pursuit of international markets, can be traced to an overreliance on political programs and an insufficient reliance on business programs. He too was suspicious of politics as a force for good, agreeing with my gut reaction that politics is like fire; a little of it warms the hearth, while a lot of it burns the house down. Most Americans intuit the dangers of politics. This is frequently summarized at the upper-middle-class cocktail party by the statement that politics is dirty and filthy. The term "dirty and filthy" is just shorthand for a more elaborate analysis of the genuinely counterproductive aspects of most political controversy, which usually revolves more around personal ambition, class interest, and economic advantage than it does around anything which could be loosely called the "general good."

Except on those occasions when the private life-styles of broad segments of the community are threatened because of economic depression, most people are willing to settle for a government which preserves the status quo and bothers them as little as possible. In the absence of war, famine, or pestilence, most voters are comparatively content. True, they probably conceive of government officials as a group of clowns and of the institution of government as inefficient and corrupt, but if nothing is hurting them, they pass their days without so much as a thought for the political structure.

The average voter is about as tolerant of his government officials as he is of his plumber, doctor, or automobile mechanic. People seldom comment on the superb, craftsmanlike job they receive from any purveyor of services. If a person's transmission stays in when he drives his car out of the shop, and if his stomach cramps disappear after his gallbladder is removed, the average consumer, like the average voter, is satisfied. But all his tolerance is conditioned upon minimal interference with his private life. In the private sector, this implies that the mechanic's or doctor's bill is not too high and that most of the time the commodity or service for which he pays serves its purpose adequately; in the government sector, minimal interference with a consumer's private life implies that his elected officials keep the government machine running smoothly and maintain a prosperous economy. When economic disaster strikes, citizens look to their government and expect quick remedies.

Democracy, in fact, is predicated upon sufficient indifference to provide a high tolerance for doing nothing. There has been much discussion about why some countries are democracies and others are not; there has been extensive discussion in scholarly literature about the protestant ethic, the English tradition, European and Western thought, etc. There is, however, only one definite correlation between democracy and anything else, and that is between democracy and wealth. No democracy in the world is poor, with the possible exception of India, and India is at best a questionable case in light of its history from 1974 to 1977. The reason for the almost perfect correlation between democracy and wealth (although not necessarily between wealth and democracy, as wealth is a necessary but not sufficient condition for democracy) is that in poor countries the economy has nothing to spare; any economic reversal immediately touches the lives of everyone. Economic disaster breeds a widespread demand for effective government intervention, and society becomes polarized about who should meet that demand. Ultimately the man on the white horse emerges, either to take the economy in hand or to quell the civil disorder caused by disparate elements trying to solve the community's economic problems. Opportunistic activists inevitably propel themselves to power on the basis of one economic platform or another, and once having seized enough power to do anything positive about the economy, also have enough power to perpetuate themselves in office. Consequently, it must be reluctantly admitted at the outset that our relatively peaceful political process with its attendant civil and political rights is not attributable entirely to the genius of the American people or to the strength of their institutions, but to the bounty of the American continent and the American knack for harvesting its fruits.

My observations about American politics assume normal conditions, that is, widespread prosperity for the majority of Americans and the absence of a major foreign war. This, in fact, has been the climate in which American political life has matured for most of the last two hundred years. Under these conditions, very few people are seriously interested in politics except professional politicians, professional commentators on politics, and that small minority who engage in politics as a hobby or with a view toward appointed office or other personal rewards. This latter group, who are to a large extent responsible for many of the current successes of the political system, includes members of party executive committees, party women's clubs, and volunteer advisers and campaign workers of major political candidates, many of whom expect to have an opportunity for creative participation in the forthcoming administration should their candidate win.

In a world in which the primary political force is indifference, the primary political asset becomes money or its equivalent, incumbency. Political candidates can be sold like soap or toothpaste, particularly where voters pride themselves on being ''independent'' and ''voting for the man and not the party.'' The higher the level of cynicism on the part of the candidate, the greater his chances of success, thanks to the media. With enough money, it is possible for a good advertising firm to build for a candidate an image of courage, honesty, perseverence, decisiveness, and diligence—to make him or her simultaneously a populist and a great defender of industry. The higher the office, the broader the area in which the person is running, the less the person is personally known by any of the electorate, the higher is the probability that a campaign run by a modern-day Dr. Goebbels will be successful.

The problem of seeking a champion reminds me of the day I asked a local resident which of two restaurants in a small town was the better. He answered that they were both about the same, but whichever one I went to I'd wish to hell I'd gone to the other. If politics is like a town, the range of choice is comparatively small; when there is a vacancy in a high elected office, usually it is filled by someone who has been a resident for quite a while. The advantage of incumbency in an office other than the one for which the candidate is running is epitomized by this book. Were I not an incumbent judge, this book would never have been written or published. Yale University Press will spend money publicizing the book and getting me television interviews to promote sales. This would greatly promote my image as a statesman if I were interested in running for the U.S. Senate. For a nonincumbent to purchase the exposure which publication of this book can potentially generate just in West Virginia he would need to spend $100,000.

Leaders who are genuinely motivated by the general good quickly become discouraged. To organize serious political activity first requires money, and getting it is the hardest part of politics. The reason that people go to court rather than to the political process to get the law changed is that courts are much cheaper. To make an impression on politicians, except at the local level, it is necessary either to elect one's own man or to organize thousands or millions of voters; to make an impression on courts requires nothing more than a good case and the comparatively small sum of money to hire a lawyer.

Absent a pre-existing issue with a built-in constituency in search of a leader, organizing individualistic citizens into an effective political machine is both a thankless and a Herculean task. Political organizers usually fail because they are unable to raise the money or exact the work necessary for success from their would-be constituency. I once attended a local N.A.A.C.P. convention where there were about three hundred members present, a prominent black national speaker, and some serious political discussion. On the last day of the meeting it came to fund raising, and the big push was to enlist lifetime members at $500 each. Notwithstanding the impressive record of the N.A.A.C.P., nobody agreed to pledge for a life membership, and, in fact, nobody even offered to take some of the less expensive memberships which required more than normal dues. The exhortations for funds continued for at least forty-five minutes; everyone was enormously embarrassed, but everyone kept his billfold in his pocket.

Not only is it expensive to organize a movement, it is almost impossible to find a real champion to enter the political foray on one's behalf, unless one happens to be Howard Hughes or some other millionaire. In order to run successfully for congressman, senator, or governor from any position other than incumbency requires in my experience about $250,000 of the candidate's *own money*.[3] Unless people have enormous inherited wealth or psychotic ego problems, they are usually not willing to part with that type of money even if they have it—especially if they count all the hours and heartbreaks they spent accumulating it. Political leadership, therefore, is largely concentrated in the hands of either the young, who will run for office on a shoestring ignorant of the miracle necessary to beat well-financed opposition, or careerists. In general, the careerists have the edge.

At the local level, where the grievances are shared by a definable constituency, it is still possible to develop a grass-roots organization financed by nickels and dimes, but on the state or national levels, effective leadership is stymied by unmanageably diffuse constituencies. At the local level, ordinary people can become passionate about building a new highschool, putting in a new park or civic center, or even providing some low-income housing and imposing rent control. How can voters become passionate about correcting youth unemployment in the urban ghettoes? There may be passionate concern in the ghettoes, but the problem is a national one, and its solution requires national passion. We know how to build a school, how to build a park, how to build a housing project; we do

3. Obviously it costs more money to run for an open seat or as a challenger for governor or United States senator, but I have known many congressional races as well which cost over $250,000. Scholarly investigations of the subject such as Gary C. Jacobson's *Money in Congressional Elections* (New Haven: Yale University Press, 1980) place the amount of personal money at a lower figure; however, scholars are often relying primarily on *reported* figures. While many people do run successfully for high office on less money, nonetheless, a real professional who does not want to lose will not feel secure in filing with less than the $250,000 I have indicated.

not know how to employ three million people and keep them *productively* employed. Passion develops around an identifiable problem and an apparently understandable solution. Shutting down nuclear plants is a much easier program to get behind than a crash effort to substitute clean nuclear fusion for dirty nuclear fission.

Not all inertia or lack of political participation is directly attributable to cynicism or frustration—much of it comes merely from recognition of the natural limits of issue-oriented politics. The most startling revelation which I had as a young member of the legislature was that government is technical 99 percent of the time and ideological less than 1 percent of the time. Hardly fifteen of the votes I cast as a young legislator had any partisan overtones—the splits, when they occurred, tended to be based on geography, types of industry in different counties, and prolabor versus antilabor philosophies. Usually legislation which reached the floor (as opposed to being killed in committee) passed without significant dissent. Government, as I quickly found out, is a mechanical undertaking. I stood in absolute wonderment when I discovered that in any session of the legislature the media will concentrate on three or four issues, such as capital punishment, legalized gambling, unionization of public employees, or sex education in the public schools, while a thousand other bills can either be passed or killed without the slightest ripple of public concern except from those directly involved. On the state and national levels, the universe of voters divides on every technical issue into sets, but the sets change for every new issue, so that there are seldom consistent alliances. John and Dave are for proposition X, while Steve and Bill oppose it; then Bill and John are for proposition Y, while Steve and Dave oppose it.[4]

There is no correlation between political rhetoric and intelligent programs to solve problems. Rhetoric is usually emotional, while programs must be technical. For example, in West Virginia it has been fashionable for almost a century to run for the state legislature on a platform of "making the out-of-state corporations pay their own way." Ironically, at the same time that recently elected members of the legislature are devising new and imaginative schemes for shifting the tax burden to national industry, the commissioner of commerce and his entire staff are actively

4. The preeminent rationale, by the way, for the Supreme Court's absolute prohibition on state support for church schools, as set forth in *Meek v. Pittenger,* is that it will encourage alliances forged along religious lines and that these alliances may be so strong that they will carry over into other areas of government. Thus, the continued changing of the sets in accord with the parade of issues is a constant, intelligent policy and not just an accident.

seeking to attract new out-of-state corporations to West Virginia. While politicians and the press have convinced themselves, each other, and the world that West Virginia is exploited, the state has an entire department of government in the business of recruiting exploiters. This paradox is simply explained. In many of West Virginia's northern counties, the industrial working force is employed in obsolete plants which were built fifty years ago, and the owners of these plants have the option of rebuilding them where they currently stand or moving them to any other state in the union. Coal mines, obviously, must be located where there is coal, but western coal, which can be strip-mined in nonunion, politically hospitable areas, threatens even this economic mainstay. As soon as a young legislator recognizes the need to entice plants to stay in his area and new ones to relocate there, his relations with industry suddenly become far more cordial, nothwithstanding his earlier populist pronouncements about doing in the "spiders from Wall Street." The voters, of course, after a hundred years of this process fully understand that notwithstanding any platform rhetoric about "making industry pay its own way" they will be sold out in the end. The problem is not usually that the legislator has been bought, but that he has promised the impossible without knowing it himself. The voter, in turn, gives up and stays away from the polls.

That, of course, is not the whole story; there is still the outright purchase of members of the legislature through retainers for legislators who are lawyers, lavish campaign contributions, seductive business deals, or expensive entertainment. Where these practices are uncovered, there have been crusades against corruption, and in the negative, crusading process the political system fired by the press works reasonably well. However, even scrupulously honest legislators frequently look like crooks, because experience informs them of the conflicting goals which are urgently felt by different segments of their constituencies. For a politician to understand this problem himself and act upon it is one thing; to explain it in a sufficiently understandable way to make it acceptable to the various sets of self-interested voters is quite another.

Voter indifference and candidate image building combine in the United States to make all of elected politics for high prestige offices a game played by rich men and incumbents. Occasionally it is possible for someone to challenge an incumbent with someone else's money, as when a former governor with many outstanding obligations to collect takes on an incumbent U.S. senator; however, that particular set of circumstances is rare. Except in a few populous states with hugely disproportionate numbers of politically interested citizens, such as New York, incumbents seldom have any serious opposition, for not only does incumbency itself provide mountains of free publicity, it also actually provides instant access to large sums of money.

Incumbency is the equivalent of money, for it provides free access to the media, speaking engagements, and a paid staff with the ability to send out, at government expense, vast quantities of personalized mail long before a campaign actually begins. Furthermore, incumbency provides two, four, or six years of free news coverage which, with a little intelligence, can be orchestrated and manipulated to create for the incumbent the same image of courage, honesty, perserverance, and so on which a good advertising firm would create around election time for the nonincumbent.

Incumbent governors, U.S. senators, and congressmen control the fate of giant industries. If, for example, a coal producer owns a mineral lease on a thousand acres of land with marketable coal in an isolated, mountainous area, it is critically important whether the state builds a road into that particular inaccessible area. The same applies to a real estate developer who wants a highway interchange adjacent to a new housing project. With a telephone call, a governor can tell the Department of Highways either to construct twenty miles of modern blacktop along a former state-maintained cow path, so that coal can be transported, or order a new interchange constructed on a state highway adjacent to the new housing project. In either event, large private profits accrue as a result of the expenditure of state funds in an inefficient manner. At election time a governor's services along these lines are remembered, particularly since the same governor, between the time he files for reelection and January, when he would go out of office (if he should lose), can with another telephone call "upgrade" the new mountain road, detouring all traffic along it via a new cow path for ten miles, or order the new interstate interchange demolished. Senators, congressmen, and state legislators can play the same game in one way or another in direct proportion to their power in the body in which they serve.

The aspirant for office, regardless of party, can make promises only for the future, while the incumbent can deliver today. People with big money to contribute to political races are usually interested in what an officeholder can do for them right now or what he has done for them in the immediate past. Consequently, the incumbent will have ready access to a "volunteer," usually a professional lobbyist, who, without any effort on the part of the candidate, will find fifty or a hundred executives to cough up $1,000 each. Two or three such creatures are the making of a successful campaign. Corporations cannot contribute directly, so in anticipation of such a demand the executives' salaries will have been raised with the understanding that they will make political contributions, and it is the job of lobbyists to round up the checks from clean, reportable sources and deliver them to the incumbent.

In 1971 I had the temerity to announce my candidacy for the United States Senate for the 1972 election. The incumbent, Jennings Randolph, who was then seventy-one years old, had given some indications that he would retire; I never believed he would retire, but I did believe I could beat him. As long as people thought that he might retire, I was accorded a cordial welcome and even raised a few thousand dollars, but when he announced for reelection a solid wall went up in front of me, and I could not even secure an audience from any major interest group such as labor, coal producers, or the Chamber of Commerce. Senator Randolph had been a fine senator and had numerous friends, but what I experienced in terms of a freeze-out was not the effect of warm friendship, but of raw power. It was at that point, as I indicated earlier, that I decided it was better to be a winning state supreme court justice than a losing United States senator, so I took my small organization and the statewide name recognition I had bought with the campaign contributions into a lower stakes game which I could win. I outspent my opponents ten to one and won the primary election for judge by 35,000 votes and the general election by 54,000. The outcome had nothing to do with my legal ability, but with inherited name recognition, the enthusiasm and charm of youth, and money—most of it either mine or my father's. My grandfather, Matthew Mansfield Neely, had been either U.S. senator or governor of West Virginia from 1922 to 1958, and his record caused the voters to be favorably disposed toward me. Consequently, I used inherited incumbency, which was the equivalent of a paid image-building program. I have watched the process at sufficiently close range to know that when I run for reelection for judge I would rather have an impecunious Oliver Wendell Holmes as an opponent than a well-financed Jack the Ripper.

Any incumbent political figure who assumes the leadership of an activist group endangers his political career in the long run. Joseph Tydings from Maryland forfeited his seat in the U.S. Senate in the 1970 general election because of his outspoken support for gun control. People who make their livings from political office quickly learn from object lessons like Tydings that leadership of militant groups will earn them so many enemies that they will become vulnerable as yesterday's enemies are added to today's. Consequently the very class of careerists upon whom society relies to ferment political action have themselves the most to lose from political action. Every political figure whom I know personally, except John D. Rockefeller, IV, actually needs his salary from political office and would suffer a personal tragedy if he were thrown out of office. The market for used politicians is not a booming one. Championing causes, therefore, is usually left to amateurs, mainly the young, who do not have any government-financed logistical support, but everything to gain and nothing to lose from being a crusader. Even a blind hog gets an acorn occasionally; enough crusaders upset well-entrenched incumbents that crusading is an acceptable political activity at the entry level. The Joseph Tydingses of the world, however, show the dangers of crusading in the higher ranks of incumbency. The relevant point of focus for our discussion of courts is not that the political process frequently works the way we want it to, but rather that much of the time it does *not* work the way we want it to.

The result of the financing process is that a hierarchy of people whom any incumbent must satisfy naturally develops. At the top are the media. If they are unhappy, they can decimate a candidate's image regardless of how much money he spends. Next are lobbyists, who can raise big cash. Finally are the broad group of indifferent voters who do not want anything and can be satisfied by rhetoric, symbols, personal charm, trips for schoolchildren, or an occasional computer-programmed birthday card. Citizens who have definite, discrete grievances find it difficult to get themselves on the political agenda because of what could loosely be called the "Tydings Syndrome." Taking stands on controversial issues generates bad publicity, may antagonize the media, and may deter large campaign contributions. In part, this is why aggrieved groups come to the courts both as a first resort and a last resort.

The Federal Election Campaign Act of 1971, as amended, has not improved this sorry situation one bit and is, in fact, a travesty of the election reform which it so loudly promised. By prohibiting contributions in excess of $1000 from any individual, while at the same time not providing for the public financing of congressional campaigns, Congress did nothing but pass an incumbents' full employment act. The biggest lie is the half truth. Since people do not want to contribute to political campaigns any more than they want to contribute to the March of Dimes, the challenger must kill himself raising funds in nickels and dimes. It is for this reason that for a nonincumbent successfully to run for high elected office requires about $250,000 of the candidate's own money. An incumbent can always extort, and I use the term literally, the seed money for a campaign from the unwilling hands of those with whom he does business. The only counterweight to the extortion process is that the constraints of election reform do not apply to a rich challenger, because by U.S. Supreme Court holding there is no limitation on a person's use of his own private funds. Of course, if a challenger is taking on an incumbent who has been outrageously hostile to well-heeled interests, the same lobbyists who usually help incumbents may assist the challenger. That seldom happens.

Money has two political functions: (1) to create name recognition and a favorable image through paid advertising and (2) to get favorably disposed voters to the polls. In the ordinary primary election (and in most states having one predominant party the primary election is *the* election), only 22 percent of eligible voters turn out. If, by hiring heads of families for, say, somewhere between $100 and $500 to drive their entire brood or entire community to the polls (and give them instructions on who "the candidate" is), a candidate can muster an additional 5 percent of the registered vote, the effect will be decisive, as I demonstrated at the beginning of this chapter. Nothing, however, will protect an incumbent from a truly outraged constituency. No amount of money could have reelected Herbert Hoover in 1932, and no advertising agency, regardless of resources, could rehabilitate Richard Nixon. When it comes to the negative aspects of participatory democracy, the myth system and the operational system are entirely congruent; it is with regard to the positive aspects that the disparity arises.

It is interesting to pause for a moment to speculate whether in a perfect world it would be possible to have an issue-oriented political process which could accommodate itself to every grievance. Probably, even if everyone at birth were given money either to run for office or to support others, the result would be almost the same as it is today. The political process addresses inflation, energy, conservation, ecology, employment, and housing; would there be time for everyone to become "politically active" on such issues as damages for the Human Rights Commission or reform of the personal injury law? If there were numerous political parties oriented to every narrow issue, we might have a government like that of Italy, which changes with the lunar cycle. One reason that there are not more forces at work to make us like Italy is that the courts are handling the problem. We need now to focus on what problems they should handle and legitimately *can* handle and what problems they should leave to other institutions.

When I was a boy I used to drive an old International Harvester

Tractor. Tractors generally have hand throttles, so that the operator can use clutch and brake simultaneously, and the throttle device is set by locking the lever along a bar of metal which looks something like a saw. There are about eight speeds, but if you need a speed between 5 and 6 you are out of luck. So it is with elected politics; there are occasions when a discrete change in the law is needed, but the change is neither so uncontroversial as to be slipped through as a technical amendment nor so universally applauded as to become an issue.

In 1967 the West Virginia legislature passed a statute outlawing discrimination in employment and housing and established a human rights commission. In the manner of these things during the 1960s, the main authority the commission was given was to conciliate or order the elimination of discrimination; it was not specifically empowered to award money damages. The result was mainly a legislative speech without any teeth to enforce it. West Virginia has approximately a 7 percent black population, most of which had no idea of the technical problem in the enforcement of its rights. Even if all of those affected had known the problem, it is unlikely that they could have mobilized sufficient political support to change the law—the effort involved would have been prohibitive. Furthermore, if any major political figure had made human rights one of his campaign issues and talked about awarding money damages for discrimination, he would have gotten the votes of the affected black constituency and lost the red-neck vote. In recognition of the frustrations to be encountered in the political process, the Human Rights Commission came to my court asking us to interpret the law in such a way as to empower the commission to award money damages; while such authority was not specifically granted in the statute, it was not specifically withheld either. We ruled that the commission had "implied" power to award limited money damages, because that was what was needed if the Human Rights Commission was to be effective. Probably the legislature had intended only to make a speech—a purposeful compromise. We knew, however, that an unorganized constituency of 7 percent needed help and could not get it from politics.

It would be misleading to imply that all issues not addressed by the political process can be addressed by the courts. I mentioned briefly the problem of ghetto unemployment and the difficulty in developing sufficient national passion about the subject to provide a political solution. Ghetto unemployment, however, is not a problem which can be attacked directly by the courts, although the courts can nibble at the fringes. Giving teeth to the Human Rights Commission was a small nibble, and other tiny bites have been taken by other courts elsewhere.

Substandard ghetto housing is an example on a national scale of an issue where courts have tried to take up the slack from the political process at the fringes, because that narrow issue was amenable to judicial attack. The original law which permitted indifferent, unscrupulous landlords to charge outrageous prices for squalid accommodations stemmed from the nineteenth century, when people who rented farm land were expected to be responsible for the outbuildings located on it—a legal structure highly unsuited to the modern apartment dweller. In urban America a person does not rent just acres, but a whole bundle of services such as hot water, heat, elevators, clean public areas, and adequate parking. Under old common law the landowner rented his premises "as is," and the tenant had no choice but to pay rent or move, notwithstanding no hot water, broken elevators, and vermin infestation.

Slowly the courts began to change the rules, so that a tenant could refuse to pay rent, do his own repairs, deduct the cost of repairs from the rent, and stay in possession against a landlord's efforts at eviction. This new judge-made law had the effect of redistributing the wealth, but the same result would inevitably have come after tortured birth pains from the legislative process. At the same time that the courts were formulating the new rules, there were bills in the state legislatures which would have done the same thing. Every year these bills gained more support, but as we shall see in the chapter on the legislature, they were successfully resisted by concerned minority opposition. In this regard what the courts did was to simulate a democratic result because of the structural hurdles to putting problems of a limited constituency on the political agenda. Critics of courts rightfully point out that the "structural hurdles" are not accidental and that they are deliberately in the system to forestall precipitous change. There is a lot of truth to this criticism, and one of the problems with defining the permissible limits of judicial lawmaking is to recognize those cases where structural hurdles are purposeful and those cases where they have an unintended effect.

Critics of the courts usually draw an arbitrary line about court lawmaking. In the area of noncontroversial legal issues, such as torts, contracts, and administrative law, even violent opponents of judicial activism have always assumed that the courts would make the rules subject to the legislatures' changing them. For example, the entire law of products liability, which makes manufacturers responsible for defective products, was court initiated, even though it completely shifted the cost of injuries from the individual to society. Early in the twentieth century, if a person purchased an automobile and the wheel fell off, whoever was injured was out of luck unless he could conclusively prove that the manufacturer was negligent. Without belaboring the point, the primary change was a shift from liability based on a theory of negligence, or moral blameworthiness on the part of the person causing the injury, to a theory of liability without fault, where the person or company in the manufacturer-distributor-consumer chain best able to protect against this type of injury through insurance was responsible. After a sophisticated insurance industry had been developed, the courts felt it appropriate to place the risk of this type of injury on manufacturers, because they could insure and pass the cost along to consumers as a class.

To support their condemnation of modern activist courts, critics like to point to earlier periods in the history of our legal system when, they claim, courts knew their place and stayed in it. They imagine an idyllic era during which courts did nothing but decide criminal cases, resolve contract disputes between individuals, and render judgments concerning oxcart accidents on bucolic English country lanes. In that distant mythical past, the solemn berobed, bewigged (and probably benighted) jurist squirmed in horror at any petition which sought anything more than the most routine resolution of disputes. This pastoral idyll may contain a kernel of truth with respect to English jurisprudence today, but there is no doubt that a serious assertion that this was the way judges acted during the important periods of legal development would be the most obscene historical revisionism. Any idyllic view of the English judiciary, at least during two periods which we will discuss here, is about as accurate as a modern academic monograph depicting Genghis Khan as the spreader and nurturer of culture. The old English judges were a wild, power-hungry, omnipotent bunch, and they were making all the law for England long before the notion of a parliament (or legislative branch) ever crossed the minds of the illiterate whoresons and churls who mobbed at Runnymede in 1215.

In England after the Norman conquest, the king was a big man, but he was not as big as he wanted to be. He aspired to centralize all power in the crown through officers of his own choosing, to improve the efficiency of taxation, and to bring the "king's peace" to all the shires of the realm. When the term "chief magistrate" is used in our modern law (for example, in the federal statute concerning the extradition of criminals from one state to another), it refers to the chief executive, either the president or a governor, not to the chief justice or any other judicial officer. Our continued use of this term is evidence of a definite historical congruency which no longer exists, for not too long ago it was assumed that the executive authority—the king—was also the supreme law-giver and the supreme judge. Henry I and his successors, at least until the fifteenth century, took this seriously and actually held "court" to decide disputes. In the early stages, the judges were deputy kings, and this meant that they came with all the powers of the king when they were out on assizes—court sessions held as a convenience to subjects in shires distant from the king's court. In a society in which hardly anyone but the clergy (including the king himself) could read and write, when all of England had fewer than three million people, when cities were only villages and villages only farms, and when the concept of law was nothing but tradition at best and caprice at worst, the king's judges made all the law. Whatever they said in individual cases became precedent, and, through this precedent, they established a law which was "common law." Clearly "common" in this context does not mean "vulgar," but "uniform." The judges made the common law, and even then people complained bitterly, particularly unsuccessful litigants.

Interestingly enough for the purpose of providing a perspective on modern criticism, the critics of that period also looked back to a golden age under mythical good kings when the judges either did not exist or decided only the most routine, noncontroversial issues. Thirteenth-century critics, for example, claimed that the judiciary was less activist under good King Edward the Confessor, a pre-Norman king noted for his morality and justice, who allegedly left the administration of justice to the landlords. The authority for this view came from an alleged collection of laws which were usually referred to as the *Lex Edwardi Confessoris*. These purported laws of the earlier period did not exist in any coherent, consistent written form, and never had existed except in the imagination of dissatisfied litigants, until the judges turned the whole idea to their own use and began spouting new law based on the supposed *Lex Edwardi*. In the final analysis, oddly enough, the *Lex Edwardi Confessoris* found its highest use in giving an aura of legitimacy to the judges' creative production of useful public policy. The *Lex Edwardi Confessoris* generated as much confusion and provoked as many diametrically opposed views in its day as the Constitution of the United States does now. Both created a Delphi in need of an Oracle.

What does all this history have to do with courts in the United States in the 1980s? The history is important to demonstrate that a system of government is evolutionary except when there are extraordinary upheavals such as foreign invasions, conquests, or social revolutions. While the judges of the thirteenth century may not spring instantly to mind in the twentieth century, they did spring instantly to mind in the fourteenth, and those of the fourteenth in the fifteenth, and so on. Even now in the twentieth century, debate rages among the American judiciary on many issues and is fueled by the experience of nineteenth-century judges whose cases are read daily and whose memory is still fresh. Gradually a pattern of judicial conduct emerges, and having withstood the test of time, is made legitimate; as with all evolutionary systems, both social and biological, it is often difficult to determine when or how a particular piece of the system entered it, or more important, why. Whenever onc sees a part of the evolved system, either social or biological, which appears to create more trouble than it is worth, the first question to be asked is whether it is a tonsil or a liver. If the former, it can be excised; if the latter, it can only be tinkered with.

One of the most important evolved concepts concerns the idea of "natural law" or principles which are so obvious that no sovereign power can ignore them. In the latter part of the reign of Queen Elizabeth I, citizens and members of the legal profession seriously debated what the "law" was. Was it the bare will of the sovereign? Most thought not, particularly if such will were exercised without any attempt to consult the estates of the realm. Was it the sovereign in parliament? Most thought it probably was, although such eminent lawyers as Sir Edward Coke believed that the law had a natural life of its own which transcended all sovereign power, either king alone or parliament alone or the two combined. The United States has chosen sometimes consciously, sometimes unconsciously, to follow Coke's natural law approach articulated in the beginning of the seventeenth century, and with our written constitution we have had the perfect vehicle for implementing the theory of natural law. As that great lawyer Aaron Burr once said: "Law is anything which is boldly asserted and plausibly maintained."

The reason that we have never had any serious problems with the idea that courts can make law is exclusively historical. Unlike Italy, whose democratic institutions were developed entirely within the last century at the high watermark of democratic rhetoric, American institutions evolved from English institutions which were originally feudal. The first lawmakers in England were the courts, and the legislative branch developed around that function—consequently, it was presumed that courts, not parliament, would make most of the laws, subject to parliament's having a veto power. The intelligence of this basic structure becomes immediately obvious to every member of the legislative branch who knows that when the state legislatures and Congress are heated by emotional issues, there is little time left for technical problems like products liability, which nobody gives enough of a damn about to organize political pressure to change. Since somebody has to think about these issues, and since the changes the courts make are usually considered justifiable because they are in response to changed economic and social circumstances, this huge area of law is considered the legitimate province of courts.

All of this is fine in theory where we are dealing with genuine routine, technical issues, but ambitious courts and energetic judges expand the definition of "routine" and "technical" to anything which interests them, while modest courts and lethargic judges find security in sedulously following precedent regardless of its wisdom. Concrete rules about what constitutes a routine, technical matter and what constitutes a major political change have never been drawn satisfactorily. While technical changes in the common law are reviewable by a simple legislative majority, generally legislative review is sufficiently cumbersome to preclude reversals of most court-initiated policy. It is difficult to get *any* technical matter on the political agenda; the same forces of inertia which impeded change of the *old* landlord–tenant law also impede legislative change of the *new* landlord–tenant law. Although common law development may be more easily integrated into the standard theory of democracy than constitutional law development because of the legislative veto power, enough people have been burned by today's fast-paced common law development that even this area of policymaking has been considered recently as a sign of an imperial judiciary.

This brings us then to the fundamental point of this chapter, namely, that one of the critical elements for evaluation in determining the appropriateness of court lawmaking in both constitutional and common law contexts is whether the change is entirely technical and can be justified by cogent analysis of economic and social circumstances (such as spreading the risk of injuries) or whether the change is highly controversial and in an area which is *actively* being addressed by the executive and legislative branches. The closer a decision comes to being purely technical, the greater the legitimacy of court action, while the closer a decision comes to being a value judgment rather than a technical judgment, the less legitimate the court's decision.

Most people are not outraged about routine court-initiated changes in legal mechanics; rather, they are outraged by courts' imposing a new value system on them. Here it is instructive to borrow a concept from economics, namely, the idea of the "modernizing elite." In the study of underdeveloped countries, there usually appears a polarization between an elite, educated in the West, which seeks a modern economy (capitalist, communist, or mixed), and a majority which wishes to maintain a traditional society. The modernizing elite has power disproportionate to its numbers, because it has a monopoly of the medical, engineering, educational, and military services. The price which the traditional majority pays for the advantage of twentieth-century life in the way of medicine, engineering, etc., is domination by a group with which it does not agree in terms of many basic values. This country has the same type of domination by the "modernizing elite" of the judicial, legislative, and executive branches.

There are certain values that are usually held tenaciously by people trained in the great universities who disproportionately staff the upper echelons of government and the media. Raw power dictates that this value system will be vindicated more frequently than any other both in government policy and media propaganda. The U.S. Supreme Court case of *Roe v. Wade* concerning abortion proves the point. That case said that the Constitution protects the privacy of the doctor–patient relationship during the first trimester of pregnancy, thereby legalizing abortion; however, the real grounds for the decision concerned quite different issues than those addressed by the judges in their opinions. Uncounted thousands of women every year were having illegal abortions, and many were dying from unskilled medical treatment. Legalization in a number of jurisdictions such as the District of Columbia, Colorado, and New York created intense discrimination against the poor, who could not afford to travel to a legal jurisdiction. Finally, there was the prospect of millions of unwanted children being brought into the world as a result of the more permissive sexual norms of the sixties. Obviously, a leadership class in a democracy whose values are too much at odds with a sizable majority will soon cease to be a leadership class. Far more frequently than not, the leadership class does reflect the values of a majority; however, the proponents of competing values do not have a fighting chance to become the majority.

Roe v. Wade offers a complex interweaving of both technical and value considerations. It is the classic marginal case for court intervention into policymaking. On the one side, there was the cost of welfare for unwanted children along with the hidden cost of increased crime and social disruption from children with no family love or discipline. The values involved, on the other side, were the most sacred a society can hold: the sanctity of life; the propriety of premarital sex; and the morality of the frustration of the divine plan for procreation. These were pure values and had nothing to do with science or social engineering. Obviously, if a majority of the Supreme Court had graduated from Notre Dame or Bob Jones University, *Roe v. Wade* would have been decided differently; as it happened, of the nine men on the Supreme Court who decided *Roe v. Wade,* only Mr. Chief Justice Burger and Justices Marshall and Douglas had not attended Yale or Harvard for an undergraduate, graduate, or professional degree. Justice Douglas, however, had taught at Yale. *Roe v. Wade* can be explained to traditionalists only as usurious interest exacted by the modernizing elite for its monopoly of power.

In terms of legitimacy we can make a comparison between change in the abortion laws and changes in the West Virginia Human Rights Commission's power or in landlord-tenant law. Abortion involved highly controversial values; the fact that abortion *had* been legalized in three jurisdictions indicated that it was a subject which was actively on the political agenda. This was not the case with regard to the Human Rights Commission or landlord-tenant law, as the value decisions had already been made. The legislature's own equal rights bill *was* the value determination regarding the Human Rights Commission, and for landlord-tenant law the New Deal decided that people should not be exploited because of need, particularly with regard to such basic necessities as housing. There was instant majority support for both human rights enforcement on the state level and new landlord-tenant law on the national level. Abortion, on the other hand, has continued to tear the political community asunder. It is an issue which enters most important political races, including the one for the mayor of New York in 1978, an office which has no power to do anything about it.

Historically, the outrage against the modernizing elite has subsided within a decade because attitudes change quickly and in the direction of the "modern" value. Also, people finally give up and move on to other issues. *Roe v. Wade,* for example, was decided in 1973 at a time when the Gallup poll showed that two out of three Americans thought abortion should be a decision between a woman and her doctor. In 1968 an earlier Gallup poll had shown that only 15 percent of American voters favored a similar proposition. By 1969 the percentage was higher, but even in 1969 there was a *majority* in favor of legalizing abortion in only one statistical category—those having a college education, again the modernizing elite.

Unlike the natural sciences, the science of law does not work with constant principles, such as gravity, but rather with human beings. No one has ever established a satisfactory theory of when courts should legislate; all we know is that court legislation has generally been favorably received notwithstanding vocal, organized, minority criticism.

Courts often pragmatically embrace a course of action which theory cannot countenance. At the heart, however, of all court legislation is the fact that the political process is no more faithful to pure theory than the courts; the political system has inherent structural defects which foreclose its dealing effectively with certain issues and as a practical, rather than a theoretical, matter is no more "democratic" than the courts.

3
THE LEGISLATURE

The structure of American society consists of interlocking privileges produced by past special interest legislation so pervasive that we accept disparate treatment for different groups as quite normal and commonplace. Almost every recognizable group enjoys some advantage which is not enjoyed by others: bulk mailers can send heavy junk for less than a housewife can send a postcard; homeowners can deduct interest on their mortgage payments from taxable income, while apartment dwellers cannot deduct any part of their rent; industries hit by strikes receive no government aid, while striking workers get food stamps; businessmen can deduct from taxable income personal cars, airplanes, and thinly disguised vacation travel, while factory workers pay tax on every cent of income; welfare recipients get a subsistence dole, while minimum wage employees receive barely more for a forty-hour week; and railroad employees may sue their employers in federal court for full damages for work-related injuries, while airline and truck workers must recover under state workmen's compensation.

Regardless of the origin of special privileges, the groups who benefit from them are wedded to their continued enjoyment. New legislation in any area will disturb the expectations of some group, even if disturbing such expectations is not the primary purpose of the legislation. There is constant warfare in the political process among special interest groups and between special interest groups and what can quite imprecisely be called the general public. Railroads are at war with trucks; coal is at war with oil; domestic producers of steel are at war with users of cheaper foreign steel; and environmentalists are at war with industry. A legislature frequently does not get credit for the thing which it does best, namely, prevent the passage of very bad law sponsored by the powerful predators of the political jungle. Most of the impetus to court activism stems from the phenomenon that a legislature cannot be designed which will pass good legislation in a timely manner and simultaneously prevent the passage of dangerous legislation. Although the legislative process is confounding to those with urgent political agendas, there is nevertheless a similarity between a legislature and a local health department which, through its routine inspections of everything from sewers to restaurants, prevents far more illness than the hospitals ever cure.

The time-tested tactic for passing special interest legislation is to create a connection between the benefit for the affected interest group and a general benefit for society as a whole. This is almost always the origin of tax shelters. Does it, for example, really alleviate the housing shortage to give real estate developers the benefit of accelerated depreciation on new apartment buildings? This particular tax incentive permits an investor with a million-dollar building to "shelter" taxable income from other sources of about $100,000 a year for ten years. The developers argue with some plausibility that in the real estate market of the 1980s it is impossible to build apartment houses at a profit without this government subsidy; however, owners of existing buildings are not given a comparable tax advantage, and when new buildings are built with the tax incentive subsidy, rents will remain lower than they would be if there were a greater shortage of available housing. Developers and renters profit, while owners of existing rental units suffer. Since there are more renters than apartment building owners, democracy dictates that subsidizing apartments is in the "public interest." The builders of new apartment units are predators in one sense; they seek to make a profit at the expense of the treasury and indirectly at the expense of the owners of existing, unsubsidized buildings. If legislation favoring apartment construction is predatory in one sense, it is in the public interest in another, so that the legislative process is called upon to balance advantages to one group against disadvantages to another. I cannot conceive of a statute which will not make someone worse off.

A legislature is designed to strike this balance among interest groups. In every session of Congress, for example, the National Association of Manufacturers and the AFL-CIO each rush to have legislation introduced that will hinder or help unions in organizing successful strikes. A recurring issue in this war of bills is the appropriate limitations on the third-party boycott, that is, strikes against employers who are not directly involved in a particular labor dispute but who do business with an employer who is. This is the whole issue of common situs picketing, which concerns large construction sites where each subcontractor has its own separate gate for its own employees; under existing law, if the union strikes a subcontractor the union can picket only its gate, not the entire job. The elimination of this rule limiting the parties affected by a strike is high on the agenda of the unions, while the passage of a national right to work law (which would make it illegal for union membership to be a condition of employment) is high on the list of priorities for employers.

Much of the subject of this book concerns the courts' arrogating unto themselves the role of lawmaker, a function traditionally thought to be legitimately the exclusive function of the legislature. However, even when the courts are going full speed at the lawmaking business, they still try to limit their lawmaking to "general interest" law as opposed to "special interest" law. The distinction between the two, as we shall see later, is not nearly as clean-cut as we would like, but nonetheless, the distinction can be made, and without it any analysis of the proper law-making function of courts becomes utterly incomprehensible. Legislatures have intentionally designed a cumbersome procedure for themselves in comparison to the fairly streamlined procedure of the courts, because they wish to frustrate the passage of special interest legislation. Judges, in general, are under no political compulsion to be solicitous of the avarice of special interests; however, since judges do have lawmaking powers, interest groups are enormously concerned with the philosophy and prior associations of any potential judge. Where judges are elected, both business and labor will put forth candidates, although usually they will do nothing for them in terms of providing the mother's milk of politics, to wit, money. The difference between judges and legislators is that judges can betray their benefactors without fear of future retribution and usually, although not always, they do. All of President Nixon's appointees to the U.S. Supreme Court consistently held against him on cases involving Watergate. If judges did not engage in universal betrayal, some other neutral force would need to be invented.

If the National Association of Manufacturers comes to federal court with a suit alleging that the closed shop, which makes union membership a condition of employment, is unconstitutional, the federal court could dismiss the matter without any political repercussions. The classic misconception about courts when they are compared to legislatures is that courts do *not* set their own agendas but rather hear all cases brought to them, while the legislatures set their own agendas in response to pressure groups. It is true that the courts do not go out to solicit cases, but courts can pick and choose those issues which they wish to address from the thousands which are brought in any given year. The courts frustrate predators by saying there are no legal grounds for relief, frequently though the classic issue-avoidance techniques of lack of standing, lack of ripeness, mootness, or because the issue is a "political question." None of these concepts, by the way, determines its own application; the men on the courts do that and through the manipulation of these concepts set the courts' agendas. What occurs is that issues are constantly put on the courts' agendas and disposed of adversely to the predators. This is exactly what happens in the legislatures, but the mechanics are different.

Unlike judges, legislators are elected for comparatively short terms, and predators are not philosophical at election time about legislators' negative if occasionally statesmanlike responses to their selfish pet causes. Since judges can retreat into the legal mumbo-jumbo of constitutional, statutory, or common law, all but the most sophisticated predators believe that they have been frustrated by some set of neutral rules rather than the public policy vision of individual judges. Legislators, however, are permitted no such luxury, and it is from the need to be able to say "no" without dire personal political consequences that the cumbersome procedures of the legislature spring. Consequently, contrary to popular conception, the difference between courts and legislatures is not procedural but substantive; both can pursue any agenda they wish. Usually the courts concern themselves with the general issue calendar, while the legislature is concerned with the special interest calendar. Both calendars are legitimate concerns of a well-balanced society, and both are necessary.

A legislature must give a hearing to every group of predators that comes down the pike. Nobody likes special interest legislation; even legislators who sponsor special interest legislation to please their constituents often dislike their participation in the process. Nonetheless, the advancement of special interests is central to democracy, particularly since occasionally the special interests are correct that there is a congruency between their interests and the general interest. The tax shelter for new apartment houses is an example of this congruency. Since legislatures must devise institutional procedures which disguise their efforts to reduce the number of successful raids by powerful predators on the common weal, the courts have been put in the business, through historical trial and error, of compensating for the inevitable inertia which the procedures of the legislature foster. In general, courts actively seek to vindicate the public interest, but that, of course, ducks the issue of whether the courts' view of the public interest is in fact the public interest. As we shall see later, even generally recognized public interest law changes have their predatory side.

The sanctions which powerful predators can impose on elected officials cause the legislative agenda to be disproportionately concerned with special interest issues. Furthermore it is the height of political folly to make a frontal attack on any proposed special interest legislation. During my tenure as a state legislator, there was a fight between the AFL-CIO and the West Virginia Education Association over teacher representation. The question came down to a definition of the appropriate bargaining unit in schools (although West Virginia does not have collective bargaining for state employees in the formal sense); the union wanted the bargaining unit set by statute to include all personnel in the schools, which would have placed cooks, bus drivers, janitors, and auxiliary personnel in the same unit with professional teachers. This would have assured an AFL-CIO-affiliated union of being chosen the bargaining representative for the entire group instead of the teachers' professional association; however, there was no sentiment among the teachers for AFL-CIO representation. Since collective bargaining was not required by statute and since it was illegal to strike, the teachers preferred to use their professional association for bargaining. I voted against the AFL-CIO-sponsored legislation, and the AFL-CIO never supported me in any election thereafter. Not only that, but to this day, after the passage of almost ten years, the leadership of organized labor has consistently given me the cold shoulder notwithstanding a sterling "labor record" as chief justice in such areas as workmen's compensation, consumer protection, and products liability. If the average voter attention span is very short, that of professional lobbyists is very long.

The AFL-CIO versus teacher fight is a good example of the private warfare which goes on continuously in the legislative process. In that case the teachers' association could deliver as many votes as the union. The problem facing individual legislators becomes much more complex, however, when all of the militant, organized groups are on one side and the unorganized consumer or taxpayer is on the other. It is only at this juncture that the salutary effects of a brilliantly designed, inherently negative process can be fully appreciated by the general public. Originally, in fact, the medieval parliaments, which were the direct ancestors of our modern legislatures, were set up, not to initiate policy, but rather to give or withhold assent from policy made by the king. The purpose of parliament was to restrain other institutions of society—king, powerful nobles, judges, and royal officers—from interfering with the complex matrix of interlocking privileges which were usually referred to as "the traditional rights of the subject." In former times people were more willing than they are today to identify with the forces of conservatism; it is unlikely that any modern political party would echo Simon de Montford's thirteenth-century political slogan, "nolumus leges Anglicae mutare" (traditionally translated, the laws of England will never change), yet people want security in the continuance of their privileged positions as much today as they did in the Middle Ages at the dawn of parliamentary development. What they often fail to realize is that an *institutional* system which gives them security in *their* vested interests also gives everyone else security in his vested interests.[1]

At the heart of the negative process of a legislature is a system which brings very few issues to the floor for a vote. Given that most legislation is sponsored by powerful interest groups, the preferred method of protecting the common weal is to "kill" predatory bills rather than to "defeat" them. The wisdom of this tactic became obvious to me *after* the AFL-CIO applied its sanctions. The difference between "killing" and "defeating" legislation is that when a bill is "killed" very few people are on record as having voted against the legislation, while "defeating" a bill entails a record vote by the entire Congress or legislature.

The fascinating mechanics of "killing" legislation begin with the committee system. Any legislative body is divided into small groups, ostensibly so that technical expertise can be developed in limited areas. The chairmanship and membership of these committees are determined in different ways in different legislative bodies; however, committee assignment and committee leadership are always some function of seniority, appointment by leadership committees, and election by the members. The most powerful officer in any legislative body is the presiding officer, such as the Speaker of the House of Representatives, unless, like the vice president of the United States presiding in the United States Senate, he is a ceremonial figurehead, in which case it is the highest officer elected by the members, the majority leader in the case of the U.S. Senate.

The West Virginia legislature is a typical example of this system. There the Speaker of the House of Delegates and the president of the Senate appoint all committee chairmen and committee members. The presiding

1. In this book I am concerned primarily with the mechanics of a legislative process which is essentially negative. The clash of vested interests is essentially a fight over income shares, and while I give a few examples of the skirmishes over income, it is beyond the scope of this book to explore the shifting alliances and complete military history of the various battles which have been fought in recent years. Suffice it to say that since the emergence of a formal, bicameral parliament in the reign of Edward III, the legislature has been the primary battlefield in England and the United States for the fight over income shares which occurs somewhere in every society. The best analysis which I have read of the actual battle being fought in the United States in the 1980s is found in Professor Lester C. Thurow's book, *The Zero-Sum Society* (New York: Basic Books, 1980).

officer is, of course, first elected by the entire membership, so that there is a continuous trading of votes in the race for presiding officer, for chairmanships, and for memberships on powerful committees. When a bill is introduced into one house of a legislature, the presiding officer or the rules committee determines to which committee it should be assigned. The committee chairman, in turn, can assign it to a subcommittee which can do numerous things from reporting it back immediately to the full committee with a favorable recommendation, to holding public hearings, to permitting the bill to languish on the calendar until the expiration of the session. Consequently, the fate of any piece of legislation depends initially on the discretion of the presiding officer (and his professional staff—a force never to be discounted) and the committee chairman. If, for example, there are two committees which could evaluate a bill, one of which is liberal and the other conservative, the fate of the legislation is determined in the first instance by the committee to which it is assigned. If the committee chairman is more conservative than the majority of the membership, he can manipulate the committee result by his selection of the subcommittee or his timing of the issue on the agenda.

The decisive power of committee chairmen is a direct result of the limited time available for considering bills. It is this time limitation which makes position on the calendar critical. Unlike private industry or the executive branch, which are ongoing concerns, all legislative assemblies meet for fixed periods and then dissolve. Death through consignment to the foot of a calendar which will never be considered in its entirety is the safest technique of bill murder. The Congress of the United States ends every two years, and legislation which has not passed at the time Congress adjourns must start all over again in the next Congress. Consequently, every moment which legislation can be delayed moves it ever closer to oblivion. In state legislatures, where there are many new members, the leadership encourages public hearings, heavy concentration on emotional issues such as capital punishment, and a lot of brief meetings combined with long weekends during the first 80 percent of a typical two- or three-month legislative session in order to limit the time available for the consideration of most legislation. The closer the end of a legislative session, the more important becomes the setting of committee agendas, the manipulation of the Rules Committee, which determines whether bills will be placed on special calendars for expedited treatment or permitted to languish on the "regular" calendar, and the conference committees composed of senior members of both houses.

The power of conference committees is utterly awesome; even when both houses have agreed on legislation in principle, the conference committees can refuse to iron out minor differences in form, which inevitably results in the sun setting on the legislation. Just to emphasize the critical effect of mechanics, in my young, freewheeling, political days, I was a party to the *physical* waylaying of messengers carrying conference committee reports between the Senate and House on the last night session, so that bills clearing conference would not arrive in time to be accepted by the House and passed. The less drastic techniques of waylaying involved engaging the messenger in conversation for an hour, feigning illness, or giving a bogus urgent message resulting in a lengthy wild goose chase. In even earlier days, when legislative sobriety was scrutinized a little less closely, it was not beyond contemplation to invite the messenger to "take a sip," thus lubricating the "engaging in conversation" technique of waylaying. If the messenger, who was always a member of one body or the other, was stupid enough to be waylaid, it was all considered fair. (I am deeply repentant now, of course.)

In Congress the committee chairmen determine the fate of a bill not only by their control over the agendas but also by their power to determine the expenditure of committee funds, hiring of staff, and the referral of bills to subcommittees. The control of funds and staff can be manipulated in a cynical way to have a chilling effect on all members who are not either of consummate integrity or independent wealth. Junkets, office space, and patronage appointments depend upon the good will of the chairman.

Many of the highly touted reforms of the 1970s in Congress were really mirages, particularly the modification of the seniority system, which was extensively publicized. The seniority rule is actually a custom and not a formal rule of Congress, but it has been observed faithfully. There is a good reason; in a body composed of hundreds of ambitious, egotistical, arrogant individuals, some mechanical rule for advancement is essential lest everyone spend all of his energy jockeying for position and power within the body rather than on necessary work. Here is our first example of the complex human engineering problems which are inherent in the running of a legislature. While the mechanical advancement which seniority guarantees may be essential to prevent member alliances based on internal politics rather than external issues, the seniority system inevitably has a profound effect on the substance of legislation. In the 1950s and 60s when over 50 percent of the chairmanships were held by southern Democrats, committee power was used to block civil rights and social welfare legislation. Reform has made some inroads into the chairmen's power; for example, they can no longer refuse to hold committee meetings at all. Now three members can request a hearing from the chairman in writing, and if he refuses, seven days later a majority of the members may call a meeting. Reform, nonetheless, has operated in only the extreme cases. In the relevant range of day-to-day legislation, agenda control, budget and staff control, and a spirit of going along in order to get along keeps the outcome of most issues still firmly in the hands of a small group in the leadership.

Since 1975 all committee chairmen in the House of Representatives have been elected by secret ballot. This procedural reform resulted in the ouster of three committee chairmen in 1975, and the Senate followed suit with other reforms which reduced the power of committee chairmen. Ostensible procedural reform notwithstanding, complex psychological and sociological factors utterly confound the reformers. For example, the more liberal and socially active legislators opt for committee assignments where they will be able to take a direct part in the writing of legislation in housing, education, and jobs. The more conservative members gravitate toward the powerful committees that control the *internal* legislative process, such as the Rules Committee or the Appropriations Committee. A liberal committee may present a bill which then languishes in the Rules Committee or is entirely gutted in the Appropriations Committee through lack of funds. Were the memberships reversed, of course, there would be no legislation to languish or be gutted.

For those with urgent political agendas who are highly accusatory when they allege that legislatures are "do nothing," it should become apparent that a legislature is *designed* to do nothing, with the emphasis appropriately being placed on the word "designed." The value of an institution whose primary attribute is inertia to politicians who wish to keep their jobs is that a majority of bills will die from inactivity; that then permits legislators to be "in favor" of a great deal of legislation without ever being required to vote on it. When constituents seek to hold a legislator responsible for the failure of a particular bill, he can say, plausibly, that it was assigned to a committee on which he did not serve and that he was unable to shake the bill out of that committee. If he has foreseen positive constituent interest, he can produce letters from the committee chairman in answer to his excited pleas to report the legislation to the floor; correspondence of this sort is the stock in trade of legislators. Notwithstanding the earnest correspondence, it is quite possible that when the legislator and committee chairman were having a drink before dinner, the legislator indicated his personal desire to kill the bill in spite of the facade of excited correspondence.

I once introduced a bill in good faith which would have permitted the aged to ride school buses free of charge, so that in rural areas they would be able to get to town during the day. The press gave the bill much favorable publicity, and the elderly were enthusiastic; however, the school authorities quickly explained to me that the elderly and school children have incompatible diseases and that the mixture on a school bus would be quite dangerous to the health of both. In addition there were other practical problems which made what sounded like a good idea quite unworkable. Consequently I had the bill killed myself, although I did not announce that fact publicly. I would not personally have cynically engineered such a result from the beginning, but the rewards of consummate cynicism cannot be lost on the reader.

There is a certain irony in the fact that in order for the democratic, majoritarian institution of a legislature to function, procedures must be designed which frustrate a democratic, majoritarian result. A few representative figures should demonstrate conclusively that the entire legislative process is designed to avoid the passage of legislation. For example, in the 95th Congress, which met from 1977 through 1978, 18,045 bills were introduced in both houses, while only 634 passed. In New York during the 1977–78 session 39,842 bills were introduced, while 1,758 passed; in Illinois in the 1977–78 session 5,345 were introduced, while only 1,518 passed; and in West Virginia during the 1977–78 session 3,270 were introduced, while only 277 passed. Certainly it would be possible to bring every bill automatically to the floor of each house for a vote, letting the chips fall where they may. Committees could evaluate bills all they wished and make reports to the floor during debate on the legislation; however, every bill would be voted upon within six months of introduction. If what a majority of legislators really wanted was to *pass* legislation, this system would inevitably have evolved. While inexperienced members frustrated by their own lack of power within the system often urge reforms which would lead more or less to this automatic vote system, such proposals are routinely voted down by large majorities. The reason is quite obvious—members who come from highly politicized constituencies recognize that if such a system were ever implemented they would either be required to vote for every predatory bill which comes up or anger so many powerful interest groups that their political life expectancy would be about as long as that of an artillery forward observer.

The conservative organization of a legislature is nothing more than a procedural system designed to achieve a substantive result. Since the alternatives in legislative organization are either to permit all legislation to come to the floor or to screen it through a system of committees, we are led to the ironic conclusion that regardless of how a legislature organizes itself, the institution will pass either too much or too little legislation; it cannot organize itself both to pass good bills and kill bad bills. If, for example, a legislature were to organize itself to bring all legislation to the floor automatically, there would be such a rush of predatory legislation that the role of the courts would be completely reversed. In order to provide balance to the structure, courts would then engage in the wholesale striking down of vicious legislation. This, in fact, was what the courts sincerely thought they were doing during the New Deal, when the Congress tended to expedite administration-sponsored legislation without extensive screening. Regardless of what one thinks of the merits of the New Deal (I still have a portrait of Franklin D. Roosevelt looking down at me in my study as I write these words), a careful reading of history of the U.S. Supreme Court from 1933 to 1938 will disclose the mirror image of today's activist courts; in that era the courts would not permit legislation which appeared in the least degree predatory to stand.

It is often argued that the courts of yesteryear were curmudgeonly, conservative agents of property owners. In fact the courts of yesteryear were probably as activist and innovative as today's courts according to the knowledge, mores, and academic economic principles of the time. In the nineteenth century, the courts grafted the vision of Adam Smith's *Wealth of Nations* onto the due process, contract, and commerce clauses of the U.S. Constitution, created both labor and capital mobility, and protected infant industry from crippling damage awards before the advent of universal insurance. While the Supreme Court of the 1930s was operating under Marshallian economic principles which later Keynesian economic principles made obsolete, nonetheless, the Court *actively* pursued its vision of proper public policy according to the generally accepted, academic economic principles of the time. When Congress rubberstamped every administrative proposal, many of them violating these principles, which dictated a sharp separation of government from the private sector, the Court felt compelled to vindicate the ancient learning. When Mr. Justice Stone argued in the 1930s for judicial restraint, he did nothing more than work backward from a conclusion on the merits of administration policy to a logical reason for the conclusion, namely, principled reluctance to have courts substitute their judgment for the executive's. The whole history of the Supreme Court during the depression, however, really stands only for the proposition that, historically, courts balance legislatures, which, as we said before, will inevitably pass too much or too little legislation. When they pass too much, the courts look negative and conservative; when they pass too little, the courts look liberal and activist.

The courts have always been concerned that the democratic process may return consummate incompetents to Congress who will proceed to dismantle machinery which has proven successful for decades or that competent legislators will be so pressured by popular outcry that they will accomplish the same result. Fortunately, the legislatures themselves are concerned with the same problem. A legislative body is composed of all sorts of people. Therefore, one of the jobs of the leadership is to prevent important decisions from being made by either outright fools or novices who mean well but lack the requisite technical experience. Getting elected to Congress does not mean that the candidate is knowledgeable about any of the issues before Congress or even about the legislative process itself. While a legislator may come to the capital with his own agenda for improving the environment or curtailing beef imports, there is no reason to believe that he knows anything about running post offices or choosing wisely between nuclear fission and nuclear fusion research, both of which may be competing for limited funds. This is the compelling reason for dividing among different committees and their paid, professional staffs the responsibility for handling legislation. The committee system makes it possible for legislators to specialize in certain fields and to develop more than a passing knowledge of critically important technical matters. There we again confront a sociological phenomenon similar to friction in physics; while the committee system provides needed expertise, its inevitable result is concentration of power and inertia.

The cantankerous Wilbur Mills, for example, who was chairman of the House Ways and Means Committee until his precipitous fall from office in the wake of a sex and liquor scandal in 1975, was always the archetype of the autocratic chairman. He did, however, have sufficient power to prevent any amendments to tax legislation within the committee, with the salutary effect that the design of what was already one of the most complex legal structures in history was in the hands of professional staff and experienced tax lawyers. His departure from office is reflected in the Tax Reform Act of 1976, which is the most perplexing piece of tax legislation ever passed in the United States. Tax practitioners unanimously agree that it would be better to pay significantly higher taxes than to try to operate under the provisions of this act, which requires impossible records and enormously expensive accounting. Even a lawyer with tax experience and some aptitude for the subject cannot understand routine subjects like capital gains. Anyone who doubts this conclusion need only pick up the 1979 tax supplement to *American Jurisprudence,* one of the two great law encyclopedias, and read the section on capital gains. While equity and complexity are almost inseparable in any modern tax scheme, there comes a point where complexity is such that no one can understand the law well enough to follow it. In technical areas like tax, the autocracy of a Wilbur Mills is almost universally appreciated, yet where a committee chairman like Wilbur Mills has the power to do good things, that very power implies the further authority to gut tax bills to achieve results which may not be consistent with the policy directions of a majority of the members.

More troublesome to the political theorist, however, is the indirect consequence of any power to control legislation, namely the power to trade for one's own account. Trading for one's own account has been with us as long as parliaments. England had one experience with a unicameral legislature during the Long Parliament and the Rump Parliament in the civil war of the 1640s and concluded from that experience that two separate houses make it more difficult for legislators to *pass* legislation for their own purposes. An active House of Lords became a pleasant relief during the Restoration, and while American democracy was heavily influenced by the philosophy of the Commonwealth, the value of a bicameral system with a Senate imitating the House of Lords was never seriously doubted. In Norway the constitution establishes a unicameral legislature, but the pernicious qualities of such an institution are so widely known that the Norwegian unicameral legislature has divided *itself* into two separate houses, which by internal rules must each independently pass a given piece of legislation.

Congress is composed principally of professional legislators. The problem of trading for one's own account is far more acute in the states, where part-time legislators come from the insurance industry, trial bar, teaching profession, and organized labor, bringing their own or their employers' briefs to the legislative process. Possibly the most pervasive and most sophisticated form of bribery in legislatures is for special interests to *retain* lawyer members ostensibly for routine legal work, but with the implicit understanding that legislation unfavorable to the client will miraculously find itself at the foot of the legislative agenda. God protect us if a legislature were designed so that individual members could *pass* legislation. The advantage of high-level courts is that while judges may be either stupid or benighted, or both, they are not for sale.[2] The committee system assures that the committee chairman, who has the power to *kill* legislation entirely, will not also have the power to *pass* legislation through both houses, because while he may have enough muscle to kill or pass a bill in his own chamber, he cannot automatically get the legislation past the committees of the other house, where the control over patronage, staff assignments, budgets, and junkets is in completely different, unrelated hands.

The institutional analysis of this chapter so far leads to a major conclusion which is critical to an analysis of the proper role of courts, namely, that the most valuable thing which legislators have to trade is inactivity, because that is the product which they can most easily deliver. This simple fact alone accounts, to a large extent, for the do-nothing tendency of any legislative body. Legislators instinctively seek out constituencies which will pay campaign money and political support in return for no legislative interference with their vested interests. This is not, by the way, the constituency which a hot, young, enthusiastic challenger seeks out, because that constituency is quite satisfied, thank you very much, with the incumbent. Once an incumbent, however, these are the constituencies who are most visible and most easily coaxed into a symbiotic relationship with any *former* hot, young, enthusiastic challenger. Three or four legislators in proper strategic positions can almost assure their patrons that adverse legislation, such as the elimination of the oil depletion allowance, will not pass. Even if public outcry pushes the legislation through both houses of Congress, delicate and cynical engineering can kill it with *everyone* voting for it. The experienced manipulator's stock in trade is guaranteeing that the bill will pass both houses in different forms—thus never becoming law.

This technique is known as "loving" the bill to death and, hypotheti-

2. There is one exception to this rule. In all states but West Virginia and Wisconsin, the legislatures set the judicial budget, which causes most courts to be circumspect about angering legislators. In the federal system, the influence of any individual member is too limited for him to have an effect on a judge, but I wonder about the states. Fortunately, West Virginia's founding fathers had the wisdom to give the judiciary authority to set its own budget, and while the legislature sets judges' salaries, it cannot cut staff, destroy offices, or eliminate programs as exercises in spite.

Nonetheless, I once decided a case adversely to a very prominent lawyer member of the state Senate. The decision changed the entire law of arbitration in West Virginia (a tedious commercial subject), and it is the best opinion I ever wrote. The senator was furious, and in the next session he spearheaded a movement to amend the state constitution to remove budget-making authority from the Supreme Court. Had the resolution passed the legislature, there is little doubt it would have been ratified at a general election, and it was only the inherent conservatism of the legislature which saved the independence of the judiciary.

cally, it involves the following technique. One house passes a bill which not only abolishes the oil depletion allowance but imposes a punitive recapture tax on previous depletion credits as well. The other house abolishes the depletion allowance but imposes no punitive tax. The conference committee deadlocks, because the house proposing the punitive tax refuses to recede from this aspect of the bill while the other house refuses to impose it. Thus everyone has voted for the repeal of the oil depletion allowance; one house is able to go home bragging that in addition they would have "punished" the oil companies for their unjust prior favorable tax advantages, while at the same time the depletion allowance remains on the books for yet another session.

The legitimate need for control, direction, and expertise which we have already analyzed causes the trading mix in any given legislature to reflect not relative power positions of constituencies or even some objective "need" for legislation, but rather the personal agendas of individual members multiplied by some factor which is determined by a member's position in the internal hierarchy. Montana, for example, has some of the largest and best-staffed veterans hospitals in the United States; the interesting thing, however, is that Montana has very few veterans to use them. When Mike Mansfield from Montana was Senate majority leader, he arranged for the Veterans Administration to build these hospitals, which now provide the major medical resource for everyone in Montana. Mansfield not only used his enormous personal power to get federally funded medical facilities to his remote constituents; he also made sure the Veterans Administration had rules for the facilities' use which permitted access to everyone, regardless of veteran status. In this venture, he was aided and abetted by the Veterans Administration bureaucracy, which was urgently aware of the imminent decline in the veteran population and, like the March of Dimes after the elimination of polio, is a bureaucracy in search of a raison d'être. The Montana example demonstrates that although the legislative process is always a log-rolling, pork barrel operation, the trades do not necessarily bear any relation to the importance of the constituencies affected. It is the internal power position of the person representing the interests which is determinative.

Since all sophisticated members of any given legislature recognize the selfish goals of their colleagues, there develops an inevitable negativism about the agendas of the other members. The inherent conservatism of a legislature is, therefore, a function of two converging forces: first, the tendency of any large organization to be negative, because it is easier to criticize the work of others than it is to do original work oneself; and second, the historically inherited structure of the body, which over the centuries has evolved its present form in response to society's need to say "no" to special pleas far more often than it is able to say "yes." In addition there is a matrix of personal rivalries which fire the natural tendency to criticize; ambition must always justify itself by philosophy, and if there are no real philosophical differences, they must be manufactured. Legislatures cannot be composed of lifeless, passionless, neutral machines; they must be composed of men and women, and the rites of passage which make it a long and expensive process to get elected to Congress or the state legislatures almost guarantee that only those with ambition and an ego drive will be elected.

My grandfather once explained to me why southerners had such disproportionate power in both the United States Senate and House during his tenure in the Senate. Southerners, he said, did not acquire power merely because of seniority; rather they acquired power because they were the only people in Congress to whom a member could talk about the *member's* agenda. According to his analysis, southerners usually came to Congress through a political machine which brought them up through the local ranks of the state legislature, local sheriff's office, county commission, or some other elected position and then sent them to Congress when it was their turn. In the more populous, industrial northern states, wealthy, ambitious men competed for high elected office and used their personal wealth to buy a one-on-one relationship with the voters through the media. While some of the southerners had either made money or came from old families with a little money, most of them entered politics as a way of making a living and had a more modest view of their own mission than those from states where every election is a contest which only dynamic image builders with insatiable egos can survive. Attractive, dynamic image builders have such an exalted sense of their own importance that they begin every sentence with the pronoun "I" and are usually not selected as social companions by their colleagues. Nevertheless, it is from social companionship that political alliances are formed. The power of the southerners was based, in part, on personal rapport and good will, which must always be reflected in the work product of the body. I remember that many of my grandfather's good personal friends were senators with a completely different political philosophy, and while friendship may not have changed votes on the Taft-Hartley Act or matters of similar import, personal rapport can go a long way toward passing or defeating less visible legislation.

The nature of elective politics is not calculated to foster cooperation and mutual aid. Members of Congress aspire to be United States senators and United States senators aspire to be president. In a legislative body, power tends to accrue to members without ambition for higher office, because they stay home and work. Ambition will cause a legislator to calculate each day's actions in terms of how many press releases can be generated or how many militant constituencies can be satisfied rather than in terms of the overall value of the collective work product. In any multimember body, it is always the unimaginative, unthreatening, plodding beast of burden in whom other members will place their trust. Former U.S. Senate Majority Leader Robert C. Byrd has often said that he has no agenda. That is probably why he was Senate majority leader. Sometimes a creative and imaginative person has enough patience and perseverence to disguise himself into a beast of burden long enough to acquire ultimate power. Robert Byrd always protests that he is a workhorse and not a show horse. History will ultimately pass judgment on whether he is a counterfeit or real beast; he will never tell until retirement.

The clash of rival ambitions and the matrix of personal friendships frequently have more to do with the product of a legislature than any issue in elected politics. Where I was successful as a legislator, it was often as a result of a chance friendship with the senior Republican member of the House of Delegates—a farmer from rural Grant County—who had absolutely no personal ambition whatsoever. His name was Larkin Ours, which is a bit ironic since *ours* means "bear" in French and Larkin looked a bit like a grey bear. He had massive hands and an inveterate predilection to chew tobacco, which is how we came to be friends. By accident we sat across from each other in the Finance Committee and Larkin would chew all morning; however, he was far too much a gentleman to spit in public, so he would hold his tobacco and spittle for an hour and a half straight without relief. That, unfortunately, precluded him from talking, so his method of interrogating witnesses before the Finance Committee was to pass me a note under the table with incisive questions which I would then propound to the witness as my own. Since Larkin had been in the legislature for twenty years, he knew more about the state budget than any other living human; *his* questions convinced the watching press that *I* was the most brilliant young legislator to come along in years. We played this game for quite a while and came to trust each other. Larkin would routinely cosponsor my bills and generate support for them among the rural membership. In return for this, I always stood willing to defend the farm interests on the floor whenever asked, so that I became an honorary member of the farm bloc.

When once I was about to announce passage of one of our bills, I asked Larkin what he wanted me to say about him in the press release. His answer was that he had been elected from Grant County for twenty years because he knew every resident of the county personally and that he was not going anywhere from the legislature. "You're the one who's running for the Senate, not me," he said. "What the hell do I need a press release for?" The result of his unselfish personal support was that Larkin could have had my vote on just about any issue which concerned him; on two occasions I orchestrated floor fights against legislation sponsored by the commissioner of agriculture, which the farmers were against, without knowing or caring about the general merits of the legislation. Both bills were roundly defeated, and the farm bloc solidly supported me in my race for the state Supreme Court.

Personal friendships like Larkin's and mine are just the top of a complex sociological iceberg. The matrix of relationships within any legislative body is almost beyond description, because it does not remain constant. Committee chairmen with extensive agendas trade bills to members of other committees in return for nudging other chairmen to release legislation on the first chairman's agenda. The members who have no leadership position often feel that they have not been dealt with fairly during a particular session, because none of their bills has come out of committee, so out of spite they frequently vote "no" on several important leadership bills just to show that they too have some power. For example, a member of the West Virginia House of Delegates from Brooke County had only one item on his agenda for many years—legalized slot machines. His bill never made it to the floor, and for the last several weeks of every session he always voted "no" on everyone else's legislation, with the exception of those who had assisted his efforts to get the slot machine bill out of committee. I never suffered from his ire, because I knew that a majority of the Finance Committee would never vote the bill out, so I voted for it, notwithstanding that I would have voted against it on the floor had it ever made it.

Each house of a legislature has a personality of its own as an organized, collective intelligence. Political theory would have it that differing lengths of terms and differing sizes of constituencies dictate different consistent tendencies, but the liberal or conservative institutional ideologies which political scientists would predict based upon these objective factors just do not occur with any predictable regularity. Frequently the senates are far more innovative than the lower houses, although they were generally designed to be more conservative. It is the personalities of individual members in significant leadership positions and not the length of their terms or the size of their constituencies which gives each house its collective agenda. While the structure of an institution determines the relative importance of inertia versus individual will along with the general types of issues with which the institution will be concerned, it is personalities which determine the level of priority and likelihood of passage of any given issue on any given legislative agenda. If a powerful U.S. Senate Public Works Committee chairman wants a particular bill providing black lung benefits to coal miners, he can put that legislation high on the Senate's agenda by making internal trades which guarantee his bill a priority position on the agenda; such legislation may be unwelcome in the House, however, and there then ensues a trade of a bill high on the House's agenda in return for the black lung bill.

It cannot be emphasized enough that getting a bill through a member's own house is relatively simple in comparison to getting a bill passed in *exactly* the same form by both houses. The process is so cumbersome that the efforts of the members alone are usually insufficient; professional, paid lobbyists are almost always necessary to monitor the progress of legislation and to prepare its way. Legislation which has paid staff in support of it has a far greater likelihood of passing than legislation which has only the support of a few members with their limited resources.

I was once asked to sponsor some enabling legislation allowing the issuance of county development bonds to finance major industrial pollution control devices. The primary beneficiaries were the public utilities, but it was definitely a public interest bill, because any expense borne by a regulated utility gets passed through to rate payers. Under the bill, companies could solicit the counties to initiate revenue bond issues which, because the bonds would be interest-bearing obligations of local governments, would provide tax-free interest to bondholders. This tax advantage would then cut the interest rate in half for financing environmental equipment. It seemed like a good idea to me, but the bill was hardly high on my personal agenda. Miraculously, I no sooner put my name to the bill than it cleared committee and was passed not only by the House, but by the Senate as well. That bill had been ''greased to go'' within the leadership; I was asked to sponsor the bill only because the leadership wanted the legislation introduced by a member who would not bring any personal animosity to the issue or invite trading by the membership on the bill to grease the way for Sunday horse racing, legalized slot machines, or higher weight limitations for coal trucks using public roads. The legislation had been drafted by the utility company lobbyists, who had it in proper form for my signature; furthermore, they had approached every important member to urge its passage *before* the session had begun and proceeded to remind committee chairmen of their pledged support during the session and inspired them to place the issue on the agenda.

In this regard it is fruitful to compare this process with what usually occurs when legislation is introduced to improve juvenile facilities or for some similar social purpose. There is no paid lobby for juveniles, so that interested members must do all the leg work in addition to urging their other bills. There is no entertainment budget, no dinner meetings with the added inducement of free, good food with appropriate accompanying liquor. There is no paid staff to gather facts, prepare paper work, or monitor progress. Finally there is no political support to be traded.

The enormous edge which legislation proposed by paid lobbyists has in the legislative process becomes quickly apparent when it is remembered that the average member has very little time to work on legislation. The professional lobbyist can devote full time to one or two bills and coordinate the efforts of all positive, but only marginally interested participants in the process. Close attention to the schedule of any senator or congressman will disclose remarkably little time to read bills, evaluate legislation, or consult with colleagues to move bills on their merry way. Between meetings with one's constituents, answering the mail, serving the ombudsman function for constituents in their dealings with the administrative agencies, speech-making, and traveling home to mend fences, the average legislator is so busy getting reelected that he has little time to do his job. Professional lobbyists not only monitor the progress of legislation and designate developing traps; they usually draft the first proposed bill and provide the legislator with detailed factual information which is the product of extensive research. Skillful lobbyists can do one further thing: permit the legislator to trade for his own personal account. Lobbyists, as we discussed earlier, are extremely good at raising money, and in the case of the labor union lobbyists, they can even deliver direct political support at election time.

This then leads us to an analysis of two related concepts, namely, agenda and access, as they relate to the legislative branch and the courts. It should be obvious from the discussion so far in this chapter that the agenda of a legislature is not necessarily dictated by the constituencies represented but rather by the legislators themselves. Anyone can get a bill introduced into the legislature on any subject; I have known legislators who would introduce a bill on anything for a constituent and place "by request" after his name as sponsor. Further, I have never known a "by request'' bill to emerge from any committee. Constituents often believe that their issue is on the agenda because a bill has been introduced when, in fact, without a militant proponent, the process itself has already determined that their issue will receive no attention at all. This is particularly true of general interest legislation as opposed to special interest legislation. The difference, of course, is the absence or presence of professional lobbyists. In the two years I served in the legislature, literally five times more attention was devoted to dog and horse racing than to the entire problem of state institutions—penal, mental health, and medical put together. The reason was that in the latter areas of concern, there was no ability to trade for one's own account. Constituencies directly affected by general interest legislation, like relatives of mental patients, are seldom well enough organized to assure positive political rewards to their friends or sanctions against their enemies; the racing interests, on the other hand, know who their friends are and are generous in their entertainment before election time and in their contributions at election times. Mental health patients do not vote. The very old and crippled do not vote. And, unless organized by a good machine and paid on election day, ghetto dwellers and the rural poor do not vote.

Any given legislator has limited credit upon which he can draw, and he tends to use it in those areas where he will get the highest political return. Some legislators specialize in general interest legislation, and occasionally they get some of it passed because they are good promoters in the press. The media are the one powerful lobby for general interest legislation which can apply heavy sanctions, because they are able to make almost any public official look foolish in his own home district. However, in the absence of unusual press concern, general interest legislation which flies in the face of well-entrenched special interests is doomed to failure until there is a well enough defined sense of grievance to generate militant, organized, financially backed, public concern.

While a general sense of outrage can force a general interest issue onto the legislative agenda, there must be some consensus as well about how to correct the problem which has caused the concern. No single issue, for example, so preoccupies the mind of the average voter as we enter the decade of the 1980s as inflation and the ancillary question of whether controlling inflation will ultimately bring on a depression. It is worth dwelling at some length on inflation, because the problem succinctly shows why courts cannot always be substituted for legislatures. In order for a court to serve a quasi-legislative function, the issue addressed must almost always have failed to receive legislative attention because of a *mechanical* breakdown in the legislative process, either in the form of minority blockage through the committee system of legislation which a majority wants or in the form of legislative oversight, that is, failure to flesh out remedies necessary to implement a legislative policy. In this latter class would fall the Supreme Court's implied individual cause of action on the federal Rehabilitation Act of 1973, 29 U.S.C. § 701, *et seq.* where § 794 provides generally that an otherwise qualified handicapped person cannot be discriminated against in any program receiving federal assistance. Since the only remedy provided in the act was curtailment of federal funds to the offending program, a draconian remedy, the Court concluded that in the absence of a private cause of action there would be no remedy for isolated individual discrimination unless the Court implied an individual cause of action in the courts.

The national legislative agenda in the fall of 1979 did not contain one serious proposal to curtail inflation. Notwithstanding the abysmal track record of monetary policy since 1974 as an inflation fighter, there were no serious proposals for an alternative policy along the lines of the type of wage–price controls we had during World War II and Korea. Already in the 1920s Gardiner Means observed that farm prices fell more rapidly and more severely than industrial prices, a phenomenon which was again observed from 1929 to 1932. The reason, not subject seriously to debate, was that the industrial corporations had the power in their markets—the power normally associated with monopoly or oligopoly—to exploit the inelasticities in the demand schedule for their own products and to control losses in revenue in spite of lay-offs and reductions in output. Gardiner Means coined the expression "administered prices" in the 1930s, and John K. Galbraith echoed the analysis by describing the workings of the "planning sector" in the 1970s. The use of monetary policy, which essentially involves curtailing the money supply in times of high inflation (which has the effect of raising interest rates), penalizes all industries which rely heavily on borrowed funds—particularly the housing industry, retailing, and small business in general. The beautiful, self-regulating model of the classical economists from Adam Smith to Alfred Marshall, which predicts that a rise in unemployment of labor, capital, and land will lead to a reduction in prices and an increase in sales or employment, applies only in some dream world of perfect competition. Monopolists and creatures which look like monopolists, namely, oligopolists (steel, automobiles, pharmaceuticals, oil, etc.), do not lower prices, but frequently even raise them in times of recession to limit their loss of revenue.

It has been seriously argued in the economic literature that there is only one alternative to monetary policy and that is a flexible fiscal policy (that is, one which increases government expenditures during times of recession and *decreases* them during times of inflation and full employment) combined with wage–price controls in the oligopolistic sector. Even ardent proponents of wage–price controls generally concede that they are needed or useful only in industries where big labor and big capital are able jointly to exploit their respective market positions; in agriculture, trade, and most small business, the competition is sufficiently atomistic to foreclose the need for regulation. For the purposes of our discussion here, however, the important question is not whether wage–price controls are the ultimate answer to inflation, but rather that the issue was not even on the congressional agenda in the fall of 1979, when the prime rate of interest was 15¾ percent and inflation was proceeding at 11 percent a year. According to former congressman William Moorhead of Pennsylvania, the reason that no responsible legislator had sponsored a wage–price control bill in 1979 was that the reverberations in the economy in response to the suggestion of such a plan would have been disastrous. Once industry thought that price controls were imminent, prices would skyrocket in response to the mere prospect, followed instantaneously by wages.

Neither big corporations nor big unions want their prerogatives limited by controls, and the unorganized middle class is sufficiently confused by the mystery of economics that they cannot understand the mechanics of the prescriptions offered by economists. Before the Reagan administration unveiled its anti-inflation plan, there was not even a serious anti-inflation movement; monetary policy using high interest rates suited the labor unions and corporations, because it left both these powerful market forces the power to redistribute wealth in their favor, and it suited the man in the street because it did not involve the creation of another government bureaucracy. The social security recipient concentrated not upon controlling prices, but rather upon raising social security to compensate for rising prices—a far more easily understood and fool-proof antidote.

The inflation problem points up one structural weakness of legislatures which usually cannot be remedied by the courts, namely, that before the legislative process can effectively attack a problem, there must be some consensus regarding the solution. Some of inflation is caused by excess government spending and excess government borrowing, taking money away from private capital markets to support such spending. However, in addition, one component of inflation is the hidden cost of commodities such as clean air, product safety, occupational safety, workmen's compensation benefits, and regulation per se which are real wealth but paid for in the purchase of automobiles and loaves of bread. Furthermore, there are approximately fifty million more Americans than there were in 1945, which puts increasing pressure on the price of scarce resources. An attack upon inflation would require such a reordering of American priorities and life-styles that the consensus has been that it is easier to live with inflation. While the Reagan administration in 1981 flogged Congress to attack the easiest part of the inflation problem, namely, the deficit in the federal budget, no attack was made in more intractable areas, like the ability of oligopolies and their unions to control prices and wages.

Constitutional scholars have argued that those affected most by inflation, namely, the older generation who are creditors, can force the courts to consider their agenda faster than the legislative process and that the courts could return to their former active supervision of economic matters and begin to force a curtailment of government spending as well as a system of wage–price controls. Increasingly the courts have permitted private causes of action on vaguely worded policy statutes or parts of the Constitution which probably were not intended to provide private causes of action. In one case where six unknown federal agents broke into a home and did a lot of violence, the Supreme Court implied a direct cause of action for damages from the Fourth Amendment right to privacy; in another the Court concluded that the attorney general did not have adequate resources to enforce the Voting Rights Act, so an implied private cause of action for private damages was allowed. If the courts were seeking a vehicle for action against inflation, they might start with the Employment Act of 1946, which establishes full employment as a goal of public policy. Since inflation does have an adverse affect in *some* instances upon employment, from this act alone an entire common law of inflation fighting could emerge in a ten-year period. Congress itself might very well like an excuse to balance the budget without constituent outrage leading to their own unemployment. Furthermore, significant inroads against inflation could be grounded on the due process clause of the Fifth and Fourteenth Amendments if it were alleged that the expansion of the money supply and excessive borrowing were a deprivation of property without due process of law. It could be argued that excessive state government regulation impairs the obligations of contracts under Article 1, Section 9, of the Constitution. The courts, however, are no more likely to act without consensus than is the Congress.

In the courts, any bright lawyer or small group willing to hire a bright lawyer can enlist the active attention of the entire judicial process. While it is necessary to get past a local trial judge, an intermediate court of appeals, and ultimately the highest state court or the U.S. Supreme Court, the highest state or federal court is the only decision maker which counts in terms of making broad policy, although the lower courts may be critical for its implementation. It is unnecessary to pass two courts in the same form. Consequently, the litigants need impress only a majority of a five-, seven-, or nine-man body, namely the highest court, to generate relief, which such a small, underfinanced group could never obtain in the legislative process.

Small groups who will be affected adversely by the policies of the Reagan administration can be expected to flock to the courts. Yet while the Employment Act or the Constitution may be out there for the courts to use to develop a new approach to inflation control, the courts cannot handle the problem any better than anyone else.

The goals of inflation control and high employment may be "general interest" goals, but the means are the highest form of "special interest" legislation, and for that reason inflation is a political issue beyond court competence. People very much wish that if sacrifices are necessary, they will be borne by someone else. Although courts might apply some "scientific" principles, there is little perceived science when oxen are being gored. Inflation can be controlled in the short run by attacking government programs for the poor, the ability of industry and unions to raise prices, environmental regulation, or consumer price pressure through a tax increase. None of these solutions is significantly more scientific than another. Furthermore, the losers will always ask why the winners should not bear the burden. Unlike the courts, a new administration can bring with it the ethic of the abattoir. If the courts respond to the liberals' pleas to mitigate the blood-letting they must then take on the whole problem, since they will then be responsible.

Notwithstanding the Reagan administration's intelligent concern about incentives for capital formation, much of this administration's early program was merely a direct attack on the living standards of the poor. This reflected only the dreams of its constituency who were not poor. While nothing could be more disastrous than a cut in the income tax for the middle class in 1981, since a portion of the taxpayer's new money would be spent on imports and the rest would press against already fully used domestic capacity—thus more strain on the American dollar, higher interest rates, and higher inflation—the decision to seek a tax cut was part of an overall political program where dreams and rhetoric created a limited consensus. The upper middle class will understand the folly of exclusively self-centered policies only after inflation becomes worse and the poor revolt by voting. The conservatives have a right to experiment with turning conservative wishful thinking into successful action. When they fail, as they will, their experiment will instruct public understanding so that the next experiment may represent something closer to equitable burden sharing. All the courts could do is experiment in the same way, but without the safety valve of the biennial election.

What I hope to have done by exploring the inflation example at such length is to demonstrate that courts cannot and do not substitute themselves for legislatures any time there is a problem which the legislature fails to address. The courts are successful only when they serve the limited function of shortcutting the cumbersome procedural hurdles which the legislature has created to protect us from predatory legislation, but which can also be used by a small minority to frustrate legislation which a majority genuinely desires. The Gallup polls almost conclusively prove that, with the exception of busing, in the great social issues addressed by the Supreme Court in the last twenty years, all were decided exactly as the majority would have decided them. Of course, many of the issues which the courts address are known to but a small affected group, and it is in this area of activism that the accusation of judicial legislation is much more justified, particularly as no one can know how a majority would decide those issues or what political compromises created the status quo which the courts are upsetting. Where predators have made a bargain in the legislative process, they are utterly confounded when the courts deprive them of the fruits of their contracts, and their complaints are justified, since the courts strike down only that part of the entire political compromise favorable to them without voiding the whole deal. Certainly political compromises are legitimate areas of inquiry in public law litigation.[3]

3. I can give one brief example of the "political compromise" problem which will illuminate how in narrow issues a court can frustrate the political process. In 1980 a case involving the discharge of a West Virginia deputy sheriff reached the West Virginia Supreme Court in which the deputy challenged the constitutionality of a proscription in the Deputy Sheriff Civil Service Act on "any political activity whatsoever" on the part of covered employees as violative of First Amendment rights. Elsewhere the courts, including the U.S. Supreme Court, have looked unfavorably upon broad proscriptions of political activity, unless there can be shown a "compelling public interest" in such limitations on the constitutionally protected right to participate in the political process.

When I was a member of the legislature, I had horsed the Deputy Sheriff Civil Service Act through the House of Delegates and remember that the quid pro quo of civil service protection for deputy sheriffs was an absolute prohibition on political activity, because the sheriffs' offices had previously been the most political offices in the state. (In fact, the deputy sheriffs had elected me to the

One good rule of thumb for determining the legitimacy of court intrusion into political decision making is to ask: "If this issue were to be brought to the *floor* of both houses of Congress for a vote, how would it be decided at that stage?" Court activism is generally not elitist from my experience; almost every time the Supreme Court decides a major issue, its decision would pass the above test. The courts are not generally concerned with issues where the democratic process is working, as, for example, inflation, where the do-nothing legislative result reflected faithfully a societal lack of consensus, but rather with situations where the bare *mechanics* of the legislative process frustrate a democratic result.

This brings us to a large subject which we shall address in much more detail in chapter 8 on the judiciary, but which should be mentioned here in the proper context, namely, the wisdom of irreversible constitutional rulings. The legislative process is such that there is a tendency to preserve the status quo; frequently what is needed is a disruption of the status quo, so that the legislature, the executive, and other democratic institutions can rethink a given problem. Often the courts serve the function of anarchists—they throw a bomb on the assumption that if the status quo is disrupted, the new status quo, reflecting the new consensus, must necessarily be better. Unfortunately, since courts have become accustomed to using the fiction of an objective, immutable, principled Constitution to

legislature, and my help on the civil service bill was the payment of a political debt.) However, the Civil Service Act had a routine "severability" clause, providing that if any part of the act were to be held unconstitutional, the rest of the act would stand. The result then, quite possibly, could have been that the state Supreme Court would have struck down the proscription on political activity, while leaving civil service protection intact.

In the final event, we ruled that deputy sheriffs held such powerful positions in their rural counties (in terms of their capacity to intimidate the citizenry if they were active in politics) that there was a sufficiently compelling state interest to justify a proscription on most political activity. We then recognized quite explicitly the political problem inherent in striking only part of the statute, even though its proscriptions were too broad under the First Amendment. Consequently we left the statute but explained that it could be enforced only in a narrow, constitutional way. We call this type of practical rewriting of the statute "the doctrine of the least intrusive remedy," and it has been used on a number of other occasions in West Virginia.

If we had been compelled to strike the political activity clause while simultaneously sustaining the rest of the statute, there never would have been a new law with an acceptably narrow provision proscribing certain clearly defined political activity, because the deputy sheriffs would have mobilized their machine to grind the legislative process to a halt. Under a statute which provided civil service protection but had no restraint on political activities the deputies would have been able to dictate who the next sheriff would be in most cases, and where they lost an election, they would still have been in place to harass and intimidate the winning candidate. Furthermore, a candidate who won over the active opposition of the deputies would never have been able to achieve a modicum of peace in his department, and we would have had the worst of all possible worlds. There would have been constant trading of political support for salaries, duty hours, and other benefits without the quieting effect which potential loss in spoils system politics has upon the intensity of political involvement.

accomplish this goal, they frequently foreclose the legislature from rethinking the problem creatively. In a different context, Professor Guido Calabresi of Yale has written extensively on "structural due process," by which he implies the very phenomenon of overturning the status quo which I have been discussing. The advantage of adopting this new term for our purposes here is that it may permit courts to bring to a conscious level their anarchist function, take pride in it, and leave the development of the new status quo to the legislative process.

I have been guilty of doing the exact opposite, namely, being too specific in my prescriptions for correcting constitutional infirmities, and have lived to regret it. In the case of *Harris v. Calendine,* the opinion which I wrote setting forth "constitutional" standards for handling juvenile status offenders (children guilty of no crime except truancy, promiscuity, or ungovernability), I wrote that it was constitutionally impermissible to incarcerate status offenders in the same facility with criminal offenders. When my court struck down about 50 percent of all the state's juvenile laws, there was no real rethinking by the legislature, because we established the guidelines. At that time there was a public interest law firm in Charleston, financed by a grant from Washington, which was lobbying for a revision of the juvenile code. When the court struck down the juvenile laws, the legislature just passed the bill which had been introduced by this group, since it conformed almost exactly to our constitutional holding. However, a rethinking of the entire problem would have led to a much more reasonable result in the next two years; as it actually turned out, the revised juvenile law made control of children almost impossible. Had I been wiser and more experienced, I might have foreseen the coming problems; in a legislature, with its diverse backgrounds and experiences, it is likely that my lack of foresight would have been compensated for.

The state had no "secure, prison-like facilities" which it could devote *exclusively* to status offenders, as *Harris* had mandated, so it chose to do nothing with them. The result was that we had two years of truancy, incorrigibility, running away, and general lack of control, because the children could actually quote the court opinion and the new statute. Had we been more flexible, a portion of the existing juvenile facilities could have been partitioned off for the exclusive use of status offenders, and a deterrent detention facility would still have been in existence. When, in 1979, the Department of Welfare was given responsibility for maintaining a "secure, prison-like facility" for status offenders, the deterrent effect was remarkable, and control of adolescents returned to something approaching normal. My mistake was in being too specific ab "proper" treatment of status offenders and grounding my own p preferences on immutable constitutional principles. If I had said that t treatment of status offenders was not adequately humane according to constitutional principles; that the status quo was inadequate; and that the operation of all status offender laws would be suspended until the legislature passed a new act, I would have forced the legislature to put the issue on its agenda, given meaningful access to the community leaders who were concerned with the problem, and forced the issue to the *floor* of both houses, where the democratic process would have worked quite well.

Once the institutional analysis of this book is taken seriously, it will become quite permissible to speak in terms of structural due process, that is, the constitutional right to have issues considered periodically by the entire membership of Congress or the legislatures, without the let and hindrance of the legislative process's inherent negativism. In this way courts become a useful aid to the democratic process rather than a substitute for it. Had the United States Supreme Court done this in the area of abortion, the final result (which probably would have ended up as abortion on demand in the initial stages of pregnancy if the Gallup poll is accurate) would have appeared a great deal more legitimate, and there would not now be the pressure for a constitutional convention.

I have dwelled at some length on the proposition that the courts do not pursue the special interest calendar. The distinction between the special and general interest calendars, of course, is that the special interest calendar is largely predatory. Unfortunately, the two cannot be separated entirely on the basis of the existence or nonexistence of predation, because general interest changes in the law usually have adverse effects upon large numbers of people. The question then becomes whether the adverse effects are morally justified, and there we enter upon treacherous shoals.

This is the story of *Bakke v. Cal. Board of Regents* and *Steelworkers v. Weber;* in the former case a white male was denied admission to medical school while less qualified minority applicants were admitted, and in the latter case a white laborer was denied admission to a training program while less senior minority workers were admitted. In spite of a twenty-five-year history of active pursuit of racial equality, the Supreme Court was finally confronted with the special interest or predatory nature of some of its own previous policies, which had been responsible initially for creating a climate in which affirmative action programs would flourish. The Supreme Court ducked the affirmative action issue in both cases by deciding each on narrow, nonconstitutional grounds. My own opinion is that the Supreme Court balanced the need for immediate, compensatory, affirmative action programs against the predatory nature of such programs and determined that they were appropriate in the short run but would eventually be declared unconstitutional, because ultimately there would be corruption of the means. These two cases merely stand for the proposition that today's public interest policies can, through excess, become tomorrow's predatory policies. While the goal may always be in the public interest, the means may themselves be corrupted and force a reevaluation of the means. A decision can be completely correct for its time and place, but its effect may become pernicious over time as other circumstances change. Means to laudable ends can easily become corrupted, abused, or obsolete.

Certainly a majority of the educated elite, as reflected by the attitudes of the faculties, trustees, and student bodies at major universities, consider affirmative action, although predatory, morally justifiable. It is just as certain, however, that a majority of Americans disapprove. There is no theoretical justification for continued court support of affirmative action other than the elitist one that the courts know from their superior education that affirmative action is necessary in the short run to achieve the generally applauded moral end of equal opportunity in the long run. That is probably not illegitimate, since judges are social science specialists and have available to them more information and have pursued the issue with more thought and diligence than the man on the street. Courts should probably be accorded as much deference in their decisions over means as medical doctors, professional architects, or plumbers.

In the Lincoln County school case to which I have previously alluded, the residents of Lincoln County wanted to force residents of other counties to pay for their schools by making school finance exclusively a state rather than a local responsibility. That sounds reasonable primarily because there is not very much money involved, but how would it work on a national level, where New Jersey paid for Mississippi's schools, or on a worldwide level, where the United States paid for Mexico's schools? At some point the predatory nature of wealth redistribution even in a good cause becomes obvious. That is not necessarily to say that it should not be done; it is merely to say that reasonable men of good will can differ about the long-run value of such a program.

The crucial question, then, for an institutional analysis of court activism is, do the courts frustrate the one function which is ideally suited to the institution of the legislature, namely, control of the volume and nature of predatory legislation? The answer depends upon whether one takes a broad or narrow view of the concept of "predatory." From the narrow view, even the desegregation decision of 1954 is predatory, because it made blacks better off at the expense of whites; with better education came the decimation of the buyers' market for servants, competition in the previously all-white job market, and competition for social, political, and economic power. While it was all done in vindication of social justice, it upset expectations of privilege on the part of a broad segment of society. Even reformation of the mental health and juvenile detention institutions can be viewed as predatory, since those reforms direct state or federal money away from highways, schools, local festivals, and support of the arts toward the mental hospitals and juvenile rehabilitation facilities. Nonetheless, the average citizen (a mystical creation like the law's "reasonable man" or Bentham's "economic man") does not, in my experience, conceptualize assistance to the least fortunate as predatory; the average citizen considers these movements, even integration, in the "general interest."

It is impossible to establish criteria for determining "special" as opposed to "general" interest legislation to anyone's satisfaction; it is essentially an ad hoc process predicated largely on the emotional reactions of the citizenry. Although any classification is an inherently subjective exercise, at a certain point there is such a consensus about which category should contain a particular issue that the subjective nature of the judgment becomes academic for practical political purposes. Courts probably classify issues as "special interest" or "general interest" more or less as respondents to the Gallup poll would do it.

To say that courts try to confine their lawmaking activities to the "general interest," while legislatures are avowedly the hunting ground of the "special interests," is merely the beginning of an analysis of whether a court has acted in a legitimate or a usurpatory manner when it intrudes itself into any particular political question. Unfortunately, just below the surface of what appears to be "general interest" litigation often lurk ominous "special interest" considerations. However, even recognizing that there is an overlap of special interest considerations in all general interest issues and vice versa, it is still possible now to formulate some criteria for when courts should play an activist, policymaking role.

The first question should be, is the court asked to perform a predatory as opposed to a general interest function? Second, does the affected constituency have access to the legislative process in any practical sense? Third, are there mechanical problems unintentionally created by the organization of the legislature which make it impossible for the issue to be placed on the legislative agenda even if there is practical access to the legislative process? Finally, how would the people decide the issue if it were placed on a plebiscite or if it were brought to the floor of the legislature without the interference of the committee system or leadership control?

The fact that we have formulated criteria does not mean, of course, that there will be any agreement on how the criteria should be applied; however, their mere articulation will make the decision-making process more rational than it would be if arguments continued to center on semantics and precedent. Furthermore, by recognizing the crucial effect which the organization of institutions has on the substantive product of those institutions, courts can admit publicly their quasi-anarchist function and by so doing make their interventions in the political process far less intrusive. While some judges would obviously characterize the desegregation and mental institution cases as predatory, most would not, and while most judges would characterize an effort by employers to eliminate the closed shop as predatory, some would not. Deciding between the two extremes requires judgment, which is why the controversy concerning whether courts are good or evil will never be laid to rest.

4 BUREAUCRACY AND THE EXECUTIVE BRANCH

Steve and Peggy Miller are stolidly upper-middle-class, midwestern Americans with three children, dog, and station wagon. In the summer of 1979, they decided to take the obligatory tour of "our Nation's Capital" with their children and went off to Washington to see "their government." As part of the tour, they went to the famous Air and Space Museum for the harmless purpose of admiring its architecture and exhibits—they did not even have tickets for any performance. Unbeknownst to them, however, on this particular Sunday afternoon the president of the United States *did* have tickets to a performance, and while the Millers were casually roaming the lobby, the performance ended, and the audience prepared to leave. Suddenly the doors to the theatre flew open, and two burly Secret Service men literally knocked Peggy Miller to the floor and shoved her larger husband unceremoniously out of the way (to the shock, consternation, and wonderment of the untouched children), so that the president could make an unimpeded departure. The president was out of sight, did not witness the incident, and departed screened by his entourage in complete ignorance of the physically wounded Peggy or her emotionally wounded husband. The whole episode was a ludicrous scene which would have humiliated the president if he had known about it.

The Millers are real people, and the episode in the museum is a real event. Not only was the president ignorant of the arrogant macho of his personal minions at the time, but notwithstanding letters to everyone in government with sufficient stature to warrant a letterhead, the Millers have yet to receive any satisfaction. The point, of course, is that if the president of the United States cannot control the members of his *personal* retinue, how can he be expected to control a G.S. 13 administrator in the Bureau of Indian Affairs in Wambly, South Dakota? The answer, obviously, is that he cannot.

When we begin to analyze the pervasive intrusion of the courts into the workings of the executive branch, the point of entry again must be the disparity between the myth and operational systems. The incident with the Millers is a microcosm of the disparity between the two systems, since the self-aggrandizing bravado of the Secret Service men is a parody of all the insolence, bullheadedness, and lack of consideration which can characterize any civil servant or even an entire agency when it determines to do something. The myth system tends to generalize to the huge federal and state bureaucracies the democratic, political control which the town meeting of Stockbridge, Massachusetts, has over the employees of the township. But it should be obvious that in the operational system, democratic control expressed through the ballot box is able to redress only widely felt grievances and not individual or small group grievances.

There are roughly three million civil service jobs in the federal merit system of which none is elected. In fact, in the entire federal executive branch, there are but two elected officials, the president and vice president. In the state governments, there are usually, in addition to the governor, a few statewide elected officials variously called treasurers, comptrollers, auditors, commissioners, attorneys general, or superintendents, all with executive duties. However, even where there are numerous statewide elected officials in the state executive branch, the majority of the state civil servants, ranging from five thousand to hundreds of thousands, depending on the state, are responsible to the governor.

The myth of democratic control becomes even more ironic when it is remembered that in addition to the ratios of elected officials to civil service employees, neither presidents nor governors select the civil service; its members are passed on from administration to administration. Jimmy Carter could have had the Secret Service man who knocked down Peggy transferred from his personal security force to the pursuit of counterfeiters, but he could not have fired him without invoking some very cumbersome formal procedures.

In addition to the difficulty of making those theoretically responsible to the executive operationally responsible, not all bureaucracies are even theoretically responsible to any elected official. The lion's share of the federal bureaucracy falls under the supervision of cabinet officers; however, in addition, there are independent boards and agencies established by Congress which, while allegedly responsible to Congress, are actually responsible to no one. Examples of the independent agency include the Federal Reserve Board, the Federal Trade Commission, the Nuclear Regulatory Commission, the National Labor Relations Board, and the Federal Communications Commission. The typical structure of these boards is that three to seven commissioners are appointed by the president with the advice and consent of the Senate for six-year terms and are eligible for reappointment. At the state level, there are state boards of regents which run higher education, state public service commissions which regulate public utilities, and state boards of health which administer the health laws. At the local level there is the county board of education, which may be either elected or appointed.

It is necessary to recognize the distinction between those parts of the executive branch (a most imprecise term) which are actually under the executive and those hybrid agencies which have quasi-legislative responsibilities to promulgate regulations and quasi-executive authority to enforce their own regulations. In the latter category of boards, agencies, and commissions, the absence of political control is even more obvious than it is in agencies under direct executive supervision. The point is only mentioned here, for further elaboration later, that one reason that the independent boards were created was *intentionally* to remove them from political control. What does that do to the theory of democracy?

Critics of the courts' function of reviewing the actions of administrative agencies are quick to point out that the power to review (allegedly to insure a certain procedural regularity and conformity to legislative mandates) also implies the power to substitute court judgment for that of the agencies. The question then arises why the agencies are in greater need of supervision from some other body than the court themselves. Certainly there are courts which throw their weight around like Peggy Miller's Secret Service agent. Even assuming that the personally abusive judge is comparatively rare, the more serious criticism is that judges substitute their own conclusions about the wisdom of administrative policy for that of agencies specifically entrusted to make that policy. Since there is no obvious reason to believe that the agencies will be wrong more often than the courts, why not let the agencies make the decisions? Where judges have strong ideological convictions, or where they have insufficient learning to understand what is going on, there is critical danger that an extra level of review will interfere with effective political leadership. The answer to this criticism is that courts are not as likely to be wrong as the agencies; while they are equally susceptible to human error, they are almost immune from institutional error. The rest of this chapter will attempt to illuminate this basic premise of administrative review.

In 1978 the United States Supreme Court spoke directly to the issue of judges substituting their policy preferences for that of the agencies in a case involving Vermont Yankee Power's attempt to construct a nuclear power plant in New England. The U.S. Circuit Court of Appeals for the District of Columbia, which handles most appeals from federal administrative agency rulings, had ordered the case remanded for further proceedings, basically, as the Supreme Court remarked, because the court did not like nuclear power. That case pointed out in no uncertain terms that the power to exercise legitimate control implies the power to exercise complete control. The Supreme Court reversed with a proper admonition, but its vituperative comments did not solve the overall problems. If the Supreme Court had been against nuclear power, it would have affirmed!

Even if we assume an institutional superiority in courts which dictates limited control, the question still remains, what control is legitimate and what control is usurpatory? The answer lies in an analysis of bureaucracies as institutions and a dissection of their inherent institutional weaknesses. The intent of the courts' supervisory role is to supply corrective balance to institutional weaknesses, although legal scholars seldom speak in terms of social structure, but rather of "procedural due process."[1] A sedulous regard for proper procedure has its rightful place, but no legitimate concept of procedure is at the heart of most administrative review. The reported cases justify court veto of administrative action in two ways. First, the court can find procedural irregularity on the part of the agency, such as failure to give notice, lack of a fair hearing, or inadequate findings of fact to support the agency's conclusion. Second, if the agency has been careful to protect its procedural flanks, the court can find the action by the agency in excess of its authority, "arbitrary," or contrary to the weight of the evidence. There are occasions, of course, where there is real procedural irregularity or where an agency does act in excess of its authority; however, most of the reversals which cause public outcry occur because the court disagrees with the agency's policy and finds some procedural device on which to turn its ruling.

It is not sufficient to say that in those cases where the court disagrees, but in which there is no legitimate procedural or legal irregularity, it is improper for the court to overrule the agency. If that were the correct rule, then our analysis of institutions would say little which is new; the fact of the matter is that there *are* occasions where a court *should* reverse agency

1. Administrative law finds its genesis in constitutional rulings which have now been codified in the federal and state administrative procedures acts. While appeals from administrative agencies now have statutory grounds, all that these statutes have done is to regulate proceedings which are based on a constitutional right of review grounded on the Fifth and Fourteenth Amendments' due process clauses. Consequently, administrative review is not outside the perimeters of this book's primary area of concern, namely, constitutional law.

policy merely because the court disagrees with it. (The most absurd results are frequently achieved through perfect procedure.) We have created independent boards and agencies in response to certain serious structural problems in the executive and legislative branches, but as usually occurs, the solution to the problem changed the problem. The new problem is how to control the vicious tendencies of the boards and agencies, and the solution to that problem, namely, court supervision of these bodies, changes the problem again.

The creation of the independent board or agency has been in direct response to two imperatives. The first imperative was the need to insulate Congress or the state legislatures from the impossible task of passing unpalatable regulatory legislation at every session. The second was the need to reduce the level of government corruption by removing critical decisions from the hands of elected officials who trade for their own accounts. When, however, both of these problems are overcome, the new problem which arises is that the bureaucracies have a life of their own as organic wholes. While they are not tempted to individual self-dealing in the same way that elected political officials are, they are nonetheless tempted to institutional self-dealing, that is, acting in such a way as to further the ends of the bureaucracy as a whole.

As the last chapter discussed in wearisome length, elected politicians are always loath to go on record as being against the vital interests of any constituent. Any type of regulation, or in fact any government program, invariably puts in jeopardy the vital interests of some group. Even the dream project of the 1930s, the Tennessee Valley Authority, forced the dislocation of thousands of families from their ancestral homes to make way for the dam to generate the power for rural electrification. While responsible elected officials are willing, on occasion, to perform a necessary castor-oil-administering function, they do not want to do it every day. Furthermore, from a mechanical point of view, it is easier to pass legislation with broad ends, leaving the means to be devised by others, than it is to give forewarning in Congress of all the ways in which the achievement of some broad goal are going to hurt.

In the second chapter I mentioned the West Virginia Human Rights Commission, which was given a broad mandate by the legislature to eliminate discrimination, but which was given no threatening enforcement power. The commission then proceeded to assess monetary damages under its "inherent powers" against people who discriminated, and the courts backed it up. Had the power to assess damages been given the commission specifically in the statute, it is unlikely that the statute would ever have passed the legislature. Once authority has been given to a state human rights commission, or at the federal level to the National Labor Relations Board to regulate labor disputes or to the Federal Trade Commission to regulate commerce, the bullet has been bitten for all time by the political branches, and a state legislature or Congress in subsequent sessions ceases to be the political enemy and becomes the potential friend. The emphasis in the minds of affected interest groups shifts from what Congress did in establishing the board or commission to what Congress can do with a new statute to *reverse* adverse action taken by the board. At that point the legislative game of being for everything while doing nothing takes over and saves all of the members' jobs.

The theoretical justification for administrative agencies is that regulation is very technical work which must be entrusted to specialists. There is, indeed, a great deal of truth to this, particularly in fields like atomic energy. Under the doctrine of nondelegation of powers, Congress and the legislatures are expected to pass enabling legislation with sufficiently detailed policy guidelines that the agencies will have adequate standards to determine whether agency rules reasonably implement legislative *policy*. While the doctrine of nondelegation tended to be strictly enforced up to 1940, it is now eroded in practical terms because of the impossibility of giving precise legislative policy direction. My court has recognized that it is means and not ends which will grind the legislative process to a halt. That was the implicit holding in the Human Rights Commission case, which, by the way, was based upon a similar holding in New Jersey. Since it is almost impossible in real life to separate means and ends or policy and implementation, the functional interplay has not been between the agencies and their legislative bodies but between the agencies and the courts. The courts have recognized that to achieve the necessary legislative consensus, the statutes must necessarily be broad. The courts then undertake, themselves, to assure that the agencies do not run wild. This is the heart of *practical* administrative law.

One of the first examples of Congress divorcing itself from a stormy problem was the creation of the Federal Reserve System to control the money supply in 1913. The Federal Reserve System traces its origins to the Wilson administration, when it was created as a compromise between a real central bank like the Bank of England and nineteenth-century American, unregulated, state banking. A two-line, eighth-grade history book summary might say that the eastern, creditor, banking interests wanted a stable money supply, while the cash-short western debtors wanted continued easy credit with its tendency toward inflation. By the

1960s the original powers of the regional Federal Reserve banks had almost completely disappeared, leaving the management of the entire monetary system in the hands of the Washington-based national Federal Reserve Board, which had total responsibility for the money supply, interest rates, and credit availability.

Today's acrimonious debate between the economists who advocate monetary policy and the economists who advocate fiscal policy is primarily fired by the political fact of life that the independence of the Federal Reserve Board, combined with its small, technically qualified membership, makes monetary policy the *only* manageable input to the full employment, stable-money-supply equation. Politically, Congress can always use "fiscal policy" to turn on federal *spending* to stem a recession, but absent the type of revolutionary fervor which launched the Reagan administration, it cannot turn the money off to accomplish anti-inflation fine tuning. In spite of monetary policy's injustices, the most notable of which is that high interest rates to control inflation penalize industries, like construction, which rely heavily on borrowed funds, it is at least *possible* to have a *rational* monetary policy. The theoretical work of eminent economists like Milton Friedman, justifying monetary policy, is interesting, but most economists believe in monetary policy the same way they believe in air when it is the only thing available to breathe. While the use of countercyclical fiscal policy, which puts money into the economy in times of recession and removes it in times of boom, is far more incisive and probably more just, it is also politically difficult. Turning off the federal money implies that people lose jobs and that existing programs are curtailed—a theoretically proper result which in practice might lead to large-scale congressional unemployment. Dwelling at length on the Federal Reserve System may be a bit tedious; however, it is the quintessential example of the pervasive tendency of elected officials to shift hard, if not impossible, political responsibilities onto the shoulders of nonelected officials better able to bear public hostility.

During the 1960s and 1970s, monetary policy was accepted as the preeminent inflation fighter (although fiscal policy was accepted as the preeminent unemployment fighter), because reduced government spending would have outraged all the constituencies affected adversely; higher taxes would have outraged everyone; higher productivity required a change in psychology beyond the capacity of government; and reducing regulatory costs would have implied unacceptable consequences with regard to the environment, occupational health and safety, and myriad other social goals. The Federal Reserve, however, did what it was intended to do—take the heat of unpleasant decision making out of the hands of elected politicians who could not act responsibly without dire personal consequences. Like the courts in similar circumstances, the Federal Reserve can retreat into its graphs, charts, and economic mumbo-jumbo and pretend it is doing technical tinkering in consonance with some set of neutral, scientific principles. Meanwhile young couples pay exorbitant rent for run-down flats and construction workers queue for unemployment checks. However, what is of critical importance, neither group blames the Congress. If the cynical political consideration of burden shifting alone were at the heart of the creation of administrative agencies, the public long ago would have forbidden such delegation. However, as is so frequently the case in similar circumstances, legitimate management considerations outweigh all illegitimate perversions of the structure. Congress and the state legislatures are not *capable* of formulating the detailed rules and regulations necessary to implement legislative policy. Quite aside from the political advantages, there is little practical alternative to broad delegation. While theoretically there has always been some value in separating "policymaking" from "administration," from a practical perspective the act of administering either gives rise to or points out the need for specific policies. It is the administrators themselves who confront problems never contemplated by the legislators. Until one gets down into the regulation mire, the solutions do not become obvious. As Jean-Paul Sartre once said, "Il vous faut vous enmerder!"

Examples of agencies which do something it would be almost impossible for Congress to do are the Nuclear Regulatory Commission and the Federal Trade Commission. Since nuclear power, both fission and fusion, are on the frontiers of science, no one can know in advance where new and urgent dangers may develop. The accident at Three Mile Island in Pennsylvania in 1979, where radioactive material leaked into the atmosphere, raised issues in the construction of nuclear power plants which could not have been anticipated by anyone, much less legislators, several years before. Similarly, the Federal Trade Commission is given authority to maintain competition and prevent collusion or unfair practices in the marketplace, but the structure of industries changes from day to day. The advent of computer technology has greatly increased the capacity of large horizontally and vertically integrated enterprises to realize economies of scale. This phenomenon has the effect of lowering costs, raising efficiency, and lowering prices; however, simultaneously it has the untoward effect of concentrating industry and causing monopoly. In both the areas of nuclear power and trade regulation the issues must constantly be reviewed and the regulations changed and updated—a task which Congress with its other time demands and inordinately cumbersome process cannot possibly perform.

The ironic thing about criticism of politicians for cynically shifting decision making from themselves to others is that they are enthusiastically encouraged in this process by the good government lobby. Not only do politicians not like political decision making, but the people do not like it either. The pervasive desire to get as many functions as possible out of politics creates board after board and converts local elected officials into appointees at an ever accelerating pace. The war cry of "democratic control" is usually invoked *after* a particular function has been "de-politicized"; whenever a function is directly in the hands of elected politicians the complaint is universally heard that a given function has become "political," by which is meant that the officials exercising the control are either incompetent or trading for their own accounts. Notwithstanding everyone's love of democracy, there is almost universal agreement that the elective process brings a higher number of incompetents and self-dealers to high positions than the appointive process.

Trading for one's own account can take a number of forms, the most obvious of which is outright graft. Graft, however, is not limited to elected officials, so that particular type of trading for one's own account is not an inherent part of the political process. Since graft can occur anywhere in government where an individual has power to affect the vital interests of others, it is no more a fit subject for continued discussion here than armed robbery. Other types of trading for one's own account, however, are inherently part of the political process and important in any analysis of institutional strengths and weaknesses.

Elected officials rely upon a certain geographical constituency for the votes necessary to keep them in office; consequently, anything which makes that constituency better off, even at the expense of others, will have a positive effect upon an incumbent politician's job security. The smaller the constituency, the greater the effect which helping individuals or very small groups will have. For example, a legislator running for the West Virginia legislature from Marion County has a geographical constituency of 61,356 persons. However, there are only 38,771 registered voters, of which 27,644 are Democrats and 10,268 are Republicans. Marion County has been a Democrat county since Franklin Roosevelt's first term, and while a few Republicans have been elected in the last fifty years, it was always because the Democrats actively went out and lost. Consequently, it is not a general election between Democrats and Republicans which is decisive in that county, because a Democrat nominee can expect automatically to win the general election. It is the Democrat primary election which is decisive, and in a nonpresidential election, only about 19 percent of the electorate, or 5,252 Democrat voters turn out at the polls. Of that group any candidate can expect to lose 250 votes because of voter ignorance, and he can similarly expect to gain 250 votes for exactly the same reason. That leaves 4,752 intelligent voters to determine one's election, of which 2,377 are required to win. At the local level, offending one individual from a large family may cost an incumbent a political office he values highly. Unlike national or statewide politics, local politics is a tedious process of picking up votes one at a time.

Trading for one's own account, then, frequently takes the form of seeking benefits for individuals or groups in one's own constituency at the expense of others, appropriating money inefficiently to local projects such as veterans hospitals in Montana, hiring more people than are justified, or getting less competent but politically active constituents hired at the expense of more qualified applicants. These are the legitimate considerations which through the past three decades have prompted what can loosely be called the "good government lobby," usually led by the newspapers, to seek to take as many routine governmental functions as possible out of the hands of elected officials.

Frequently depolitization works quite well. In 1968, for example, the West Virginia legislature removed control over the state's colleges from the legislature and placed their control in the hands of a board of regents. Before this change the budgets for West Virginia University, Marshall University, and the seven state colleges were made separately by the finance committees of the House and Senate. This tended to make the continued solvency of any given college depend upon the position within the internal power structure of those interested in that institution. Thus it was essential that there be legislators "interested" in any given institution, and that opened up endless possibilities for trading for one's own account. The critical personal quality sought in any college president in those days was political acumen—one element of which, for example, was an ability to strike a happy compromise and hire legislators' constituents only into jobs where inefficiency would not seriously damage the entire institution. At the undergraduate level, admission policy was not particularly important, but in the medical, nursing, and law schools there was constant political pressure to admit persons recommended by legislators, and the president of West Virginia University had to walk a tight line between maintaining legislative good will and not turning his professional schools into institutions to receive political patronage incompetents.

The creation of the Board of Regents went a long way toward eliminating these problems. The board consists of nine members, each of whom is appointed by the governor with the advice and consent of the state Senate for a nine-year term. Appropriations for the state colleges and universities are made to the board, which is then empowered to set the budgets for the individual schools. The board hires its chief executive officer, the chancellor, and he then hires a staff to allocate money with some semblance of reason among the competing institutions. A strong governor, of course, exercises a certain moral suasion over policy, and the legislature can condition appropriations upon promises that certain policies will be adopted, but the political control is indirect and confined to the truly powerful governor and a few members of the legislative leadership. I believe that today the chairmen of the House and Senate finance committees can get one applicant a year into the West Virginia University College of Medicine who would not otherwise be accepted; however, the rank and file can get nothing but polite letters promising "every consideration." As chief justice I *know* that I cannot get a candidate into the College of Law; I have more influence at Yale than I have at West Virginia University! It is exactly this lack of *personal* influence that the legislative leadership and concerned citizens (read "newspapers") envisaged when they took education out of the hands of politicians and placed it in the hands of bureaucrats.

The general lesson which the history of the Board of Regents teaches can be applied to most other regulatory responsibilities, the Nuclear Regulatory Commission or the Federal Trade Commission, for example. It should be obvious that in addition to practical problems which make it impossible for Congress to do its own regulating, the very purpose of the regulatory scheme would be defeated if every powerful legislator could trade for his own account in the interactions between Congress and its own employees who, under any other regulatory scheme, would be called upon to do the day-to-day regulating.

It is at about this point in the analysis that the courts begin to intrude themselves. Although the creation of the nonpolitical, independent, technically competent board or agency may contain to manageable proportions the vice of *individual* self-dealing, such a scheme also diminishes legitimate political control. The reason that courts have imposed themselves upon the regulatory scheme is that the bureaucracy is also capable of self-dealing. It should be remembered that "self-dealing" is *not* the same as graft—it is an integral and inevitable outgrowth of a particular institutional structure. The self-dealing to which I have alluded with regard to politicians is generally legal, and the self-dealing which must be feared from the bureaucracy is even more thoroughly legal.

While the bureaucracy does not engage in the type of vulgar self-dealing associated with elected officials, its peculiar brand of self-dealing is even more insidious, because it is the more difficult to isolate and combat; it is self-dealing for the institution of bureaucracy as an institution. In 1978, average pay for federal nonmilitary employees was $18,304 a year, while for nonfarm private employees it was $13,323. Over 7.5 percent of the federal workers received more than $25,000 a year, and although the basic top salary was pegged to presidential appointees' $50,000, the Civil Service Reform Act of 1978 created the Senior Executive Service, in which high-level employees could, with merit incentive bonuses, earn up to $66,000 a year. At the state and municipal levels the figures are substantially lower, but generally when inflation-proof pensions are included into the bargain, state and local employees do better in terms of both outright cash and job security than their counterparts in the private sector. These figures should quickly make it apparent that any bureaucracy which is in place has an enormous vested interest in continuing to exist.

Several years ago as a newly elected judge I received one of life's great awakenings when I discovered that the bureaucracies of the various federally funded legal clinics in West Virginia spent considerable time fighting one another for a greater piece of the poverty action. There were three agencies involved, and not only did they fight, but they made vituperative ad hominem attacks on one another. In order to attract attention to themselves, they solicited "public interest" law suits where, for all intents and purposes, the plaintiffs were manufactured. Instead of defending the poor in their routine brushes with everyone from employers and landlords to the government itself and waiting for the big-issue law suits to develop as a natural result of such confrontations, the public interest lawyers placed routine legal services low on their agenda and concentrated disproportionate effort on attempts to enlist the courts to legislate. In all fairness, they did a lot of good, but somehow I had the distinct gut feeling that it was not "good" which was uppermost in their minds. Defending the poor had become a business in which poverty was bought wholesale and sold to the federal government at retail. The point is that even in a bureaucracy with an urgent mission, staffed primarily by committed people, there is a tendency to place the health of the bureaucracy first and the mission second.

Much of the apparently ridiculous action of the courts is calculated to contain bureaucratic self-dealing to manageable proportions. When the courts take defensive action against bureaucracy's self-aggrandizement, they often find themselves having a difficult time explaining in *legal* terms why they are interfering. The ludicrous nature of a process which requires the control of complex institutions to be explained in a slave language code is no better illustrated than in a Tennessee Valley controversy where the popular press, including such reputable commentators as the editorial staff of *Time* magazine, had great fun in 1979 pointing out that a multi-million-dollar dam was halted in midconstruction to save a three-inch fish of the perch family known as the snail darter. It required a last-minute amendment insinuated into the Energy and Water Development Appropriations Act in June 1979 to authorize the Tennessee Valley Authority to complete the Tellico Dam near Knoxville, "notwithstanding the Endangered Species Act or any other law." The snail darter, which was merely an excuse for the courts to call the project into question, trivialized a heated local controversy between the Tennessee Valley Authority and thousands of local residents.

The area to be flooded by the Tellico Dam was rich in archeological treasures from the distant past of the Cherokee Nation; the doomed valley was both beautiful and populated by farmers who had been born and raised there, with roots going back to 1817, when the Indians were driven out. Some Indian burial mounds in the flooded area may be as old as eight thousand years, and when the controversy was raging over the necessity of the dam, after the courts had stopped work there, a review committee including the secretaries of the interior, agriculture, and army agreed unanimously that the Tellico project was economically unsound. The chairman of the Council of Economic Advisors at the time, Charles Shultze, pointed out that the total projected benefits of the dam amounted to less than the cost of its completion.

The point, of course, is not whether the Tellico Dam project was in the public interest; I could not presume to judge a controversy which has produced books of its own. The point is that the snail darter was but the excuse demanded by the absurdity of the legal reasoning process for a court to delay a bureaucracy which had its *own* reasons, above and beyond public benefits, to expand its dominion. Since judges do not usually write in terms of social structures, tiny technical issues like the snail darter become the visible fulcrum by which Archimedes-like judges are able to move the world. If, indeed, the snail darter is the fulcrum, the unseen lever is either a finely honed academic understanding of social structures or merely an intuitive grasp of the nature of man, economics, and practical politics.

The question of bureaucratic self-interest is a legitimate one in administrative law, but it is seldom mentioned even tangentially in the reported cases. It is considered both impolite and impolitic for the courts to cast aspersions on the institutional integrity of other agencies of government. Yet to say that bureaucracies have institutional, organic imperatives is not to call into question the integrity of individuals. Each institution of government has "institutional" weaknesses independent of the men and women who staff them. When a bureaucrat becomes a judge he acts like one, and when a judge becomes a bureaucrat he acts like one. It should be obvious, therefore, that the development of a body of "law" based on the sociology of institutions is a fit and proper undertaking and does not necessarily imply a *power* struggle between the courts and administrative agencies.

In a way, a body of law developed to control government bureaucracies is the mirror image of the reforms of the 1930s designed to control private business. With 36 percent of the gross national product dedicated to government, it should be obvious that government is big business. If it is accepted, as Gardiner Means first pointed out, that by 1930 big business was dominated by a technostructure (to use a Galbraith word) whose primary goal was not profits but upward mobility for middle management and continued security for the corporation as an entity, then political and legal reform since 1932 has been directed primarily toward control of this group. The result, however, as demonstrated by the institutional actions of legal aid societies, has been for the controllers to develop the exact organizational qualities of the business institutions they have been built to control.

Certainly government is not singled out for any particular censure, since large business organizations and government bureaucracies have most characteristics in common. The Social Security Administration, for example, in many ways resembles General Motors. Small business, on the other hand, does not look very much like a government bureaucracy, because small business is in the "market" or "competitive" sector of the economy. Big business with its attendant technostructure is either a monopoly (public utilities), an oligopoly (that is, very few producers, such as steel, oil, or automobiles), or a business/government partnership (defense contractors). People who think that the employees and management of General Motors consider its primary function to be maximizing profits for stockholders are wrong, just as people who think that government workers and agency heads are primarily interested in delivering cost/benefit-effective services to taxpayers are wrong. Upward mobility for middle management is the real raison d'être of both the corporation and any government bureaucracy, and it is control of this phenomenon which stretches almost to the breaking point the legal reasoning of administrative decisions.

The problems which the self-dealing proclivities of government imply can probably be seen most clearly by looking at similar structures in business, where the contrast between what the organization is supposed to be doing and what it actually does is more obvious. General Motors, for example, like any other large corporation, thinks of its stockholders as an annoyance and seeks to keep them satisfied only to the extent necessary to preclude a stockholders' revolt. The point is probably best illustrated by the following short article from the May 31, 1978, "Tax Report" section of the *Wall Street Journal*:

> Congress has practically ignored a proposal to end "double taxation" on dividends: once as corporate income, again as dividend income to stockholders. One reason the measure has gone nowhere is the quiet opposition massed against it by some big corporations, Sen. Bob Packwood (R. Ore.) suggested to a group of tax accountants last week.
>
> Many companies question the idea because "it wouldn't help them," a Packwood aide said. Companies fear that easing taxes on dividends would mean increased pressure to pay out more of their earnings as dividends, Sen. Packwood told the accountants. "Corporate managements don't have shareholders' interests at heart," a congressional committee aid asserted. "They take a fairly arrogant attitude."
>
> "Corporate managements are separate and apart from shareholders and seek to perpetuate themselves by holding onto earnings and pay only what dividends they have to," said the committee aide, who works on tax matters.

From 1970 to 1980, for example, General Motors did not pay the maximum possible portion of its profits to the stockholders as dividends. Instead, profits were reinvested, allegedly for the purpose of improving the market value of the stock. This is a fine theory, except that the market price of General Motors stock barely increased in that ten-year period, and if one took the small increase which did occur and added it to the yearly dividend, the total return, dividends and capital gains, would hardly have kept pace with the 7 percent or higher compounded annual average rate of inflation. A group of new investors looking for a way to make money certainly would not elect to create a General Motors-type enterprise.

Who then benefits from this huge corporate structure? Obviously it is the executives, management, workers, vendors, consultants, lawyers, distributors, dealers, and ultimately perhaps even the consumer, who gets a hell of a car for his money. Now, if an institution which is democratically controlled by stockholders, which is in business for the sole benefit of the stockholders, and which has a measurable criterion of performance (profits) can get along basically running the entire show for almost everyone in the world except the stockholders, what chance does an average citizen have of getting a government bureaucracy to think about eight-thousand-year-old Indian burial mounds, ancestral family farms, or valleys of unspoiled splendor? The truth of the matter is that the typical government bureaucracy does not care whether a project which would destroy all of the above has an excess of public benefits to public detriments. What are the benefits to the bureaucracy? That is the crucial question.

When General Motors builds a new plant, establishes a new division, or diversifies into a new field, it is not giving the stockholders a higher return than they could get if the company simply paid them their share of the money earmarked for expansion and let them invest it in new, dynamic, growth industries. What General Motors is doing is providing myriad channels of upward mobility for its middle management, since every hierarchy, corporate and government, resembles a pyramid in which there is not as much room at the top as there is in the middle or at the bottom. An average college-educated manager's working life extends from age twenty-three to sixty-five, or forty-two years, during the better part of which he would like to be close to the top. But, alas, the fact is that on the mathematical average only one out of forty-two people ahead of him will retire in any given year. Furthermore, since there are fewer and fewer positions at each successive step up the pyramid, it is not even possible to move up one forty-second of the way to the top each year.

The obvious way to overcome the sociological, demographic, and mathematical impediments to upward mobility is to create successive, parallel hierarchies, each dominated by someone who found advancement blocked in the original organizational structure. This is known in economics as horizontal expansion, and when the new business complements the original structure it is known as "horizontal integration." A variation of this process is "vertical integration," where the existing structure acquires either its suppliers, its distributors, or both.

The same forces militating in favor of the creation of successive, cloning, parallel hierarchies in private enterprise exist to an even greater extent in government, because there is practically no way to measure the cost/benefit effectiveness of what a particular department of government does. Outside routine housekeeping functions such as providing water, garbage collection, and ambulance service, where utilization rates can be easily measured and customer satisfaction easily ascertained, there is seldom any attempt to assure that every tax dollar expended generates satisfaction for someone, somewhere, roughly equal to the satisfaction the same tax dollar could have generated if it had been spent elsewhere.

One significant curb on government expansion does exist in legislative resistance to new appropriations. In general the legislative branch *is* solicitous of constituents' desire to pay lower taxes, although at the same time many individual legislators favor any bureaucratic projects which might be located in their districts. Even a well-entrenched and popular bureaucracy will find that annual budget increases are insufficient to feed its voracious appetite, and when no amount of pressure can convince individual legislators to open the purse, the bureaucracy must look outside government to the self-sustaining, profit-generating, private sector of the economy. A bureaucracy instinctively fights defeat by legislative resistance through fiscal conservatism. If the bureaucrats are a little clever, they will arrange for government resources outside the effective control of the legislative process to be at their disposal as they expand into activities which generate their own "profit." Such resources as tax-free local bonds, established government loan programs, private loans with government guarantees, and so on can help fund the construction of, for example, a parking garage or electric power plant, both of which, upon completion, ought to generate sufficient revenue to relieve the inconvenient financial dependence on the legislature.

Former Secretary of the Treasury William E. Simon estimates that in 1975 70 percent of all long-term capital funds available in private money markets was being borrowed by the federal government and 80 percent of all funds available by government at all levels. By 1975, $11 billion was owed by "independent" agencies like the TVA and the Export-Import Bank. Government-sponsored enterprises such as the Farm Credit Administration and the Federal Home Loan Bank Board owed $88 billion while $237 billion in loans was guaranteed by the Federal Housing Administration, the Veterans Administration, the Farmers Home Administration, and others. The proliferation of government bureaucracy borrowing or administering private funds is borne out by the simple fact that the United States has the lowest *private* capital investment rate as a percentage of GNP in the industrial world, including England, which is considered a borderline socialist country. From 1960 through the early 1970s, in times of both peace and war, the United States averaged a private investment rate of less than 18 percent a year of our GNP, while Japan averaged 35 percent, Germany 26 percent, and France 25 percent.

The significance of the fact that government borrows about 80 percent of available capital is that bureaucracies can expand with borrowed funds without untoward consequences to their political sponsors. At the state and local level, bonds on which the interest is exempt from federal taxation may be issued by a public authority. This usually cuts in half the interest rate payable on these bonds and places any public authority at a distinct advantage vis-à-vis any private developer. With government's monopoly of the taxing power, its authority to exempt itself from its own regulations, and its freedom from the necessity of showing a profit, government is capable of putting everyone else out of business. Once everyone else is out of business, how do we measure the cost/benefit effectiveness of an operation which is the sole supplier of a particular market service, such as electricity? This, by the way, was the lesson Britain learned after World War II, when the Labour government nationalized railroads and steel. Those industries have both been disasters ever since, a fact which even the Labour governments recognize, since they have never extended the policy to other industries. Part of the problem in Britain aside from efficiency was that both levels of employment and wages ceased to be labor relations problems and became political problems. The same phenomenon probably accounts for many of the problems of New York City, where government employees can back up their demands for salaries and pensions with an organized vote.

There has been a long history in the United States at both the federal and local levels of court scrutiny of government incursions into the private sector. The basic standard in the law, still standing unmodified from its original version in Adam Smith's *Wealth of Nations,* is that government action must be for a "public purpose," which implies that private enterprise is either unwilling or unable to accomplish the same result. Adam Smith, by the way, illustrated the requirement of a "public purpose" by reference to the building of a fire wall, a necessary undertaking which he allowed would never be accomplished if private cooperation were relied upon. Urban renewal is a good present-day example of legitimate government intrusion into an area in competition with private developers. Without the power of eminent domain, urban renewal is impossible; therefore, either government or a regulated private instrumentality must be called upon to do the job. I am sure, however, that the conservative reader would question this conclusion, since urban renewal makes more social sense than economic sense.

Determining a "public purpose" has always been an ad hoc undertaking. Consequently, what may be a "public purpose" for one time and one place may not be a "public purpose" for another time or place. The crucial question for the courts is whether private resources are adequate to do the job; the political actors determine whether the job is worth doing. Principles of economics as well as law are never set in stone; what applies at one stage of industrialization may not apply at another. Since 1938 the courts have been quite liberal in favor of government agencies with regard to the question of "public purpose," because we lived in an objectively Keynesian world. The United States was characterized by underemployed plant capacity and adequate raw materials. Interest rates in the 1960s and early 1970s (except during the Vietnam war) reflected limited competition between government and private borrowers—that was the time for the Interstate Highway Program, urban renewal, federally sponsored home construction, and cleaning up the environment. While part of the comparatively low interest rate phenomenon was attributable to increases in the money supply, reflected in inflation, it is questionable whether before 1973 a more conservative policy would not have led to widespread unemployment. Government's share of gross national product went from 12 percent in 1930 to 36 percent in 1976, but the result appeared to be general prosperity, shared particularly by the poor, which is why a modest level of inflation was acceptable.

Reconciling the needs for full employment, economic growth, private investment, income distribution equity, and political freedom is a hit or miss proposition. One of the values which social and economic policy seeks to further is personal freedom, through decentralization of control, so that a word about the political ramifications of substantial bureaucratic control of the economic system is in order. The nature of totalitarianism is obviously, by definition, the totality of its control over all diffuse, hierarchical, social, and economic structures in society. The consequence of such organization is that there is nowhere for eccentrics to flee, because wherever they go, the same power structure from which they are fleeing will be waiting for them. In a country like the United States, where political and economic power are in separate hands at least throughout a substantial part of the political and economic spectrum, freedom of thought and expression are not greatly curtailed.

Politics is dangerous; being on the wrong side can cost a person his job, his business, admission of his children to professional schools, or personal bankruptcy, depending upon how much hard ball the local, state, or national political machine wants to play. However, in a free market economy, where the government does not control all the gas stations, bookstores, art shops, restaurants, hardware stores, and television repair shops, there is always some way a person can feed his family while enjoying his First Amendment rights. When we talk about prior restraint on freedom of the press and the chilling effect of libel suits or censorship on expression, we forget about the preeminent chilling effect, state ownership. In fact, nothing chills anybody's anything quite as much as being hungry, out of work, and without hope for the future. Totalitarian powers face very little real dissidence (except that instigated or supported from outside), precisely because the state is totally organized. This same phenomenon was experienced to a lesser but sufficiently chilling extent in the American South during the heyday of segregation—civil rights movements required outside agitators exactly because all of the internal power structures were aligned on the side of segregation.

Somehow, at this point, I hear my late grandfather turning rapidly in his grave, because this is the type of prattle which used to emanate from the mouth of Ohio's conservative Senator Robert Taft in the 1940s. Republicans of the Roosevelt era always appeared to be quite pleased to take bread out of the mouths of the hungry if the result was dictated by the impersonal, if imperfect, forces of the free market. It can be argued forcefully at this point that free speech, free association, free mobility, and free enterprise are exclusively middle-class values which are fundamental only to that class. Authoritarians of either the right or left argue that the right to a job, security from criminal violence, and a more equal distribution of the wealth are far more "fundamental" values to the working class. To the extent, therefore, that courts restrain government involvement with the economy in consonance with "liberal" middle-class values, courts merely force their own values on society. The only answer to this is that the pursuit of middle-class values furthers economic development, security, and wealth equality.

The experiment in judicial restraint since 1938 is a recognition of the urgency of the Keynesian agenda—a recognition that an exclusively "liberal" economic model will not fulfill any fundamental values, middle-class or other. Excess in anything, whether it be economic freedom or government control, is unhealthy. Much of the lawmaking activity of the

American courts for the last two hundred years has been directed toward achieving a golden mean, a mean which is, by definition, unsatisfactory to both liberals and conservatives alike.

Appellate judges must make decisions about the legitimacy of government incursions into the self-sustaining, profit-generating sector of the economy. The question is usually framed in constitutional terms, namely, that government competition with private enterprise constitutes a "taking of property" without "due process." This takes us back to the rule that the government can enter the private sector only for a "public purpose." Judges insensitive to economic issues can look to what courts in similar circumstances have done elsewhere; a whole body of precedent has grown up around urban renewal, parking authorities, industrial parks, and local development bonds to do everything from building factories to installing pollution control devices. Even with extensive precedent, however, the law is difficult to apply, because behind every legitimate public purpose lurk numerous, ominous private purposes.

In my first eight years as a judge in West Virginia, I voted only once that a proposed project failed to be for a "public purpose." The case involved a motel developer who wanted to use tax-exempt, county development bonds to finance a convention center in Marion County. It appeared to me that while some conventions might be brought to the city of Fairmont, the primary effect would be the construction of a large motel near Interstate Highway 79 which would compete unfairly with existing motel accommodations in the area because of the low, government-subsidized interest on its construction loan. The ad hoc nature of the determination is illustrated by the fact that if Marion County had been a large enough market area to support a center with continual, year-round conventions, with the attendant attraction of nonresidents to the area to spend their money, I would have ruled in favor of its construction.

As a state judge, my vision is far more parochial than it would be if I were a federal judge; I will always approve the use of development bonds or other government–private sector partnerships to bring industry to West Virginia regardless of the effect of such policies on other regions. State judges are usually not concerned with their own residents' competing "unfairly" against private industry in other states—that problem is what the federal courts are paid to solve. Consequently a convention center which draws from a national market and makes the West Virginia economy better off at the expense of Pennsylvania or Maryland I consider a legitimate West Virginia "public purpose"; however, a convention center, constructed with government subsidy, which permits one group of West Virginians to compete unfairly against other West Virginians is inappropriate and illegal.

Military historians are fond of pointing out that generals are usually prepared to fight the last war, and I have concluded that the same is often true of politicians, economists, and judges. In the area of administering the proper economic balance, the issues today are not the same as they were during the Roosevelt, Truman, or Eisenhower administrations. A great deal of the debate over government involvement in the "private sector" is phrased in the rhetoric of the 1940s and 50s; it is as if two generals massed opposing armies on the ancient battlefields of the Levant dressed and armed like those of Darius and Alexander to do battle for the mastery of a world in which the atomic bomb had been discovered! It should have become obvious by now to the heirs of Robert Taft that the free enterprise economy is not capable of maintaining anything approaching full employment; that private enterprise cannot possibly undertake to provide all of the necessary social services, including such fundamental programs as social security, because, like the building of Adam Smith's fire wall, there is a need for compulsion.[2] It should also be obvious that without government regulation the strong will exploit the weak, and social costs in terms of pollution, job accidents, and monopoly practices will skyrocket.

The heirs of Roosevelt, on the other hand, must recognize by now that the self-dealing tendencies of all government bureaucracies are *real* dangers and not merely an exercise in the imagination of the heirs of Robert Taft. Most of the constitutional law cases of the nineteenth century, which so confound law students today, merely evince policies, clothed as legal rules, to establish a free trade zone among the sovereign states and to curb government control of the private sector. While occasionally the courts were "owned" by the business pirates of the nineteenth century, the law generated at that time was overwhelmingly serious law which gave voice to a *common* political judgment. The due process and contract

2. The apparent paradox that there is a *valuable* service which the government, rather than private enterprise, must provide comes from the distinction between private costs and public costs. While a bus fare which would make public transportation profitable to private enterprise would induce individuals to drive their own cars, the public cost in roads, garages, traffic police, and pollution which private cars cause makes it more economical to subsidize public transportation. All humanitarian considerations to the side for the moment, the same rationale probably applies to public housing, as slums breed crime, encourage welfare culture, and reduce the tax base which new construction in blighted areas would augment if slum property were condemned and its tenants moved to other quarters.

clauses of the Constitution provided the necessary lever. Unfair government competition with private enterprise was held to be taking private property without just compensation, and excessive state government regulation of industry was held to be an impairment of the private right to contract. It is unfair to judge nineteenth-century courts on the basis of the liberal writings of political activists of that century. Political activists never voice the political philosophy of the silent majority; otherwise they would not need to be activists.

The last economic war, namely, Roosevelt's war in the 1930s, gave a distorted view of the battlefield. Even Adam Smith admitted that while most govenment bureaucracies, most of the time, tend to promote their own selfish ends, occasionally a substantial, competent service is provided to the citizenry. By 1933 the number of things which government could efficiently do had far outstripped the number of things which the United States Supreme Court permitted government to do. While the Supreme Court in the early 1930s may have been correct as a matter of principle to recognize the threat of government expansion, it failed to comprehend that technology had created a legitimate reason for new government responsibilities in certain specific areas. The existence of telephones, almost universal literacy, trains, airplanes, efficient mails, primitive data-processing facilities, and similar technical advances made it possible to inaugurate programs like social security because *for the first time* a bureaucracy could actually manage it.

Could we really imagine a hundred years ago, when the average employer had difficulty reading and writing and the average bookkeeper had difficulty with long division, establishing the reporting, record-keeping, and disbursement systems necessary for a national old-age and survivors insurance fund? How, by the way, would the claimants have gotten their checks, and how would they have cashed them? Technology not only made government involvement possible, but made it necessary. As we progressed into the 1950s and 1960s, it became obvious that with the geometric growth of industrialization, environmental control was essential. In the area of trade regulation, it likewise became obvious that the computer age generated enormous economies of scale with the invitation to monopoly. The point of this is that the learning articulated during the nineteenth century should be taken seriously; the principles were correct, but the case-by-case precedent, created by individual factual contexts, is almost useless, because everything has changed. The vituperative criticism of nineteenth-century courts sprang from our need to dissociate ourselves from the prison of precedent, which included both principles and factual contexts to which those principles were applied. Their principles, based on an understanding of institutions, were correct in the abstract.

The operative principles of government did not dramatically change between 1932 and 1963. The main difference from previous periods was simply the presence of a vast store of pre-existing, unused technology, which made almost anything government did cost/benefit effective. It was like an ancient, inefficient steamboat which lost 96 percent of its power from the boiler to the paddlewheel. If cheap wood were available for fuel, and if it were the only machine capable of moving cargo up the Hudson River to Albany, it could not lose money no matter how inefficient, in terms of thermodynamics, the machinery was. Government fit into that model between 1933 and 1963, convincing two generations that everything we had previously learned about the market economy, free enterprise, and the separation of political from economic power in the nineteenth century was rubbish. This whole way of thinking was aided by competing stereotypes: the first of the fat, arrogant, capitalist plutocrat indifferently gorging himself in the midst of a starving world; the second of the eager, young, dedicated government administrator in his one eight-year-old tweed suit. What the courts understand is that today both the plutocrat and the administrator are men in grey flannel suits. We have left the age of pirates, plutocrats, autocrats, and crusaders and entered the age of organized, collective intelligences. When the professional managers are graduated from college, they are arbitrarily assigned to the plutocrat Blue Team or the crusader Red Team.

The learning which prominent liberals such as Charles A. Reich in *The Greening of America* and John Kenneth Galbraith in *Economics and the Public Purpose* are expositing today about the social dynamics of bureaucracy was understood by Adam Smith when he wrote the *Wealth of Nations* in 1776 and by the nineteenth-century courts which made American economic policy. It was a lesson learned from centuries of feudalism, mercantilism, or just plain oligarchic bad government running under the flag of whatever "ism" people in the history business chose. In the course of recorded history, government in all its permutations has basically operated first and foremost for the benefit of those running the government and only secondarily for the benefit of the governed. The reason that administrative law makes so little sense in terms of its "standards of review" and its "procedural due process" is that it is absolutely forbidden to bring this underlying question of social dynamics to a conscious level in any published opinion. The procedure by which the actions of administrative agencies are reviewed by the courts is usually conceived as a process where agency actions are forced to conform to the law. On occasions when agencies arrogate unto themselves authority which they are specifically denied, this may be a correct statement; however, the more accurate general explanation is that policymaking is transferred from the agencies, which have an institutional interest in their own decisions, to a neutral body. This is the way we have reconciled the urgency of the Keynesian agenda with the learning of Adam Smith about the dynamics of governmental self-dealing. We have replaced the nineteenth-century courts' proscription of government involvement in the private sector with a type of court supervision of that involvement.

The incapacity of the political organs of society to control the bureaucracy has forced that function on the courts. There is a great deal of slippage. Frequently the courts reverse perfectly legitimate and necessary actions; frequently court procedures delay government actions to the point where costs become prohibitive; and frequently courts have an insufficient arsenal of weapons to attack the most wearisome problems of bureaucracy.[3]

Notwithstanding all of these problems, the control of bureaucracy must be undertaken, and it breaks down into two components: The first is the control of institutional self-dealing, which we have already discussed in terms of empire building and incursions into the private sector. The second, and far more difficult component, is the control of individual civil servants. It is into this latter category that this chapter's opening scene with Steve and Peggy Miller falls. As we saw with Steve and

3. In the last category it is amusing to observe that empire building frequently prompts the creation of new bureaucracies with numerous new management positions but with absolutely nothing to do—or at least nothing to keep employees busy. Bureaucracies abhor vacuums, however, and soon idleness, which raises in the bureaucrat's mind the specter of unemployment or transfer to Omaha, Nebraska, is displaced by activity. When the bureaucracy has nothing to do, it usually begins to do "research" into its general area of responsibility and asks questions which another, possibly overworked, bureaucracy must answer. When the process becomes very well developed, whole new bureaucracies spring up for the purpose of answering inane questions posed by other bureaucracies. When one of the unwilling participants in this absurd process is private industry, particularly industry competing with protected foreign producers or more efficient domestic producers, the game becomes so expensive that jobs may be endangered and whole communities threatened. I have always thought that private industry should at least have a right to "substantive due process" review of government reporting requirements, where the crucial question which the courts would answer is whether a particular reporting requirement bears a reasonable relationship to a legitimate public purpose. So far, to my knowledge, no ingenious group of lawyers and judges has undertaken to develop this particular weapon. I have addressed the subject at bar association meetings, yet there seems to be little enthusiasm to use my court to develop such rules on the state level.

Peggy, the whole theoretical construction of democratic control through a political hierarchy is a fiction, an impossibility.

Even though executive branch employees may not read business administration journals, it is no secret to them that the chief executive has a limited span of control. Many employees take advantage of this limitation to render service which might be characterized at best as deficient. The thoughtful concern and responsiveness of many agencies is similar to the thoughtful concern and responsiveness of the U.S. Post Office. You've been there. You stand in line forty-five minutes in front of a window where a clerk allegedly sells money orders. But as you finally see daylight before you and the hope flickers that before nightfall you may indeed be able to purchase a money order, the clerk snaps down the little shade, on the customer's side of which is written "Closed." In such circumstances the natural law principle giving citizens the right to overthrow unjust governments takes on new meaning.

The problem, however, is not just the simple one of span of control, which might be solved by creative administration. Even if the chief executive of any bureaucracy could exert tighter control over his subordinates, he could not compensate for their inherent limitations of immaturity, low level of experience, naive value judgments, and potential for economic or social co-option. Most of the first-rate people at the higher levels of federal and state administrations are young—very young—and a large number are lawyers. While first-level senior officials are comfortably middle-aged, their itinerant assistants are frequently under thirty, and most share a somewhat uniform vision of the universe based upon the current philosophy of the universities which they attended. But a university is not an accurate representation of the United States as a whole and does not teach about the problems of Small Town, U.S.A. Yet the affairs of much of the country are inevitably managed to some degree by a group of people who consider areas west of the Hudson, except California, as Indian country. Unfortunately, the crucial question in government is not, "Who is the secretary, or the assistant secretary, or the department head?" but rather, "Who is the yahoo doing the real staff work for any of these speech-making politicians?"

In 1968 during the height of the Vietnam war when I was a twenty-seven-year-old army artillery captain, I was made staff economist for one quarter of South Vietnam. I worked for one of the State Department's finest professional foreign service officers, Charles S. Whitehouse, who later served as ambassador to Laos and Thailand. He had eminently little knowledge of what I did in economic development because he was in charge of twelve provinces. I got the job because anyone outside of air-conditioned Saigon with any pretense to economic knowledge was a rare bird. By virtue of being military, I could be assigned to dangerous areas, while the better-trained civilians were content to supervise from afar. On those occasions when I consulted Ambassador Whitehouse about major policy, my own approach was wrong 50 percent of the time. I have always held a surpassingly high regard for Charles Whitehouse as a commander, because he routinely gave his young officers a fair hearing and then explained to *their* satisfaction why what they were doing was stupid; however, the crucial point is that most of the time I did important things without consulting him. I went my merry way like a bull in a china shop devoid of the least idea of the country, people, or language.

By the time I had been in Vietnam about a year, I began to become a bit efficient; yet at that point my tour ended and I went home, leaving a new young officer to remake all my mistakes. Economists were so rare in Vietnam that at the age of twenty-seven I wrote the economic development section of the 1969 pacification plan for all of Vietnam—a plan which expressed my *own* policy of shifting emphasis from social service projects to cash-income-producing projects. No one ever questioned that such a policy change originated in a twenty-seven-year-old mind whose economic experience was limited to undergraduate training at Dartmouth and a few years of teaching undergraduates in New Haven. The plan was rubber-stamped because very few people were at all interested in economics in the middle of a war, and since the people who approved the new policy did not know about the old policy, they had no idea that the plan involved a major policy shift. While the location for my personal experiences happened to be Vietnam, what I did is business as usual for every agency of the executive branch right here in the continental United States.

The executive branch provides incalculable permutations and combinations of lack of experience, self-dealing, naiveté, and incompetence, which can all have disastrous consequences on the government work product. What happens, for example, when a talented young administrator concludes that it is time to move out of government into a higher-paying private sector post? If, over the past several years, he has been regulating a particular industry, it must dawn on him that his highest value is in that industry. The problem then is to make some "friends" who will pay off later in terms of job offers. Similarly, if the top regulators are former members of the regulated industry, where do their loyalties lie? What happens when an administrator comes from the industry but decides to do penance for all of the meretricious actions which the marketplace forced him to commit in his former life? What happens when high staff positions are filled with the inordinately arrogant graduates of the Yale and Harvard law schools who have been trained that they have a monopoly on, not only all the intellect, but all the morality as well?

Finally, it should be noted that there is a pervasive lack of political experience among the employees of the executive branch. Regardless of what else one says about elected politicians, they are experienced. They may be experienced in the same way Moll Flanders was experienced, but they are where they are because they have learned how to keep most of their constituents happy most of the time. They understand the concept of compromise, the middle way of the half-loaf, and have a healthy sense of the mix of incompatible, selfish, irrational interests of which society is composed. With the young graduates of the great universities, unfortunately, everything is a matter of principle; their likes, dislikes, emotional attachments, prejudices, and vision of what is right and wrong inevitably get translated into questions of morality. (Moral commitment and inflexibility might be forgivable if their analyses were not so simplistic.)

We frequently hear of the case where the regulators come from the industry, leading to a co-option of the regulators by the industry which they purport to regulate. We seldom hear, however, of the equally oppressive converse problem, namely, administrators who feather their own power nests within an agency by exerting tighter controls over the regulated industry. Yet these types of problems at the top of the regulatory pyramid are only exacerbated at the bottom where all the staff work, investigations, and supervision are carried out. The most obvious staff problem is the drafting and promulgation of complex rules and regulations which the drafters frequently conceive in ignorance. The young have no experience on the battlefield, though they have been hired to run the war. As often as not, those being regulated cannot understand the regulations until they commit a violation. My favorite example is the application to family-owned and -operated restaurants of the Occupational Safety and Health Administration requirement that separate restrooms be made available for male and female employees. I have heard some very funny stories about families which have used the same restroom at home for twenty years but were forced to have palatial restrooms at work. Once the administrative system gets a rule like this on the books, however, it requires an act of God to change it.

Executive department employees' pervasive lack of political experience, bringing with it an arrogance spawned by too much power at too early an age, is the structural concomitant of lack of effective span of control. This staffing pattern constitutes the primary structural deficiency of the executive branch, but there are other, compounding deficiencies which make the doing of daily, routine business a terrible chore. The first of these is laziness. A commonly heard expression among government employees in and around Washington is "It's good enough for government work," and a substantial number of executive branch employees mean it. A person with a problem—for example, the need to obtain lost or misplaced records for social security purposes—must penetrate layers of administrative personnel to find some responsible, conscientious employee who can make things move. Often the average citizen must resort to a letter from his congressman, which sometimes shakes the bureaucracy a bit and raises the priority. The bureaucracy has become so independent, however, that as the years pass this technique becomes less and less effective.

Creative thinking which finds a way to meet the citizen's need requires a detailed analysis of the request, an understanding of the various possible avenues of help, an honest desire to be of help rather than to take an early lunch, and a comprehension of how programs and facilities operate. All this is work, and work is one thing which almost everyone is hesitant to supply in large amounts. All civil servants are "at work" during the normal day, but work has two dimensions—length and intensity. The length dimension is easy to measure, but the intensity dimension eludes effective control. Consequently, the ultimate criterion for judging the acceptability of a civil servant's performance is whether his output is "good enough for government work." The whole civil service system with its insurmountable obstacles to discharging an employee for stupidity, lack of resourcefulness, or just plain laziness is designed to make sure that tenure, income, and even to an extent promotion, will be based on the length rather than the intensity dimension of the work function.

The deficiency which compounds laziness is avoidance of responsibility. The effect of this employee tendency is to preserve the status quo. If employees take absolutely no responsibility outside their daily routine tasks, they will make no mistakes which might cost them promotions. Supervisors, branch chiefs, division heads, and undersecretaries do not like to receive bad news, particularly when it may force them to do extra work or call into question their prior job performance. Employees who bring problems to the attention of their superiors are as likely to be punished as advanced. The army suffered from this problem in Vietnam where, if a staff officer continued to tell his superiors that the war was going well, he could count on continued good assignments—often to an air-conditioned office in a rear area. However, once a subordinate began to relate bad news, he suddenly found himself out in the middle of a rice paddy doing "further research into the matter." If he lived through the research project, it became obvious to him that the proper course for survival was to tell people what they wanted to hear. I was always relating bad news about the state of the economy in Vietnam, and I used to pray that Charles Whitehouse would not get shot down in his helicopter, because he was almost unique in understanding that an officer had a moral obligation to bring bad news. Had he suffered an untimely demise, the people directly under him would have shipped me out to some area of low life expectancy in the twinkling of an eye.

It is actually dangerous for a career civil servant to short-circuit red tape, because occasionally this process can be embarrassing to an employee's superiors. If the superiors are small-minded people, they can fire or discipline the creative civil servant for his one mistake, when commendation for all the times he successfully made government work as it should is what is really in order. I remember once in Vietnam having a Filipina secretary who was continually ill. Once we thought she had hepatitis, and I took her to the Second Field Evacuation Hospital in Saigon, one of the finest hospitals in Asia at the time, where, because she was not an American, she was not entitled to be cared for. However, I blustered my way past the military police at the hospital gate—it was difficult to throw sick people out once they got in—and was confronted inside by a master sergeant in the Medical Service Corps, who asked who would pay the daily rate which the army exacted from non-Americans in such emergency circumstances. I asked him how much the rate was, and he said $42.00 a day. I told him that the girl worked for me and had no money and that I would have to be responsible. Thereupon he took out a table of rate schedules which looked something like an airline's foreign fare chart and began mumbling to himself. After five minutes he reported that I would be eligible for the $1.52-per-day rate and would need to pay $1.00 in advance. The girl got well; I never heard from the sergeant or the Medical Service Corps again; and I have always considered him to be among the world's truly superior civil servants.

All of my experiences with the executive branch in Vietnam merely reinforced what I had learned at home as a young man. For many years my father was generally responsible for fraud prevention in the Social Security Administration. His area of expertise was relatively specialized, but he always had an intense sympathy for the average claimant who was shunted about from computer to computer, department to department, and office to office. Occasionally he would get a call from someone with a problem who had been mistakenly connected to his office or had called after referring to the directory, not realizing that the term "investigations" did not mean "investigating lazy civil servants," but investigating fraud. Invariably my father either solved these persons' problems by unclogging bureaucratic bottlenecks or gave them a definitive negative answer. As I was growing up, I heard these stories day after day, and I concluded that about the only thing which can loosen clogged bureaucracy is an intelligent, resourceful, and concerned human being.

It is exactly the need for the intelligent, resourceful, and concerned human being which prompts increasing resort to the courts to force the engines of bureaucracy to *decide* issues. Often what frustrates the average citizen is not an adverse decision, but no decision. The procedures of a court are ideally suited to give a final resolution to any administrative issue, because both everyone and everything involved in the decision can be subpoenaed to appear at one time. It is, for example, frequently a nightmare for a developer to get a permit from a state health department for a subdivision sewer treatment system. It takes months for anyone in the state agency to look at the project plan, and then the plan may be rejected without specific comments about what the developer should do to comply with applicable health regulations. When the developer and his architect are finally convinced that they have complied with the applicable regulations, they may find their only recourse is to bring an action in mandamus to require the health department either to give them a permit or explain why the permit is being denied. If the agency is predicating its disapproval upon its own studies, the subpoena power may be relied upon to bring those studies forward, along with their authors, for cross-examination, and the court will decide whether the agency has legitimate grounds to string the developer along. At least the developer will get some idea of what he must do to have his system approved.

The advantage of a court is that it has a "docket" which moves along automatically, taking the first case filed and going through the cases more or less in order. Unless there is a problem of case backlog which precludes an expeditious hearing, all parties concerned know that on a given day not too far in the future, the matter will be brought on for full hearing, by which time briefs and records must be filed and witnesses brought for examination. Furthermore, the judge has no association with the bureaucracy involved and, subject to review by a higher court, he can enter any order he thinks appropriate to make the government work.

When a person goes to court and files a complaint against an administrative agency, a copy of that complaint, along with a summons requiring the agency to file an answer within thirty days, is served on the agency. The beauty of this is that the agency must respond within thirty days in some intelligent way and ultimately send a *living human being* into court. The agency cannot answer on a form or be represented by a computer. That very requirement often shakes things loose, because all the earlier vital steps in the decision-making process may have been controlled by low-echelon employees who have "not gotten around" to doing something. By bringing an action in court, the control of the entire matter *within* the agency passes immediately from the hands of glorified clerks into the hands of lawyers, who may quickly see that the petitioner is correct and direct their client, the agency, to take such steps as are necessary to resolve the dispute without court proceedings. The very action of going to court establishes a time perimeter around what is otherwise an open-ended process whose slow workings are dictated by the chosen pace of life of the bureaucrats. Here it is worth pointing out that courts are not effective because of the issues which they decide, but because of the issues which they do not decide. Whenever anyone goes to court, he loses even if he wins; the real winners are those who get justice because their adversaries *fear* eventual court proceedings and design their systems to avoid court confrontation.

Implicit in the whole structure of court control of administrative action is society's desire to remove important decision making from the hands of administrators and place it in the hands of politicians. To refer to judges as "politicians" may seem silly in light of the lengths to which we go to "depoliticize" courts, but the term politician in this context does not connote partisan or ideological politics, but merely experience with the entire body politic. Judges are judges because of politics, either by being elected or by being appointed. Furthermore, most judges are first appointed in their late forties, which means that the majority of sitting judges are in their middle fifties. They have seen a great deal and had considerable experience: they have defended innocent people against a corrupt system; they have represented struggling businesses against arrogant regulators; they have represented the consumer against the powerful predators of American industry; they have represented the government against organized crime; and, frequently, they have represented organized crime against the government.

The day-to-day practice of law is an inherently unintellectual undertaking, which may be why the results in reported cases are frequently more satisfactory than the reasoning. Good judges often intuit the correct result, although they may not be able to articulate their reasons in terms of theoretical structures which would be satisfying to law professors. By the time a good trial lawyer has practiced for twenty-five years, he has about seen it all. If he is any good, the stereotypes which he learned at university no longer impress themselves upon his imagination, and he understands that there are *two* sides to every issue. Concisely stated, he has learned to hate a little less.

The same, of course, is true of elected politicians and high appointed officials; however, they are not in control of the day-to-day operation of government. A G.S. 15 government executive is almost, by definition, devoid of broad based experience, because if he had not spent his entire life in a particular bureaucracy, he would not be a G.S. 15. The purpose of placing ultimate responsibility for administrative action into the hands of the courts, therefore, is to protect everyone outside the government *from* the government itself. The cases in the 1960s establishing "due process" rights for welfare claimants are examples of the courts' attempting to curtail precipitous, catastrophic action by very low-level civil servants. Merely by imposing the requirement of notice, hearing, and review, the courts raised the level of personnel who could make the final decision to cut off welfare payments. Similarly, in the cases handed down by the Circuit Court of Appeals for the District of Columbia in the 1970s protecting business from the Environmental Protection Agency (and I think particularly of the *International Harvester* case), there was an effort to reconcile industry's legitimate need for time both to do research and to overcome consumer resistance to environmental control devices with the agency's need to carry out its congressional mandate.

Young government administrators who have become drunk on the university wine of regulation as the summa bona take more lightly than their older counterparts in the courts the serious adverse effects on employment and production of draconian governmental schemes. The social and economic class of the regulators, their philosophical disposition, and the jobs they have been assigned make government and business natural enemies—adversaries from the word go, notwithstanding that such a result was not intended. To permit either party full sway would be like sending the foxes to guard the chickens.

Frequently, courses in administrative law teach that the theory of administrative review is that society cannot guarantee the quality of any substantive decision, but it can at least guarantee the rationality of the process by which any particular decision is obtained. It is assumed that by requiring notice of proposed agency action, affording a hearing to all parties, and providing some mechanism of review, the action of agencies will be better considered and the result more rational. Once, however, the agencies know how to protect themselves from reversal by the use of proper procedure, they can still be as arrogant, arbitrary, and self-dealing as they wish. The legitimate benefits of proper procedure in routine cases should not be discounted, but the procedural justifications for reversals are largely overrated.

Once an agency makes up its mind to do something, the most sedulous attention to refined procedure becomes nothing but window dressing. The courts, therefore, must be able to reverse agency action merely because the action is wrong, and this is what they do most of the time. The method which courts choose, however, to achieve substantive results is usually to veil their substantive determination in procedural garb. The classic reasons are that "all the evidence was not considered," "all affected parties were not adequately represented," or "the agency's opinion did not adequately illuminate its conclusions on all issues fairly raised." No matter how it is phrased, however, what the court is saying is that it disagrees with the agency and would prefer the status quo until the agency undertakes the time-consuming ordeal of doing the whole thing over again, by which time the personnel and policy may have changed.

The fact, of course, that courts have the power to review does not necessarily mean that they always use it wisely; frequently the agency is correct, and the court is wrong. I have seldom engaged in such acrimonious debate with my colleagues as in teacher discharge cases. From 1975 to 1980, the court on which I sit was loath to permit teachers to be fired for any reason and reversed almost every discharge which reached the court. Judges, too, have their passions and prejudices, and this particular majority just happened to be seized with surpassing sympathy for anyone who was about to lose his job. My own conclusion, memorialized in numerous dissents, was that since the teacher tenure laws make it almost impossible to fire a teacher, a board of education which undertakes to do so usually has good grounds. Since the schools are arguably run for the benefit of the children and not the teachers, I think that my court imposed an undue hindrance on the local boards' executive authority. The point, of course, is that although courts are superior institutions for reviewing policy, they may be just as wrong as any administrative agency. The difference between a court and an agency, however, is that the court does not have any *institutional* bias; it merely has the bias of the individual men and women in the judicial system—trial court, intermediate appellate court, and supreme court.

Any analysis of the proper role of courts must weigh courts as *institutions* for making certain decisions against other, alternative *institutions*. Overall, the reason that we have entrusted the courts with administrative review is that there is a lower probability of institutional error, even though the probability of human error may be as high. In our quest for improvement in the system, this may be the fundamental epiphany—that court performance is the resultant force of two vectors: institutional competence and human competence. Most criticisms of court performance confuse the two and conclude that the courts are either doing too much or too little. When courts make consistently wrong decisions, the cry goes out that "courts are too activist," and when the courts decline to pursue certain liberal goals, such as welfare reform, they are accused of being too "conservative."

The fundamental question with regard to the proper role of courts is, what functions are they most suited to perform as an institution? As we saw in the last chapter, they are peculiarly suited to passing certain types of general interest legislation (the conservative reader may phrase it howsoever he wishes), and this chapter should lead us to conclude that the courts are peculiarly suited to combatting bureaucratic self-dealing. In addition, courts have historically demonstrated a peculiar competence in protecting the private, free market economy from obliteration or absorption by the government sector. Finally, courts are able to shift the responsibility for truly important decisions away from young, Ivy League-trained but inexperienced lawyers and administrators into the hands of older, more experienced, and more truly representative persons from all over America who have no institutional stake in the outcome of any given issue.

It should be noted that all of the functions to which the courts are institutionally suited in this supervisory role over the bureaucracy are essentially "nay-saying." The court *prohibits* government involvement in the private sector; the court *strikes down* agency rules; the court *modifies* or *reverses* particular adjudicatory decrees. Although we found that in their interactions with the legislative branch, the courts were generally *positive,* to compensate for the inherent negativism of a legislature, in their interactions with the executive branch they are basically negative, to compensate for that branch's inherently *positive* orientation. The essential mission of the courts in bringing the myth system and operational system into alignment involves supplying balance. Our look at court positivism with regard to legislatures and negativism with regard to the executive should prove, at least, that courts are performing a balancing role. Furthermore, the balance has nothing to do with philosophy or ideology—it has only to do with the structural defects of other institutions. Obviously there are certain values which are being imposed by the courts, but they are generally the shared values of the society. When administrators or legislators are appointed to the courts, their opinions reflect no deviation from the mainstream of previous court philosophy.

Of course, no matter how legitimate the institution is for achieving balance, if it is staffed by fools the results will always be foolish. For the die-hard critics of the courts, the emphasis should shift from condemning court involvement in national affairs toward improving the performance of the institution. Part of this process is raising to a conscious, articulated level all of the institutional functions which courts perform. What is wrong with questioning the TVA in an open hearing about its *own* institutional reasons for wanting a dam? We are now a mature enough society that we can be open about the discrepancies between the myth system and the operational system. We should be able to address openly all of the shortcomings of human nature and the institutional structures we have created to mitigate those shortcomings.

5 THE POLITICAL MACHINE

The difference between the amateur and the professional in politics is that the amateur is concerned with ideas, while the professional is concerned with mechanics. Often it is difficult for the well-educated, suburban American to grasp that from Heartland America to the inner cities, day-to-day politics is not about ideas, but about money. Government is the largest employer in the United States, and state and local governments are usually the largest employers in any given locale. Government provides unskilled jobs for people who lack skills, interesting jobs for people who want something interesting, powerful jobs for people who want power, and nonjobs for people who hate to work.

If every person voted for every office in every election, the job of political technicians would be far more difficult. That, however, is not the case—only roughly 22 percent of the voters turn out in a typical primary election and 35 percent of the voters turn out for the typical off-year general election. A political organization is predicated upon low voter turnout combined with control of the machinery of the electoral process. For example, in about half the states there is one predominant party which has been in control for years. In the South it is the Democrat party, while in some of the conservative, midwestern states it is the Republican party. But even in states like New York or California where one party is not in complete control, major enclaves such as New York City are controlled by one party and can serve as significant political power centers based upon local patronage.

Political party affiliation, like religion, is largely a matter of inheritance. Although there is less straight ticket voting today than there was forty years ago, a person will usually vote according to his party registration when he is unfamiliar with the candidates or uninspired by the issues, which is usually the case. An area dominated by a particular political party will tend to remain dominated by it—the political equivalent of Newton's law of inertia. Where the minority party has been frozen out of office for years, it lacks leaders with impressive records to take on high-visibility incumbents. I have most frequently heard this phenomenon expressed in back rooms as "you can't beat something with nothing," implying that the incumbent will win notwithstanding a less than spectacular record merely because there is no one to run against him who is demonstrably better. The key to political success in most places, therefore, is not attractiveness to a majority of all voters, but rather nomination by the majority party either at a primary election or in a party convention. In most places nominations are made at primary elections.

The reader who has never been involved in local politics should not generalize to local races from his or her experience in presidential, gubernatorial, or senatorial races. In national politics, both the candidates and the issues have high visibility. The candidates are given extensive coverage in the media, and the issues frequently generate emotional responses among people whose only political involvement is the exercise of their vote. None of this applies to local politics, because local candidates for prosecuting attorney, county assessor, city council, district judge, and county commission are not media stars. Locally there are remarkably few emotional issues—people may be stirred by busing and integration, construction of new public works projects, or poor quality schools, but these issues are not within local control. Except when there are allegations of widespread corruption, local elections do not involve issue-oriented campaigns. When there are no issues and no media stars, the average voter does not bestir himself to go to the polls.

If the crucial party primary which determines election has a routine turnout of between 19 percent and 23 percent of the vote, all that is required for success is to get a little less than 12 percent of the registered vote to win. A good political machine devotes most of its time and attention to being able to deliver this 12 percent of the vote on a routine basis. When local issues heat up and a large, hostile voter turnout is expected, it then becomes possible for the local political machine to lose an election. At that point it can either attempt to make itself more attractive to the voters, or it can resort to certain election-stealing techniques which are available to it by virtue of its control of the election process. The important thing to remember, however, is that powerful political machines exist on the local or state level, not the national level. While national politics may have a monopoly on the interesting, emotional issues, it is local politics which have a monopoly on putting the screws on the average citizen. General Motors may take a beating from the federal government, but the man in the street has his run-ins with the local health inspector, local constabulary, and local zoning board. Most of the cases in the U.S. Supreme Court which make big constitutional law arise from some two-bit infighting between enormously uninteresting small-time parties.

The key to controlling the electoral machinery is political patronage and money. Although much government work is civil service, that fact alone does not protect employees from political machine bosses. Civil service may keep a person from being fired, but it usually cannot prevent him from being transferred, put in a windowless room without a telephone, or kept in the same grade and salary for twenty-five years. Only where government is really big, and civil service employees are centrally located in a city where they have no effective political power (such as Washington), can a person working for the government view politics with the same peace of mind as a college student or someone working for private enterprise.

Everyone who works for the incumbent political machine has a vested interest in its perpetuation, giving the machine an instantaneous numerical voter advantage over any challenger. While the challenger's wife, children, and mother may consider it crucial whether the challenger wins, nobody else in the system cares. The incumbent machine candidate, on the other hand, has tens, hundreds, or thousands of employees for whom his reelection is a matter of personal concern and not just civic interest. In most local governments, notwithstanding the facade of civil service, most employees initially get their jobs through political contacts, and they usually expect to receive promotion through the same contacts. With the low voter turnouts generally experienced in primary elections, an immediate 5 percent of all registered voters—that is, everyone who works for the local government unit concerned (city, county, state) and their families—translates into 15–20 percent of the vote cast in any given primary. This will almost always provide the margin of victory for machine-backed candidates. The decisive number in any given election, therefore, is not the number of citizens, the number of registered voters, or the number of candidates, but rather the number of voters who actually go to the polls on election day. In the 1940s when my grandfather was governor of West Virginia, the State Road Commission trucks used to go up the rural hollows to fetch the voters to the polls, and every one who was produced voted the correct way. Any machine is long on logistical support to get its people to the polling place.

Government jobs, however, are only the beginning of a power matrix based on patronage and economic symbiosis. Where it is necessary to overcome aggressive challengers who may be able to activate the media or purchase an effective election day organization, money is always available to the machine through its power to allocate government contracts. Every person who sells typewriters, office supplies, computers, asphalt, fire trucks, school buses, textbooks, architectural services, medical supplies, or anything else wants to do business with the government. State and federal statutes requiring competitive bidding have curtailed the more shocking abuses of friend-to-friend contracting, but having the good will of the purchasing authority seldom fails to be good for business. When the purchasing department writes the bid specifications for typewriters, what is to keep the specifications from being written to conform exactly to the design of an Underwood typewriter, while conformity would require a modification of a Royal typewriter? Specifications for office furniture can be drawn to conform exactly to a particular product line, requiring competitors to figure in the bid price the expense of tooling up to meet the specifications. Very few companies which make significant campaign contributions to winning political organizations fail to realize a significant return on their investment. Compared to the stock market, the political market is always bullish. This, partially, is why business backers are usually winner pickers rather than winner makers. Since business is interested in business and not ideas, it will usually support the favorite, which always gives the incumbent the edge even if he acts like Attila the Hun.

During Governor W. W. Barron's administration in West Virginia from 1960 to 1964, there developed some truly refined techniques for chilling competitive bids. My favorite example occurred at Weston State Hospital at the beginning of the administration, where the preferred bidder made artificially low bids on meat, bread, and other staples, while permitting his competitor to make the successful bid on radishes. After three months of driving a company truck two hundred miles every week to deliver $47.82 worth of radishes, that particular "successful" bidder determined that doing business with the state was not the way to get rich—thus the favored bidder could raise his prices confidently predicting no further competition. Since this was exactly the result which the purchasing authorities wanted, they took no action to encourage bids or to avoid subsequent single bids at high prices. They merely followed the written procedures set forth in the applicable statutes; if there was only one bidder, that was too bad for the people but good for the machine.

Money is the ultimate weapon on election day, because money guarantees that a candidate can get his voters to the polls. In 1978 West

Virginia's incumbent United States senator, Jennings Randolph, then seventy-nine years old, defeated former Governor Arch A. Moore, Jr., by 4,717 votes out of 493,351 votes cast, because he had approximately $100,000 more to spend on election day than Governor Moore. Governor Moore was a dynamic, fifty-five-year-old, high-visibility candidate who had a fair record as governor and was a star on television. Senator Randolph had been an excellent senator, but he made an uninspiring appearance and was going to have a tough time beating the standard mortality tables to finish out his term. Nonetheless, the southern West Virginia counties were all Democrat, and once voters in those counties were hauled to the polls, they were expected to vote a straight Democrat ticket. Fortunately for Senator Randolph there was rain on election day, which meant that the unorganized middle class stayed home in large numbers, and the $100,000 used to hire cars and drivers in the south provided the necessary margin of victory. Since the advent of election reform, federal investigations, and conspiracy statutes, the state road trucks are no longer used. The hired car and driver, however, have taken their place. Why could Senator Randolph raise more money? The answer is simple—he was chairman of the Senate Public Works Committee and had lots of friends. People in business remember their friends, because they want to do business again sometime. In all fairness, Senator Randolph was the better man, and I voted for him myself, but that was not why he won the election.

The Randolph–Moore race merely demonstrates that if a candidate is aware of the age, occupation, geographical location, ethnic background, or party preference of his natural supporters, sufficient money will guarantee that each and every one of those supporters will actually get to the polls. Free baby-sitting service, cars to transport supporters to the polls, free food and drink (often alcoholic) at "voter rallying points," and other amenities can increase the turnout from 22 percent to, say, 28 percent of the registered vote. The additional 6 percent which the candidate or slate of candidates pay to have turned out will vote the way they are expected to vote to a man.

Sometimes a good organization is not sufficient to carry the day, and then the machine must resort to a number of election-stealing techniques. The lore of these techniques would fill several volumes, but it is worth sketching the highlights here. Since the outright buying of votes is looked upon with disfavor by the federal authorities, the preferred and legal method for accomplishing the same result is to hire heads of households to "transport voters to the polls." In West Virginia this is an enumerated, statutory, permissible expense and is reported on the appropriate form to the secretary of state. This is a routine procedure everywhere and is generally accepted as a necessary evil. When, however, this innocuous technique is combined with the outright illegal technique of the "chain ballot," the results are sufficiently spectacular to send any undergraduate political science major off to medical school.

Under the "chain ballot" system, a member of the election team enters the polling place first when it opens in the morning and picks up his official paper ballot. For those unfamiliar with the paper ballot, it should be remembered that voting machines are expensive, and rural America votes with paper. Instead of depositing it in the box, however, he puts it in his pocket and deposits an empty envelope or bogus ballot in the box instead. Emerging from the polling place, he takes his clean ballot off the grounds where he marks it "properly" for the machine's slate. When the first householder, who has been paid $200 for carting his family in, shows up, the precinct captain hands him the marked ballot and tells him to deposit it in the voting box and bring out a clean ballot. The clean ballot is then marked for the next voter, and the process continues throughout the day, until the last person, who is usually part of the election team, deposits two ballots in the box as he leaves. When this technique is employed, the people on the "inside" of the polling place will also be members of the machine who will fail to notice that an empty envelope was deposited at first or that two votes are cast at the end. In this way, all the electorate can safely vote, and the machine rests assured that not one slip will be made in putting its candidates in office. Twenty such votes are easily worth $200, or $10 each, because every bought vote is potentially two votes—it is a vote for the candidate and a vote which has been successfully denied his opponent.

When I speak about people on the "inside," I am referring to the official poll-watchers—frequently wolves who have been sent to organize deer. Almost all elections are monitored by political appointees named by the Republican and Democrat executive committees. It is at this point that control of the mechanics of an election can have a decisive effect. Let us assume for a moment a typical Heartland American county in which the Republicans hold all the local offices in a state where the Republicans also hold most of the state offices. As is usual in such a county, there is a feeble Democrat executive committee which performs all the vain functions of the loyal opposition; however, they never win a general election. Under this set of circumstances, the Republican organization in control is not a bit concerned about the Democrats in the county.

The only thing which the Republican hierarchy fears is in-house opposition in the primary from other Republicans. Consequently, what the approved machine candidate wants to do is to steal the primary election, a process which has been well developed in this county since the party primary was invented.

One of the crudest, but most effective, methods of stealing an election is to "draw a full house." Since the election laws provide that each polling place be manned on election day by appointees of the respective party executive committees, party infighting often begins with a battle for control of the executive committee. Since the winning faction gets to name its own people to be *paid* poll-watchers (the per diem in West Virginia is currently $50), and the poll-watchers will vote for the candidates of the faction which appointed them, the winning faction starts out with three to six votes at every precinct before they ever open. Of far greater importance to the machine, however, is the fact that the poll-watchers have control of the mechanics of making the vote count.

In machine counties, most paid poll-watchers are about as honest as Fagin. Crucial, however, to our Republicans' being able to steal the election is the indifference of the Democrat poll-watchers to the whole issue of who wins the Republican primary. The only incentive to the Democrat poll-workers to be honest is the ability to cause embarrassment to the Republicans in a general election by exposing vote fraud. That inconvenient possibility, however, is easily overcome, since in politics silence is literally golden. In primary and general elections, there are both Republican and Democrat poll-watchers. The Republicans are usually appointed by the Republican County chairman and the Democrats are appointed by the Democrat County chairman. If the Republicans want to steal the election, they must find some way to corrupt the Democrat poll-watchers. Many people are willing to be poll-watchers for either party as long as they are paid off, and in that capacity they are also willing to do exactly what they are told, regardless of how legal.

Obviously all the political patronage in our typical locale is channeled through the Republican hierarchy, and while the Democrats may be out of office, like everyone else they would like a little piece of the action. To whom, then, does the Democrat party chairman go for at least a little patronage which he can dispense? Naturally, to the Republican party chairman, who may quite possibly be a close personal friend. In return for golden silence, the Democrats will get a few school-bus-driving jobs (boards of education are very political), school cafeteria jobs, state liquor store jobs, and state road jobs. There may even be a few juicy contracts let to Democrats or friends of the Democrat chairman. In a truly well-run machine county, the opposition party becomes merely an appendage of the controlling faction of the majority party.

In return for the sweetheart deal in the dispensation of patronage, at election time the Republican chairman asks the Democrat chairman to appoint the Republican chairman's people (who can be either regular Democrats or Democrats registered only for the occasion) to be the Democrat party election officials. The Democrat chairman gladly agrees to appoint the machine-sponsored election officials, who demonstrate a remarkable indifference to what is going on at the counting board on election day.

It may appear to some that this scenario is too crude to be true; however, I can assure the reader that the combination of the paper ballot and the average voter is a wondrous thing to behold. The average voter does not vote for all offices in an election; he usually votes only for the offices, like congressman or sheriff, which interest him, leaving the others blank. Admittedly it is a bit obvious to erase one mark on a paper ballot and replace it with another, even though the fact that voters can legitimately do so themselves might keep erasures from being suspiciously regarded. Erasing, however, is usually not necessary; all that normally is required is to give the machine-sponsored candidate all the votes on ballots where that office was not marked. This is done by the poll-watcher assigned to the counting desk. As most contested primary elections are won by 2 or 3 percent of the total vote cast, fifteen extra votes in each precinct are usually sufficient to assure a smashing victory. In this situation, what the incumbent Republican machine has achieved is a "full house"—its people have been put in charge of the mechanics of administering the election, and they have used the mechanics alone to manipulate the result. The same effect can be achieved using voting machines.[1]

1. Another version of the "full house" involves the election officials' marking the ballots for the voters. In many precincts, the voters are so indifferent to politics that they actually have no independent choice and are quite happy to have friendly election officials cast their votes. The flavor of the whole process is given in a West Virginia case called *Brooks v. Crum* arising from the May 1972 primary election. The trial court in that case stated the salient facts as follows:

> The Court finds that of the total of some 232 persons who testified they voted at that precinct, 121 of them received assistance in voting by election Commissioners Wellman and/or Marcum, the evidence in this regard being undisputed, except that a very few of the 121 persons testified that only one of those election officials was behind the curtain of the voting machine when such assistance was rendered, while those Commissioners both testified that both of them were always behind the curtain thereof when assistance was being given any voter. There is no evidence that any of the other election officers at that precinct rendered assistance to any voter in casting his vote. Those two Commissioners further testified that they rendered assistance to all voters request-

Some of the techniques which I have just described are becoming museum pieces. When I was first elected to office in 1970, there were many places where these tactics were business as usual, but increasing supervision by the federal government through the United States attorneys has curtailed some of the more colorful abuses. While outright vote fraud may be on the wane in all but a handful of remote rural counties or in the heart of the inner cities, a description of hardball machine politics illuminates much of the law generated in the nineteenth century concerning government intrusion into the private sector. Control of political machines requires a very well-developed civil service, an independent, outside authority like the Department of Justice, and a number of independent media agencies which cannot be either bought or intimidated. All during the nineteenth century and up until 1938, when the U.S. Supreme Court was limiting the degree to which government could intrude itself into the private sector, it had in mind the enormous potential power of a *combined* political-business machine. Television, education, and sophisticated institutions have decreased the danger of this type of unified power slightly. Far more to the point, however, is America's shortage of skilled labor, which makes political patronage jobs less attractive than they were when day-to-day American society was characterized by widespread un-

---

ing it, which may have amounted to 75 per cent, though they believed it was not over 50 per cent, of all voters who voted at that precinct, and that they did so without first ascertaining, as is required by *W. Va. Code,* 3-4-21, before assistance in using a voting machine may lawfully be requested by a voter, either that any voter had a physical disability which, in the opinion of those Commissioners, prevented him from operating the machine, or that the voter had indicated on his registration record that he was unable, because of illiteracy or physical disability, to write, and did so without requiring any voter to present a doctor's certificate that the voter was blind, as is required by *W. Va. Code,* 3-1-34, which deals with the rendering of assistance to blind persons in the use of paper ballots.

By the court's count, the registration records of only 4 of the persons who were assisted by the Commissioners indicated that they were illiterate, namely, Ester Matthews, showing her to have signed the registration record by the use of a mark and having noted thereon "Can't write"; Smith Vance whereon he was indicated to be "Illiterate"; Thomas Marcum on which he is shown to have signed the registration record by his mark; and Maggie Porter on which she is shown to have signed the registration record by her mark.

The reasons for requesting assistance given in the testimony of another five of the 121 persons were that they could not see, could not see to vote, could not see good and could not read or write, though none of the registration records of those five persons so indicated, and the remainder of the 121 persons gave reasons for their requesting assistance such as that they could barely read, or could read only "printing" and not "writing", or that they failed to bring their eyeglasses to the polls, or were unfamiliar with voting machines, or were in a hurry and did not want to take the time to familiarize themselves with the ballot, and the like. The court finds a great many of the 121 persons were actually illiterate for all practical purposes. One junior in college requested and was given assistance.

employment or employment in the private sector under arduous and unpleasant conditions.

When my grandfather was in the United States Senate intermittently from 1922 to 1958, senators had far more control of the local state machine than they do today, because they had direct control of numerous patronage jobs through such agencies as the Post Office and the Works Progress Administration (WPA). Furthermore, they virtually named all the federal judges and United States attorneys, which gave them substantial control of the federal government's ability to intervene in local affairs. Where United States senators were in bed with the local and state machines, they could instantly chill any effort by the federal government to enforce honest elections. Today the U.S. Senate is impotent only because it has decided to be impotent; when it acted like a club, it had a club.

Today television has eroded the influence which political machines have on statewide senatorial elections—money is still the primary ingredient for success, but it is money to buy an image. Since United States senators now owe their election to either their independent wealth or their ability to raise money on a broad base, there is less incentive for the United States Senate to keep control of the machinery of federal enforcement. That, however, was not the case before television. Fifty years ago the incumbent political machine frequently controlled the local newspapers, and there were no competing media. Newspapers which were dependent upon adequate advertising for survival could be bullied in the same way that a good machine bullies everyone else, so that a United States senator could not go over the heads of the machine—he was dependent upon the machine's good will. The existence of national media, and regional media in television, has made it difficult to control information. Furthermore, the federal government has become so big that the bureaucracy is sufficiently insulated that federal officials can overtly challenge congressmen and senators without fear of retribution.

Today election officials who have been cowed by the agents of the Justice Department may be less willing to break the law overtly than they were twenty years ago, but they can achieve the same result under ordinary circumstances through more subtle means. Assume, for example, that older voters are disenchanted with the existing political structure and that their votes would be decisive in a primary or general election. If all the polling places are located on the second floors of buildings, and the buildings themselves are selected because they are on hills or have long entrance stairways, an older person will not be able to get to the polls with ease. Hardly anyone believes that his one vote is crucial, so if his doctor has advised him against going up stairs, he will just not vote.

On the other hand, let us assume that it is young voters whom the machine fears. All counties have money set aside for "county recreation," and there is no reason why a free, all-day rock concert with a conspicuous policy of nonenforcement of the marijuana laws cannot be scheduled on election day. While that may not keep all the kids away from the polls, it will probably keep enough of them away to make a difference in the outcome of the election.

One of my earliest political memories was of my grandfather on the evening of the 1948 general election between President Truman and Governor Dewey. I was barely seven years old and it was pouring rain—not just an ordinary fall rain, but literally torrents. My grandfather was to make the speech at the Marion County Courthouse in Fairmont to the assembled Democrat faithful as had been his habit on every election eve for over a third of a century. I was unhappy, because rain interferes with the pastimes of children, but my grandfather was absolutely elated, because rain is wonderful for organization politicians. The 1948 presidential race was the election in which Dewey was such a front-runner that the *Chicago Tribune* had already made up its early morning edition announcing a Dewey victory—thus the election was not a sure thing even in Democrat West Virginia, where the Democrats had taken such a beating in 1946 that my grandfather was returned for two years from Washington to the private practice of law.

My grandfather's good cheer as he came in soaking wet from the rally emanated from his recognition that rain keeps ordinary, middle-class people *away* from the polls. The trick, however, is that it does not keep the organization away from the polls. When the organization comes to pick you up to go to vote, you go—rain or shine—or somebody near and dear to you loses his or her job. The organization makes it both easy and pleasant to vote—friends and relatives apply a certain peer pressure to do one's civic duty. Since the only significant organization in West Virginia in 1948 was Democrat, with a Democrat governor in control of all the state patronage, the result had to be more favorable than if the sun were shining and *everyone* came out to vote.

Natural rain, however, is not indispensable, since when it is impossible to arrange for the necessary rain there are some substitute techniques which will decimate the unorganized vote. The best is to move all the polling places. People get used to their neighborhood polling places; frequently they have voted at the same school, fire hall, or state road garage for twenty years. But the location of polling places are not set in stone, and the place where each precinct votes is determined by some authority—county court, city council, or board of elections. If two weeks before an election there is a little "election reform" designed to make polling places, for example, more accessible to the handicapped, most voters will arrive where they think they should vote only to discover that they must travel ten blocks to cast their ballots. If they are old, crippled, uninterested, tired, or late, their franchise will have been obliterated. The organization, on the other hand, will have paid cars and drivers who will make sure that all the favorably disposed voters who can be targeted will make it to the polls.[2]

These few examples of the workings of a political machine in modern, twentieth-century America should give some indication that in order for the concept of one-man, one-vote to be more than window dressing, the franchise must be protected by some machinery outside the control of the existing political authority. It must be remembered, however, that so far we have been focusing on machines capable of perpetuating themselves in *normal* times by capitalizing on voter *indifference*. In a way, that fact alone implies that most citizens feel fairly treated and that government is proceeding with some modicum of efficiency and justice. While all of the enumerated techniques are confounding to vapid challengers who wish to run on colorless platforms like "honesty" or "returning the government to the people," when the voters in America get serious the elective political machinery will work well, notwithstanding attempts to frustrate

2. I tend to dwell on West Virginia examples because they are the ones I know in great detail; however, the practices I describe exist everywhere. In sophisticated New York, for example, the race between challenger Allard Lowenstein and machine incumbent John Rooney in the Democrat primary in 1972 put to shame anything we have had in West Virginia in recent years in the way of dirty tricks. Lowenstein mounted such a strong campaign that the local machine had to resort to truly crude election-stealing techniques to beat him. Among these were losing the "buff cards" that voters were required to sign; failing to inform voters that their registration had expired because they had not voted in two general elections in successive election years; changing the polling places less than ten days before the election with no notice to the thousands of voters affected by the change (the postcards informing the voters of the change arrived after the election); and delivery of broken voting machines to pro-Lowenstein areas.

Lowenstein contested the election, and when the case reached the New York court, the court ordered a special election. Now, however, comes the rub; with only twelve days to campaign, from the date the decision was handed down to the date set for the special election, the insurgent forces of Lowenstein were soundly defeated by the Democrat machine, because the machine could turn its "regulars" out even for a *special* election—the New York equivalent of the proverbial trip by state road trucks. While the margin of victory in the regular election had been very narrow, even with every election-stealing technique being played to a fare-thee-well, in the special election Rooney defeated Lowenstein by nearly two to one.

the electoral process, primarily because the techniques which really gum up the works have been foreclosed by the courts. Why does the electoral system with its commitment to one-man, one-vote work so well in the United States and fail so miserably in Uganda, Chile, the Philippines, and almost everywhere else in the world where it has been tried? Obviously part of the answer has to do with the bounty of the American continent, our early commitment to public education, and our lack of serious social problems on the scale of other multiethnic and multiracial societies—but a great deal of it has to do with our courts and our pragmatic constitutional law.

The cynical techniques described above are child's play compared to what goes on in other countries. What would happen in this country if every state machine through its majority in the legislature could employ any techniques it chose for organizing elections or, at least, any techniques not specifically outlawed by Congress? The first method of disenfranchising people is the selective literacy test. Since most of the poor in the United States are also grossly undereducated or speak something other than English as a first language, a test requiring an extensive reading knowledge of English will disqualify most poor people from the voting process. One person in five in the United States has serious problems with reading. Historically, until the Warren Court struck it down, this was the method of disenfranchising those who threatened the existing distribution of wealth. For those trustworthy team voters who happened to be illiterate, there was always the friendly county clerk or recorder of elections who winked at a few mistakes and gave a passing score for "substantial compliance."

The poll tax was another good way of keeping the poor at home on election day. A two-dollar poll tax, which, by the way, existed in enlightened Massachusetts when I was a student there in 1956, is comparatively insignificant to the middle-class household, but it is a real sacrifice for the poor. For trusted members of the political machine, there was always money available to pay the poll tax, but the challenger who might be a champion of the poor found that his natural constituency was discouraged from turning out. The Supreme Court struck this technique down during the Warren Court in a case coming out of civilized Virginia.

An effective opposition is predicated upon open discussion of the strengths and weaknesses of parties and candidates. Any control of the media—newspapers, radio, or television—can have a decisive effect on the outcome of elections. The press is primarily in the business of hustling a buck—television and radio stations along with newspapers are in the private sector and must show a profit. The media are crusaders because it is profitable, not because they are civic charities. Since unearthing corruption, treachery, and incompetence in government brings an audience, all news media and all elected officials are usually portrayed as natural enemies. Readers of small-town, local newspapers, however, know that the newspaper is frequently an ally of the incumbent machine. It has been my experience that, generally speaking, the media will be on whatever side is most profitable. There is nothing which a serious political machine would like to do better than to stifle criticism in the press, and this can be done in any of three ways. The easiest and cleanest way is to buy the media by routine payoffs to top and middle management. I have seen numerous examples of this technique. Failing that, threatening the media with a loss of advertising from private firms who are either in the pocket of or at the mercy of the machine is always very effective. A glance at most local newspapers will disclose that they are not very controversial. Where a newspaper already has a monopoly of a market, its management is loath to make enemies, which is an implicit part of any partisan activity in any local controversy. The staff, of course, likes to be controversial, but the managements are usually successful in tempering them, partially because good investigative reporting is expensive, and where a newspaper already has a monopoly these costs cannot be recouped. Finally, if the first two methods both fail, resort may be had to the passage of strict libel laws and bankrupting law suits.

By far the most dangerous threat to the honest media is the last, because newspapers frequently distort the facts in a case, usually because they are misinformed. Consequently, with the right laws and sufficiently high punitive damages for injury to reputation, papers can quickly be put out of business. This process of putting newspapers out of business when they are negligent has been characterized by the U.S. Supreme Court as creating a "chilling effect on First Amendment [freedom of the press] rights," and in fact there are few things more chilling than the prospect of bankruptcy. If this particular scheme were permitted, papers which are currently energetic in pointing out political problems would become like most small-town rags and would be reduced to carrying noncontroversial national news, local social events, sports, and the lonely hearts column, because they could not afford to risk the consequences of their own negligence. A similar technique, of course, can be used against political opponents directly—they can be sued for libel and slander whenever they exaggerate anything. In fact, more to the point, they can be sued even when they do not exaggerate anything. Litigation itself is enormously expensive—the threat of a law suit itself will chill anyone's First Amendment rights. Thus we have the miracle of the First Amendment defense and the expeditious, cheap device of the summary judgment, by which the trial court can dismiss a complaint before the defendant has to mortgage the family farm to pay his lawyer.

Other even less subtle methods of maintaining machine control are: (1) the establishment of complicated voter registration procedures for members of minority parties; (2) discrimination against those with eccentric or minority views who seek public employment, defense industry employment, or graduate education opportunities in the state system; and (3) discriminatory licensing or regulation of the exercise of a common calling or profession for those who threaten the existing power structure. None of these techniques is precluded by a requirement for ''majority rule,'' and they have all been tried in this country in one form or another with varying degrees of success in their time. In the early nineteenth century, there were the alien and sedition laws designed to curtail open discussion in the press; after the Civil War, there were the literacy test, poll-tax, and voter residency requirements; and finally, in the 1950s, there was the Smith Act aimed at destroying the Communist party.

So far, only the political machine's potential restraints on voting have been discussed. However, an entrenched political machine can do more than just mismanage government; it can also destroy or distort the economy, leading to stagnation and the inevitable frustration which limitations on economic upward mobility always causes. It is impossible to stress strongly enough that aside from the ego and power drives of office-seekers, economic interest is what primarily motivates people to be active in politics. The enormous power of government makes the possession of political power a mighty engine for self-enrichment. When I was economics officer for a quarter of South Vietnam, I had a constant fight with the professional economists on the staff of the Agency for International Development in Saigon, because they were wedded to post-Keynesian government regulation as a legitimate means of developing an economy. They believed that it was a great insight of the twentieth century that an economy could be *regulated* by government, and they encouraged the creation of South Vietnamese bureaucracies to regulate everything from the manufacture of fishing boats to the cutting of timber. I tried to explain that it was simpleminded to generalize from the experiences of a postdepression, highly industrialized United States to a preindustrial, agricultural, peasant Vietnam. Out in the boondocks where I spent most of my time, I knew that wherever there was a checkpoint on a road or a permit which needed to be issued by the government, there was someone in uniform with his hand out. In primitive countries, people join the government for the purpose of knocking down the populace for bribes. It is a natural way of life.

One of the bitterest battles which Queen Elizabeth I fought with the Commons came during the lord chancellorship of Sir Nicholas Bacon, in the twilight of her career, when her policy of granting monopoly patents not only created the greatest political hostility to the crown known in her reign, but also got the courts into the common law manufacturing business. The courts became engaged in a course of passive resistance to the allocation of economic benefits to those with *political* influence, that is, the granting by the crown to its favorites of exclusive rights to manufacture or distribute certain necessities. This experience has its counterpart in the pattern of perverting the government to private ends which is so prevalent today in primitive countries. The emergence of a broad-based middle class and the English civil wars of the seventeenth century were required to point out to our civilization that corruption is not inevitably a characteristic of government. It was not until 1776 and the publication of the *Wealth of Nations* that it was recognized that the best way to curtail government corruption (at least in a primitive society) is to forbid the government to control anything. Adam Smith's doctrine of laissez faire was a radical, revolutionary doctrine of the Enlightenment; the fact that it was used in the twentieth century as a justification for a system which no longer worked in an advanced civilization should not detract from its legitimate insights into the tendency of the political process to subvert the economic process.[3]

3. One of my good friends and protectors in the state legislature when I was a young, newly elected member was a coal and gas mogul from southern West Virginia named Harry Pauley. When I went to the legislature in 1971, Harry was an ordinary member from McDowell County who sat right behind me, which is how we came to be friends. In 1960, however, he had been Speaker of the House and at that time the most powerful man in the legislature, but he had a hankering for the executive mansion, so he left to run for governor. Harry was an honest, but highly conservative southern Democrat, only slightly to the right of Ivan the Terrible on most social issues. He had started with less than a high-school education and by sheer business intelligence had made millions of dollars and educated himself to the point where he was the most witty and eloquent speaker in the legislature. Having decided to run for governor, he was sitting one day in his Speaker's office when a janitor from a large downtown Charleston office building appeared at his door with a shopping bag. The janitor said that he had been sent up to the capitol by a group of coal operators to deliver the bag, which it turned out contained $200,000 in twenty-dollar bills. This was before the days of serious election campaign reporting requirements and indicates the intensity of interest which can be generated in industry to secure candidates who are favorably disposed to business. Harry withdrew when he heard that his opponent had lined up the AFL-CIO and the United Mine Workers (who had their own janitors and shopping bags). He observed to an intimate that even a massive spending campaign might result in his finishing second. The only thing that ever made Harry a serious candidate, however, was money.

It is possible to organize the disadvantaged, the old, and even the young, but the sustained interest of any of these groups usually depends upon a promise of some substantial economic benefit. While the young are more likely to become involved for fun and frolic, the old are usually concerned about real estate taxes, homestead exemptions, public transportation, and better medical care. While the "public interest" is allegedly the campaign platform of every political candidate, the "public interest" is not conspicuously represented on election day in the form of big bucks, and outside of enclaves dominated by small ethnic groups, American foreign policy questions have never manned a polling place. What is present on election day are large contributions from every special interest group which the elected official could possibly help. Consequently, unless he is independently wealthy, any elected politician, regardless of the political line which he talks, must necessarily give some consideration to financing the next election. As one old politician once advised a young man who was preparing to file for statewide office, "Son, talk left and buy right!"

The quintessential political machine develops when political forces grow so strong that they can dominate the business forces and require them to align their power on the side of the political machine. Usually the process is perceived as the other way around, namely, the business interests become so powerful that they can dominate the politicians. In general, however, business would just like to be left alone by government, and it is the members of government who actively go out to knock down business for logistical support. The Watergate scandal of 1973–74 disclosed that the initiative to create a Republican machine financed by business was taken by President Nixon and his aides; the testimony does not disclose that business came to the president with contributions in the hope of co-opting the government. At best the business contributors were reluctant, partially because under the prevailing election laws it was difficult to get sufficient cash out of corporations to make the contributions and the management did not have access to the quantity of funds demanded. One aspect of the potential business-political machine is graft, but I shall not dwell on it here for the same reasons which caused me to omit it from the last chapter, namely, that it is as illegal as armed robbery and not an exclusively political problem. Far more to the point in this chapter are all the marginally legal opportunities for political machines to benefit from collaboration with business forces other than by merely lining politicians' pockets.

For example, while government has many jobs, the private sector as a whole has many more. In fact, roughly 66 percent of all persons in the private sector are employed by small business—the type of firms which qualify for loans from the Small Business Administration. Small business is so easy to bankrupt through the tightening of the regulatory screws that the opportunities for blackmail boggle the mind. This is why cops eat free at restaurants and munch unpurchased fruit as they walk their beats. On a higher level, control of the regulatory screws means that a politician can place his surplus machine members, not in government, but in industry, which happily, for particularly favored employees, can often pay a great deal more than government. Thus, if a politician wants a $100,000 a year job for his brother-in-law who routinely makes a $25,000 contribution to the war chest, he can find him a job in industry. A strong state politician can—if he has a mind to do so—also dictate which law firms, contracting sources, and distributor outlets *private industry* will use merely by "suggesting" that certain facilities be used. Many big-time politicians who inconveniently find themselves out of office have business sugar daddies who pick them up as lawyers or consultants for four or eight years until they can make a comeback. It is implicit in the social contract between businessmen and big-time politicians that when politicians lose elections they will be employed at attractive salaries by business. Other politicians, even the enemies of losers, watch how the fallen are treated, because a business's past record in this regard is the surest clue to its future intentions. I once knew a race track which for many years had a state senator on its payroll at the track as a steward. Obviously one of the things which this senator did was to watch out for the racing interests; however, in 1972, when the senator lost an election, his employment continued uninterrupted, a fact which did not go unremarked by other senators.

It makes a great deal of difference to business whether it is routinely audited by the state tax commissioner, whether the local United States senator will go to bat for it before federal regulatory commissions, and whether the state will invest in social overhead capital, such as roads or flood control, in and around its facilities. Once a political machine is in control, it can extort an entire catalogue of concessions from private business, which will certainly raise the price of goods and services to the average consumer.

Not only is business compelled to trade cooperation with the machine for relief from regulation, but business also likes to enlist the positive support of government in order to gain a competitive advantage. Of all the schemes I have seen, my favorite is the proposal to build a municipal parking garage with five hundred parking spaces and one hundred stores.

The simplicity of this one is what makes it attractive. The developer enlists the urban renewal authority, pursuant to state law, to condemn a piece of prime downtown land for the construction of a parking garage of his design and specifications. The developer then offers to lease the garage from the municipality for ninety-nine years at a set rent which will be sufficient to retire all the bonded indebtedness incurred to construct the facility. The developer arranges for the urban renewal authority to issue tax-exempt bonds for construction, which cuts the interest rate in half from what it would cost in the private sector, and the developer agrees to maintain the building, provide the parking facilities, and pay 1 percent of the gross receipts in addition to the fixed rent to the municipality in return for the concession.

On the surface this looks like a perfectly legitimate deal, but what the developer has just done is use his machine connections to support his exclusively private purpose, which is not to provide the city with five hundred parking spaces, but to create a downtown mall at public expense. The one hundred stores which will be located in the mall will have a powerful competitive advantage over other businesses in town, because they will be conveniently located next to each other and to their own parking facility. The developer has succeeded in doing through eminent domain what he could never have done by private means, namely, acquire an entire city block at an artificially imposed fair market value, rather than at the value which obstinate landowners would demand.

By the terms of the developer's lease, he accepts the risks of depression, economic reverse, etc., and must pay the fixed rent to the city every year regardless of conditions. Ordinarily, however, the developer will protect his personal assets by doing business in corporate form, limiting his total liability for business reverses to the total sum of the corporate assets, which would be negligible. In return for taking this so-called risk and for low charges for parking, the developer is given the right to set the rents for stores at whatever amount he desires. Everyone knows about inflation, and everyone knows that a store which rents today for $1,000 a month will rent for $2,000 a month a few years from now. The object of the scheme is that this profit will accrue to the developer and not to the municipality, which has used its authority to condemn the land and issue the bonds. When a favored developer, through the smoke screen of a public authority, can borrow at one-half the effective interest rate and purchase land at condemnation prices, he can drive everyone else out of business.

The government is an awesome force to compete with, but if it is on the side of whatever business venturer happens to be in partnership with the existing political machine, it can be a potent force for personal gain. At first blush, the parking authority scam looks so outrageous that any newspaper would play it for the scandal of the year, and the voters—no matter how generally indifferent—would turn out to a man to throw the rascals out. The reader must remember, however, that all the pieces of the puzzle have been put together here in a relatively condensed form. In the real world the pieces emerge separately, and it is difficult for the average newspaper reporter to comprehend the whole scheme from the pieces as they come to light one at a time.

Here's how to do it if you wish to avoid a scandal: First, the urban renewal authority makes a declaration that additional downtown parking is necessary and requests proposed plans from the business community and interested citizens. A few plans are submitted, including the one of the favored developer, and duly taken under advisement. Then an announcement appears that it will be necessary to incorporate certain rent-paying tenants into the building to keep the parking fees down. Obviously nobody except competing stores will object to that. Then it is announced that bids will be accepted on the management of the building in compliance with specifications available at the office of the municipal authority. Ah, there's the rub!

Frequently there will be only one firm in the business of making a killing from this type of deal, and there will be only one serious bid. However, it is possible that some other bidder may smell a sweet deal brewing and consider bidding. At this point the political machine steps in. Unless the deal-killing prospective second bidder is in the game merely because he likes to see government well managed, he will get the message that "open bidding" was not actually contemplated. If, for example, the outside bidder happens to run a chain of stores or movie theaters, the municipality may suddenly find it necessary to do some extensive "street repair work" outside his premises with attendant jackhammer noises, traffic diversions, and inconvenience to pedestrians (to say nothing of potential interruption of electricity and water) for the next several weeks. If the outside bidder still does not catch on, health inspectors, building inspectors, fire marshals, occupational safety inspectors, and even Internal Revenue agents will begin to appear on his doorstep until the message finally sinks in.

If these Neanderthal methods of delivering the message have become unfashionable, there are more subtle ways of deterring outside bidders. One is the manipulation of the requirement that bidders be declared "responsible,'' a term which means that the bidder must have some experience in the business and have sufficient financial assets to meet any unforeseen obligations. Obviously, the concept of the ''responsible bidder'' is susceptible to result-oriented application, so that our friend who has hatched this scheme will obviously be ''responsible.'' In any sweetheart deal, the surprise bidder may find that he is not ''responsible'' enough to bid on the project, although he may be responsible enough to incur $100,000 in legal fees contesting the decision in court.[4]

If a ''surprise bid'' appears, the urban renewal authority will postpone the opening of bids on the pretext that certain changes in the specifications must be made, thus permitting the necessary time for the delivery of messages. In the end, there will be only one bidder, and it will be our developer who initiated the scheme, although a truly skillful, public-relations-conscious machine might well arrange for two or three other outrageously high bids to be submitted for window dressing. When the local paper begins hearing complaints from the business community, which is slowly perceiving the dim outline of the scheme, the authority replies that it duly gave notice to all potential bidders by letter, and to the public by publication, yet nobody wanted to bid. The interesting paradox for our form of government is that democratic government invites rather than discourages this type of deal in the operational system. The preeminent beauty of democracy in comparison to other forms of government is that it tends to spread the fruits of corruption around a little more.[5]

The one group likely to protest the parking garage scam is the business community, which will be forced to compete with the government-assisted project and to relinquish its prime land to the authority under compulsion of the eminent domain power. There is absolutely nothing wrong with an urban renewal authority's building a parking garage; that is obviously a public purpose. What is wrong is the incorporation of the hundred stores, which makes the whole enterprise not primarily a parking

4. Sometimes the local political machine can get preference for its patrons enacted into law. In both Kentucky and Ohio, for example, local bidders are given a preference over out-of-state bidders and may bid considerably higher than their out-of-state competition and still be awarded the contract.

5. When I was serving in Asia in 1968, I was sent to the Philippines to study the workings of that country's Agricultural Development Bank. In the days before the Marcos dictatorship, the Philippines was a corrupt, but robust, democracy, and I was the guest for several weeks of the elected governor of Batangas Province, Feliciano Leviste. We ate every night upstairs in the governor's private apartment in the executive mansion; however, in the downstairs dining room the governor fed anyone off the street who came looking for food. There were routinely twenty people, often strangers, eating at every meal. ''Democracy in action,'' I thought at the time and have not changed my opinion. I doubt that Marcos feeds anyone.

garage with a few ancillary stores, but primarily a shopping mall with a few ancillary parking spaces.

The reason that we do not have more deals of this type is that the courts stand ready to strike the whole scheme down at any one of a number of stages. First, if a landowner protests the condemnation of his land, a court can restrain the municipality from taking the land for a project involving a substantial private purpose. Second, the nature of the project can also be the project's undoing in the routine proceeding before the highest state court to determine the constitutionality of the proposed bond issue. The court can strike down the issuance of government bonds for the scheme if it serves no legitimate public purpose. Finally, if no opinion is obtained from the highest court in the state at the planning stage, the court can strike down the payment of interest and principal on the bonds at some later time at the instigation of any taxpaying citizen—a dangerous business for bondholders, which is why they insist beforehand on an opinion from the highest court in the state concerning the project's legitimacy.

The courts' power in this area, while occasionally codified in statutory law and made a part of the whole urban renewal authority law, is justified by reliance upon the Fifth and Fourteenth Amendments to the U.S. Constitution and their state constitutional counterparts which provide, at least through interpretation, that private property shall not be taken except for a "public purpose." In the United States, careful court supervision can potentially break up cozy deals involving the grant of government support to money-making enterprises in exchange for financial support to the political machine. Accordingly, the scenario just presented seldom occurs, because everyone knows in advance that any citizen whose family home happens to be part of the proposed project can kill the deal by contesting the eminent domain proceeding. Furthermore, as is more likely the case, any business affected adversely can contest the validity of the project at hearings on the constitutionality of the bond issue, so that the courts are capable of giving a satisfactory answer to an economic problem which none of the adversely affected litigants could possibly achieve through the political process. It is ironic and paradoxical that the democratic process can be successful only if it is supervised by a nondemocratic institution. This particular epiphany is crucial to an understanding of why democratic institutions elsewhere have failed so miserably throughout history and continue even today to fail elsewhere in the world.

If there is no wholesale buying of elections, disenfranchisements, or restraints on publicizing abuses, the political process will take action against graft, corruption, and other forms of self-dealing. The political process, however, does not accomplish this on its own. The courts strike down elaborate schemes of government-business partnership and prevent the building of political-business machines which have such a monopoly of the economic power that they can extort continued political support through the manipulation of bank credit, large-scale private employment, government benefits, access to public services, and all other critical aspects of life.

The Constitution does not protect society from a perversion of the democratic political process any more than a hundred-dollar bill protects the integrity of the American monetary system. The fact that a hundred-dollar bill alleges that it is legal tender for all debts public and private may help a person pay off an old debt at a ridiculously low real cost; however, it does not inspire a renter of property or a seller of bread to accept any given amount of money as adequate compensation for his product. Many pieces of paper money in other countries similarly inscribed have been carted to the store in wheelbarrows to purchase goods transported home in pockets. The integrity of the American monetary system is attributable to the actions of numerous institutions, among them the Federal Reserve Board, the Department of the Treasury, and the Comptroller of the Currency. In exactly the same way, it is the *institution* of the courts which guarantees the procedural integrity of the democratic process and not anything which has ever been written in the Constitution. The battle between the "interpretists," who believe that the courts should apply only those principles squarely set forth in the Constitution, and the "noninterpretists," who believe that the courts should apply fundamental values *implied* by the Constitution, both miss the point. The courts provide an institutional supervisory role which responds to the abuses of other institutions. The Constitution and the courts cannot be separated; together they form one institution.

The practical problem for those who must live with court intervention into the most trivial issues of everyday life is that this institutional role is open-ended. Cases do not come to the courts with huge signs on them reading, "I am a threat to the Democratic Process." In the course of routine litigation—for example, an eminent domain action similar to the one in the hypothetical parking authority case—a subtle issue of the proper relationship of institutions to one another (that is, a constitutional issue) might be raised which entirely changed what everyone thought was a run-of-the-mine law suit. The procedural integrity of the economic and political system cannot be guaranteed by deciding ten or twenty or even a hundred big cases a year with the issues squarely presented, but only by deciding ten thousand cases a year with the issues presented in little pieces. The complaint, of course, is that the courts are into everything, but when every law passed by a legislative assembly and every action of an administrative board, commission, or department is a potential threat, all these matters must be reviewed.

The need for review provides an irresistible temptation to those avoiding or delaying perfectly legitimate, but nonetheless personally adverse, administrative actions to use the courts as a refuge. It is always hoped that a particularly stupid judge will misunderstand the nature of the question and render a judgment against the government. This tendency to delay urgent decisions by placing tedious, costly, and difficult obstacles in the path is a problem which has become worse over the past ten years. The answer to the problem, however, is not to attack the courts' *right* to review, but rather their *method* of review. If all the critics of the courts focused their attention on methods of expediting court review and limiting court consideration to the legitimate issues of institutional propriety and balance, the whole process of court review would be both faster and less intrusive in its effect upon other agencies of government.

For example, when a public utility appeals a public service commission tariff schedule, there is only one central issue with which the courts should be concerned, namely, whether the utility is making a fair rate of return. Methods of accounting, special fuel adjustment credits, life expectancy of certain types of property, and the whole host of issues which are argued to the courts are interesting for the public service commission but quite beyond the competence of judges. The only ground for appeal by any utility is that the utility is not making a fair rate of return, and the only ground for appeal by consumers is that the utility is making too much. Once it becomes known that this is the only question which the court will address, there will be fewer appeals, and where there are appeals, the judicial process will be much more expeditious.

I resolved when I started this book that at some point I would digress from the workings of the American court structure in order to show the enormous implications elsewhere in the world of the system we have devised over time. This is the place, for want of a better one. Most emerging nations are multiethnic, with cultural and racial hostilities which will lead ineluctably to impasse absent some principled institution to referee a free-wheeling, corrupt political process. The vicious tendencies of political machines are at the heart of why democracy has not worked in the emerging nations. Democracy, unfortunately, does not bring stability or stability prosperity; rather, stability brings prosperity and prosperity *may* bring democracy. As I pointed out earlier, no democracy in the world, except India, is poor. Throughout the underdeveloped world, the great desert maker is the war of all against all, which is a day-to-day reality in most multiracial, underdeveloped nations.

The preeminent mistake which we made with regard to the emerging nations, particularly in Africa, was to focus on political institutions rather than on legal institutions. For example, the war of all against all is accelerated everywhere in sub-Sahara Africa by the ubiquitous Westminster constitution, a constitution modeled on the British government at Westminster. While Amin's Uganda was a caricature during the 1970s, Kenya was not. Yet Kenya followed Uganda's example in 1973 in threatening its own 140,000 native citizens of Asian ancestry with expulsion. Many, fearing for their futures, fled. In Britain, Parliament is supreme. There is no written constitution protecting minorities, nor is there a system of courts articulating any principled, constitutional law superior to the caprice of the mob as represented by a majority in Parliament. In Britain proper, the monarchy, House of Lords, and a well-developed hierarchical party structure aided by a sophisticated civil service all have traditional roles which temper this absurd structure. In Africa and elsewhere, when the former colonial powers withdrew, leaving "democratic" institutions, they mindlessly exported the Westminster model in its strongest democratic form, but without the ancillary, balancing institutions.

In any country where a bare majority of 51 percent has absolute and complete control, the war of all against all is inevitable. The paradox is that American civil libertarians, who are primarily concerned at home with the protection of minority rights, frequently support one-man, one-vote under a Westminster constitution abroad. They miss the point that when we talk about majority rule the issue is not whether one-man, one-vote is desirable, but rather what that one vote gets a man. More frequently than not under the Westminster model, what it gets a man is one-vote, *one-time*.

The plight of the Asians in Africa brings home the economic consequences of unchecked majority rule.[6] In societies where there is very little wealth, one of the quickest methods of palliating universal poverty for a fleeting moment is redistribution, particularly redistribution at the ex-

6. V. S. Naipaul, an Oxford-educated writer of Asian provenance who grew up in the expatriate Indian community in Trinidad, writes eloquently on this subject. I recommend Naipaul's *The Bend in the River* (New York: Knopf, 1979) to anyone who wants to *feel* the extent to which a political machine will be rapacious to all who are not within its ranks.

pense of another ethnic group. This was essentially the history of the Asian community in Uganda in 1974. When we think about a settlement in the Republic of South Africa, for example, which will provide economic and civil rights to nonwhites, at the outset we must think about law and not about politics. In South Africa the major groups are: 4.3 million white (Afrikaner, British, other); 2.4 million colored (people who are the products of early interracial unions between Hottentot and Malay stock with the infusion of some white blood); 740,000 Asian (Indian, other); and 18.6 million black (Zulu, Xhosa, and other nations consisting of literally scores of tribes). It is not that whites are potentially at war against nonwhites; it is that everyone is potentially at war against everyone else. The great nonwhite family of man is a myth of the naive imagination of limousine liberals—the political machine based on blood relationships is the reality everywhere. The fact that whites consider all nonwhites to be alike does not mean that nonwhites consider all nonwhites to be alike. It was safer to be a black in Mississippi in 1936 than it will be to be a South African of Indian ancestry in South Africa in 1990 unless the Western powers begin to pressure South Africa to create modern legal structures in addition to democratic political ones. The black African national groups, particularly Zulu and Xhosa, frequently hate one another more than they hate the whites.

A structure that provides economic, political, and civil rights in South Africa, to stay for a moment with this example, must start with a realistic program which, at the outset, evaluates the concept of one-man, one-vote and answers the question, "Vote for what?" While the power of the legislature in the United States to impeach judges is plenary, the first five chapters of this book demonstrate that elected officials are greatly circumscribed by the courts. Neither Congress nor the legislatures can redistribute wealth, except through the taxing power, which must apply uniformly to all persons of the same class. While government regulation may greatly circumscribe the use of private property, nonetheless the courts have been vigilant to prevent wholesale redistribution. Furthermore, regardless of the distaste of the majority for any minority, Congress cannot pass restrictive laws against them, expel them from the United States, or deprive them of their civil rights. Thus in the United States we do not have one-man, one-vote on most of the crucial issues of society's survival and never have had. What we have is a rule of law growing out of a nine-hundred-year Anglo-American tradition giving us a *total process* of institutional balance of which one-man, one-vote is an integral part. What is called "American democracy" is really remarkable for its nondemocracy, that is, its protection of minorities, dissenters, incompetents, misfits, and social outcasts.

The complex system of law in America depends upon certain uniquely Western ways of looking at the world: the belief in reason as a key to the understanding of an ordered universe; the belief in the uniqueness of the individual; the belief in the binding nature of voluntarily entered (not only blood-related) communities; and the belief in the need to draw a line between individual will and communal needs by a *legal* statute. In South Africa, among 18.6 million Zulus, Xhosas, and other nations, these ways of looking at the world are shared by only those very few who have been exposed to modern life. They do exist among the coloreds and Asians, at least to the extent necessary to permit the development of legal as well as political institutions. Of the elements listed, the most important is probably the belief in voluntarily entered (not only blood-related) communities. Tribalism is the repudiation of any constitutional democracy predicated on sophisticated, issue-oriented, political alliances. Tribes are the quintessential political machines.

At the heart of constitutionalism is the notion that minority rights—economic, political, and civil—are protected by a rule of law from a political machine and that when disputes arise with regard to those rights, there will be a neutral arbitrator making a principled decision. The upshot of all of this is that the enfranchisement of developing peoples can work only if there is some check on political machines, particularly tribal machines, through the creation of a powerful judiciary. In South Africa, a good constitution would probably begin by granting broad economic and civil rights in open-ended terms, with a strong multiracial judiciary to enforce these rights. In any society where one minority ethnic group (in this case the whites) have a monopoly of economic ownership *as well as* crucial technical and administrative skills, multiracialism will proceed with less disruption if it starts in the judiciary. This is particularly true because developing societies have acute economic problems which exacerbate political, social, racial. and religious antagonisms.[7]

7. When Blair Clark was editor of the *Nation,* he solicited an article from me on the use of judicial structures to substitute for political structures during a transition to majority rule in South Africa. Before the article was finished, however, Mr. Clark left the *Nation,* and the article was rejected. The letter of rejection itself reflects the enormous controversy surrounding any attempt to find a balanced solution to the political machine/majority tyranny problem in the developing world. The *Nation* gave a very fair and balanced review of the article but evidently concluded that the subject was so emotionally charged and my approach so speculative that it was not worth the expenditure of their limited credit carrying that particular load of water. Since the *Nation* is a good and serious magazine

In South Africa, by the standards of other sub-Sahara nations, the nonwhite population is faring well in terms of per capita income. This is conclusively proven by the number of black Africans who come to South Africa from other countries to work every year. Tribal blacks are drawn to the South African urban centers, the largest in Africa, because of their

---

which carries a lot of water in good causes, I do not fault them on this account, since I have done the same thing with regard to hopeless political issues where my support would be unavailing.

The difficulty involved in developing any temperate approach is no more elegantly demonstrated then by the rejection letter itself, which in its entirety is as follows:

Dear Justice Neely:

I can't remember when more memos have been written about a manuscript than on the enclosed. We talked about it once more—and a consensus, more or less, emerged that it should be turned back to you with extreme apologies. We do feel badly about the long delay. Apologies, apologies, apologies.

Due to the long history behind this decision, I want to take an unprecedented step by quoting from some of the memos that contributed to the decision. Roughly in chronological order:

1) "This would be a nice plan were South Africa a nation just finding its own strengths and stability. But for a country on the verge of severe upheaval, Neely's plan seems a little slow paced."
2) "I recommend this piece. Everyone tends to take an apocalyptic view of South Africa. But perhaps palliatives should be at least considered before the storm. He will be accused of gradualism or something worse, but as he makes his argument you get the idea that he's sketching a complex legal structure which might just work. I think readers would be interested in a thoughtful American judge's hard look at the situation, however Utopian they may judge his solution to be."
3) "What disturbs me about this piece is not so much what he says, but the political vacuum in which he says it. I disagree with his fundamental premises, but in any case believe his argument—while worth serious consideration—can only be made from the perspective of the failure of South African liberals. This is not Neely's perspective . . . He points out that the judiciary has no control over police actions under the Terrorist Act, but he never asks why this is the case and ignores the obvious political motivations."
4) "What's Neely's time table? How much impact would his multi-racial judiciary have upon black demands and feelings of deprivation? What about the forced resettlements? Why Neely's plan—to the exclusion of voting rights for non-whites, i.e. a political solution?"
5) "I don't know enough about South Africa to be dogmatic about this, but I'm suspicious. It reads to me like what might pop up in *Encounter*—a *benign* proposal for kicking blacks in the teeth. The idea that legal rights mean much without political power won't wash—as any American black will be quick to tell him. I think he's whistling Dixie in Pretoria—and I suspect he knows it."

Despite all this contention—we almost ran the piece. But it finally came down to a judgment that by the time we finished outlining what would be necessary in the way of additions, cuts and revisions it would be another story.

I hope our own frank evaluations are taken in the friendly spirit which has marked our phone conversations.

Please do keep in touch.

Regrets—and warm regards,

Kai Bird
Assistant Editor

relative prosperity. However, the urban centers cannot support all who would come, any more than the United States can support all of the people abroad who would like to emigrate here. Only 9 million out of a potential 18.6 million native blacks live in nontribal areas. Consequently, there is a need for a principled decision maker to determine the pace of economic integration.

In the age of Xerxes, at the zenith of the Persian Empire, the plain around Persepolis was remarkable for its fecundity and verdure; under weak-willed Darius, when Alexander destroyed Persepolis, the area became a desert and remained one for twenty-three hundred years. It requires very little political skill to begin a war and even less economic skill to make a desert. Stability is the precondition for prosperity, liberty, and justice, which is probably why almost all of mankind live under authoritarian regimes. But if a certain authoritarianism is essential to avert the war of all against all in countries like South Africa, then it makes a great deal of difference what form that authoritarianism takes. Toqueville, that eminent purveyor of quotes for all occasions, once observed:

> Experience teaches us that generally speaking the most perilous moment for a government is when it seeks to mend its ways. Only consummate statecraft can enable a king to save his throne when after a long spell of oppressive rule he sets to improving the lot of his subjects. Patiently endured so long as it seemed beyond redress, a grievance comes to appear intolerable once the possibility of removing it crosses men's minds.

Courts are inherently authoritarian and undemocratic, exactly like Xerxes, but the difference between the two is that the courts are principled and enforce their mandates in a neutral and uniform manner. It is interesting to remark that South Africa's infamous Terrorism Act, the statute which permits the police to confine "dangerous" persons indefinitely, is utterly outside judicial control, and the writ of habeas corpus does not run to such incarcerations.[8] The reason that it is outside judicial control is that judicial control would imply principled application. One must control real terrorism, but it does make a difference whether the control is principled and aimed at *terrorism* or is unprincipled and aimed at dissent against the established political machine.

8. That, however, may not always be the case. It would appear that the South African judiciary is struggling to create a body of law resembling our own constitutional doctrine. In 1978 Mr. Justice Didcott of the Supreme Court of Natal entertained a writ of habeas corpus on behalf of a confined black and made an independent investigation regarding his conditions of confinement and the grounds for confinement. The decision, while in favor of the government, established the principle of court jurisdiction over Terrorism Act confinement, although the case was not appealed to the highest court.

In any multiracial society proceeding simultaneously at multiple educational levels, there are numerous hard decisions which must be made, none of which can satisfy the political agenda of anyone, unless the legitimacy of majority tyranny is accepted. The courts are able to evaluate such issues as the pace of migration to urban areas, the proper allocation of funds for education among differing population groups, and the legitimacy of politically dictated restrictions on the use of the franchise (the equivalent of the American poll-tax cases), so that some balanced yet controlled reform can occur.

The courts, of course, will voice predominantly middle-class values, even if they are manned in high proportion by black, colored, or Asian barristers, since barristers are inherently middle class. Principled decisions are not always acceptable decisions, nor are they necessarily morally correct decisions. An authoritarian junta running under the flag of a "court" and applying judicial procedures might be better than a regular junta running under the Jolly Roger, but it is a junta nonetheless. Constitutional engineering seeks balance—courts need to be nudged by the political process, which is essentially a one-man, one-vote operation. But the machine needs to be controlled as well. Possibly it was all said quite succinctly by an old boy named Cohen in a 1916 issue of the *Harvard Law Review:*

> We urge our horse down hill and yet put the brake on the wheel—clearly a contradictory process to a logic too proud to learn from experience. But a genuinely scientific logic would see in this humble illustration a symbol of that measured straining in opposite directions which is the essence of that homely wisdom which makes life livable.

An examination of political machines demonstrates that elective politics creates "democratic" institutions which can be a threat to the integrity of the democratic system. American courts enjoy greater prestige than any other American governmental institution, and I believe it is because the average American intuits the functional justification for court intervention in the political process. The average American may not be able to explain the mechanics of how a political machine can cheat him of his economic, civil, and political rights, but he knows that the machines are out there ready to take him to the cleaners unless courts or some other institution besides elected politicians provide protection. Basically the average American hates politics, just like everybody else, and he intuits that courts protect him from a political process which he knows can be as vicious as it can be benevolent.

6

COURTS AND THE INSTITUTIONAL DIALOGUE

PART I: CRIMINAL LAW REFORM

Courts are successful political institutions for about the same reason that the typical military junta of a banana republic is successful. The same dissatisfaction with democracy's corruption, lack of decisiveness, and lack of action which supports juntas prompts popular acceptance of an ever expanding political role for the courts. The obvious difference between the American court and the Latin junta is that we have a formal procedure for removing American judges short of a shoot-out. Ultimate democratic veto power gives what is an inherently authoritarian institution its legitimacy.

Since neither the executive nor the legislative branch establishes the perimeters which circumscribe court power, the courts must do that themselves. Once the courts elevate an issue to "constitutional dimensions," both executive and legislative branches must cede jurisdiction, short of impeachment or constitutional revision. Except in circumstances where the courts are taking the heat off elected politicians, as with the court resolution of the abortion issue, the other branches do not like to cede jurisdiction. In fact, the other branches of government do not like the courts very much at all, and they devote much of their spare time to devising new schemes to punish the courts. Historically, the other branches have restrained judicial intervention by the simple expedient of keeping the number of judges very small and judicial staffs quite lean.

Politicians know that by keeping both the number of judges and the sizes of their staffs small, the judiciary will need to conserve its energies, avoiding "political questions," because judges will not have the resources to administer the government. Furthermore, excessive court interference in other branches' decisions will lead to a guerrilla war if not impeachment or constitutional revision. Congress and the legislatures can make the lives of judges miserable by refusing to raise their salaries, cutting their office and staff budgets, and refusing to provide the other logistical support necessary to run the courts.

There have been cases in the last ten years where courts have found the treatment of mental patients below constitutional standards (Judge Johnson in Alabama) or the treatment of juvenile offenders below constitutional standards (Judge Justice in Texas) or school desegregation inadequate (Judge Garrity in Boston), where resistance to the courts' orders from the other branches of government was so intense that the judges placed state institutions into receivership. This meant that suddenly the courts were in the business of running hospitals, prisons, and schools through their special, court-appointed commissioners, making the judges superadministrators. "How many rolls of toilet paper should go in each eighth-grade bathroom, Judge?" A judge who does very much of this in addition to his routine judicial duties will very quickly find himself tired, sick, and old before his time. Furthermore, no man should be judge in his own cause, and once a judge begins to "administer," he takes on all the characteristics of an administrator. Who then is to provide the balance? I have always argued that if Earl Warren had been made a deputy sheriff in McDowell County, West Virginia, within six months *he* would have been beating up suspects in the back of police cars. It is not the quality of men which makes temperate judges, but the contemplative nature of the institution.

There is no point trying to formulate a theory of when and how courts should intrude themselves into politics in the abstract, because sanctions from the other branches are very real. In Massachusetts there are not even enough courtrooms to hold state district court. By failing to appropriate money, a legislature can grind the entire judicial process to a halt. That is the greatest limitation on rule by junta. I spend an inordinate amount of my time with the legislature. I write to every legislator four times a year and maintain constant personal communication when the legislature is at the capitol. I entertain legislators at my house and spend evenings in suite 1105 of the Daniel Boone Hotel, where there is a legislative "hospitality room" in progress all winter (and I do not even drink). Inevitably, courts do things which are offensive to the legislature, so judges must make up in personal rapport what they lose on the merits of issues. In the winter of 1981 I stayed up nights trying to pry twenty-two additional deputy magistrate court clerks and fifty-five civil process servers out of the parsimonious legislature. Court systems, like armies, run on their stomachs.

No serious judicial system can really afford to be managed by people who lose sight of the enormous power the legislature has over the courts. In one magistrate court alone in Kanawha County (West Virginia's largest county, containing the capital city of Charleston), there were 20,000 backlogged cases in 1980 attributable to lack of supporting staff. Courts are not worth a damn if all they do is political stuff, leaving routine litigation to go to the dogs for lack of sufficient legislative rapport to buy typewriters. Everywhere in the United States, an intense guerrilla combat goes on between the judicial and legislative branches; while the American system may be based on balance of power, no power, particularly the legislature, wishes to be balanced very much. As every student of elementary physics knows, for every action there is an equal and opposite reaction.

At the judges' conventions, my observations on practical legislative relations are received with the same enthusiasm that the bastard son is received at the reading of the will. Whenever I admit that a substantial portion of my January, February, and March is spent smoking and joking the legislature, other judges stick up their noses because I insufficiently appreciate the pristine Olympian function of the judiciary. Nevertheless, I usually get my clerks, typewriters, and process servers without being too much of a whore in the bargain. (Anyway, I have four virgin colleagues.) It is from this daily contact with legislators, however, that I understand that the courts, as a policymaking agency, are rationed a certain amount of eccentric conduct each year and that exceeding their ration precipitates a reaction which adversely affects the total performance of the courts. It is one thing to enter an order which requires extensive action by the other branches and quite another to enforce that order. Courts have a certain moral authority, much of which is the natural offshoot of their high prestige as arbiters of private, nonpolitical disputes. Their strength in the political arena is predicated on this prestige, which prompts voluntary compliance. When the other branches begin a hot war of active resistance, however, the courts have the rifles, while the other branches have the heavy artillery.

All competent commentators on constitutional law have intuited that there is some limit to court rule, but no one has, to my knowledge, successfully analyzed the practical limits which are placed on the courts. The commentators, as I pointed out in chapter 1, start with certain results which they would like to see achieved, such as greater redistribution of the wealth through the welfare system or less court activism in poverty law or civil rights, and work backward from that result to some theory of activism or restraint. My own conclusion is that the legitimate value (if not the originally intended purpose) of the courts is to supply balance and apply certain scientific principles, like principles of economics, to a system with a huge capacity for imbalance and irrationality. The practical limits to this function do not emanate from constitutional principles, but rather from either the incapacity of the courts to administer governmental activities (as opposed to articulating principles) or the dire consequences of adverse reaction from the other branches.

Since economy of court intrusion into politics is dictated by personnel limitations, adverse sanctions from the other branches, and popular reluctance to have pervasive rule by junta, it would be nice to know a correct formula for rationing court activity. When we talk about supplying balance, we are returning to the problem of the myth/operational disparity. While theoretically it is possible to separate the issue of balance in the abstract from the substantive results which that supposed balance is to achieve, no judge with an ounce of conviction about anything is willing to forebear from achieving substantive and really quite unbalanced results in deference to some vague and perhaps vapid theory. A judge who was born and bred in the union movement will always manipulate legal principles to help the union, and the die-hard, Republican, antiunion judge will always figure out a way to put the union on the sucking-hind-tit side of any decision. It is a recognition of the effects of personal political conviction which has caused us to make all appellate courts multimember bodies. It is hoped that on any five-, seven-, or nine-member court, *only* two of the judges will have strong ideological convictions on any given subject. Certainly once this fact of life is recognized, there is strong practical justification for the active recruitment of minorities for judicial service. Blacks, women, Hispanics, Asians, and men from Mars if they ever immigrate, need to know that when the court adjourns to chambers, there will be someone representing them ideologically to offset all those who look like William Buckley.

Since on all momentous issues some activist minority of any given court will always have their minds made up in advance based on the result to be achieved, it is to the ideological middle that all rational argument must be addressed. A neutral theory based on the myth/operational disparity will always make some sense to the ideologically uncommitted. The theory of the myth/operational disparity, however, is not tight and neat; it is sprawling and unmanageable. In the United States, there is no political decision or condition which is so beyond democratic control that it cannot be changed by the concerted action of the voters, nor is there a political decision or condition which is so much the product of the democratic process that it is completely beyond any challenge as being illegitimately discriminatory and the result of "class tyranny." What the courts must do, therefore, is to concentrate their limited resources on the most egregious cases of discrimination and myth/operational disparity.

Consequently, we return to the framework which I established in chapter 1, namely, that there is a spectrum which ranges from one to ten on some imaginary scale in which the number assigned to any given issue is some indication of the extent to which the democratic process fails to work fairly in the operational system. As I indicated earlier, a perfect ten would be given to *Baker v. Carr*, where the politicians had apportioned the state legislatures on the basis of geography rather than population and refused to reapportion lest they lose jobs for themselves and power for their constituents. On the other side, so to speak, the perfect one can be given to any imaginary case involving the validity of the municipal laws of the town of Stockbridge, Massachusetts, where all major decisions are made annually at the town meeting, which may be attended by every interested adult who is qualified to vote.

In order to analyze the criteria for judging where a given case should be on the scale and whether it is an appropriate case for court intervention, the rest of this chapter and the next will take two controversial examples. The first, which will concern us here, is the criminal law, where judges have sought to control enforcement officers through complex procedural rules in criminal trials. The second, which will take up the next chapter, involves the courts' involvement with the finance and administration of public education. The purpose of selecting these two examples and of exploring them at length is to illuminate the script of what is essentially an institutional dialogue, or the process by which the courts call attention to the myth/operational disparity and serve as a catalyst to the proper operation of other institutions. By taking civil liberties as affected by the criminal law process, which I would rank rather high on my scale of appropriateness for court involvement, and dissecting what has happened in other institutions outside the courts, we can see the requirements for success in court-initiated reform. Furthermore, it is possible, using this example, to catalogue some of the political factors which make for an egregious case of myth/operational disparity and to show a concrete example of a problem which only the courts could cure. If the analysis of criminal law reform points out the factors which make an issue ideal for court-initiated reform, the school finance case should show the opposite. While school finance is not completely beyond the capacity of the courts to generate reform, a dissection of the problem should show the limits to successful court action and how the courts can bite off more than they can chew.

Americans generally believe that our criminal law is not working; that the guilty roam the streets free to commit new crimes pending their trials; that more concern is shown for the criminal than for the victims of crime; and that most criminals, even when caught red-handed, "get off" because of smart lawyers and soft courts. There is a certain legitimacy in at least part of this criticism. Criminal law, and perforce the safety of the streets, is tied inextricably to civil liberties, and so far we have not conceived a Rhadamanthine criminal law system which does not inherently threaten civil liberties in general.

Criminal law involves two distinct elements: proof of guilt by competent evidence before a jury and adherence to a set procedure for obtaining the evidence presented to the jury. This second aspect includes the manner in which the defendant was arrested, the type of legal representation the defendant had at trial, and the way the defendant was treated after he was arrested but before he was tried. The first aspect of the criminal law process—determining guilt or innocence before a jury—presents relatively few problems; it is the essence of the truth-finding function of courts, and everyone concedes that only the guilty should be punished. A jury is a wondrous creation, and the average American on a jury where he must decide the question of guilt reflects in his own cautious actions the heart of the entire system. He agonizes. He bends over so far backward to be fair that the typical jury is out for hours in a case which, to a trained observer, is open and shut. The same barber who regales you with his law-and-order theories in the shop is the first to be responsible in the jury room. Consequently, there is usually no complaint about the jury process—most Americans condone its solicitous regard for the rights of the accused where the question is one of truth, guilt or innocence, fairness or unfairness.

Less understood and less approved, however, is the second aspect of the criminal process—the close examination by courts of all the procedure attendant on bringing the defendant to trial. In most criminal proceedings where an unquestionably guilty person is set free, the defect which has caused his release has nothing to do with a jury determination of his guilt, but rather with the manner by which the state brought him to trial. The entire area of criminal procedure has been developed primarily through constitutional interpretation, and when a guilty defendant is released because of a procedural error, it is almost always because of a violation of what have come to be called the defendant's "constitutional rights." Other than the Fifth and Fourteenth Amendments' due process clauses, the primary vehicles for creative development of constitutional principles in the criminal law field are the Fourth and Sixth Amendments to the Constitution. Both amendments are remarkable for their brevity:

> *Fourth Amendment*
> The right of the people to be secure in their persons, houses, papers, and effects, against unreasonable searches and seizures, shall not be violated, and no Warrants shall issue, but upon probable cause, supported by Oath or affirmation, and particularly describing the place to be searched, and the persons or things to be seized.
>
> *Sixth Amendment*
> In all criminal prosecutions, the accused shall enjoy the right to a speedy and public trial, by an impartial jury of the State and district wherein the crime shall have been committed, which district shall have been previously ascertained by law, and to be informed of the nature and cause of the accusation; to be confronted with the witnesses against him; to have compulsory process for obtaining witnesses in his favor, and to have the Assistance of Counsel for his defence.

Around these simple statements has grown up an entire body of law concerning when a search warrant is needed and when it is not, how a warrant is to be obtained, and what happens if a person is arrested or his house is searched without a warrant. Until the 1960s, the Supreme Court did not supervise state court criminal prosecutions very closely; occasionally it intervened when there was a particularly egregious miscarriage of justice, but the Supreme Court's revolutionary development of complex procedural rules dates basically from *Escobedo v. Illinois* in 1963, a case involving a defendant's right to counsel under the Sixth Amendment.

Today the average citizen complains that crime in the street is ever increasing and that this serious problem is lost on courts overly concerned about criminals', rather than law-abiding citizens', rights. Complex criminal procedures require sedulous attention to arrest and search warrant requirements, universal availability of competent counsel, exhaustive warnings to the defendant about his right to remain silent, and the execution on his part of detailed waivers of this right before any confession can be used in evidence. Widespread criticism of the courts in the area of criminal law is given added credence by the generally observed fact that judges, lawyers, and law professors are not "average people." The class which is so concerned with the rights of criminals, people correctly point out, lives in ritzy suburbs or quiet academic communities, drives to work in air-conditioned cars during daylight hours, parks in private underground parking garages equipped with private elevators, and sends its children either to private schools or to affluent neighborhood schools where there are no other pupils who extort, knife, and rape in the halls. This privileged class, critics say, does not know what it is like to take public transportation, to live in urban environments next to the most Dickensian slums, to work odd shifts involving after-dark commuting, and to work in all-night grocery stores, gas stations, or fast food establishments where itinerant armed criminals are always on the prowl. Since the danger which criminals pose to the general population is obvious to anyone but the outright fool, it is very difficult to explain the justification for criminal law reform other than as rank indifference by one privileged class to the sufferings of another class. Yet there is a justification, and that justification concerns controlling social institutions which can be controlled only through criminal procedure.

Any analysis of the body of civil liberties law surrounding criminal procedure must consider the institutions in American society in the early 1960s, when the reform of criminal procedure began to gather momentum. If you were an average American driving alone in the sixties through a rural town in almost any state, from California to Massachusetts, and for some reason ran afoul of the law, your life was not worth a plugged nickel unless you had either money or friends. Even the simple offense of speeding frequently landed a normal, law-abiding citizen in some filthy county jail from 10 o'clock Friday night until at least 10 o'clock Monday morning, when a local, one-gallused, tobacco-spitting, non-law-trained political hack of a magistrate appeared to conduct the typical local proceeding, which was a caricature of itself. Not only were you liable to be fined and to have spent the weekend in jail to boot, but it is possible that you were also assaulted in jail and mistreated by the cops who made the arrest. Even after twenty years of reform, police brutality is an everyday occurrence everywhere. It reaches my court in some form once a week, which means that its incidence is very high, since far more trespasses are perpetrated than are ever reported. Much of this is probably beyond the experience of solid members of the middle class who never traveled twenty years ago in the military or to see the country, but humiliating experiences were frequently visited upon soldiers and sailors on leave, students in unconventional modes of dress traveling back and forth to school, and poor people driving 1946 Fords with bad mufflers and fenders tied on with baling wire.

Television's version of the criminal process always features either the FBI or the comparatively well-trained and well-equipped police departments of major cities. In most of the United States, however, police departments consist of nothing more than a bunch of country boys who found work pinning on a badge, strapping on a gun, and riding around in a patrol car. Not so long ago, the average policeman in a medium-sized city had no training other than on the job, and the rural police force, usually composed of deputy sheriffs, was not only untrained, but changed every time there was an election. Frequently people were attracted to police work because they were bullies to start with, and I have known small groups of state policemen who got their jollies entering local beer joints to beat up on the locals. Many a small-town policeman, although he never heard of Suetonius, imitates in his own small way the techniques of Caligula. It is not accidental that the United States Supreme Court started its dramatic crusade against what had to be appalling conditions under the leadership of Earl Warren, who had been a prosecuting attorney in California. He knew what the institution of criminal law enforcement was like on the ground, and while he may have abused the process himself when he was young, when he put on his black robe and was thereby translated to sainthood, he set about cleaning up the system.

The criminal law system to a very large extent consists of the members of one social class putting members of another social class in jail. All crime can be classified in two distinct groups: "natural law crime," which everyone agrees is horrible and must be punished for the protection of society (murder, rape, arson, armed robbery, larceny, and assault) and "positive law crime," which involves things which are illegal and punishable only because the state says so (income tax evasion, public intoxication, stock fraud, and antitrust violations). The second type of crime, involving the violation of criminal statutes but not the perpetration of violent trespasses, attracts an enormous amount of press attention, particularly because of nonenforcement against "middle-class" criminals. There are a lot of middle-class criminals out there, quietly embezzling from federal banks, designing schemes to pirate the assets of publicly held corporations, or conspiring with one another to raise prices and limit output in some form of monopoly. They do not frighten us. The proverbial little old lady is not nearly so horrified by the prospect of losing a few thousand dollars to a stock swindler as she is by the prospect of three armed teenagers entering her apartment, tying her up, tormenting her, and stealing several thousand dollars' worth of jewlry, appliances, paintings, and silver. Middle-class crime is outrageous, but not personally threatening, while ordinary, natural law, dangerous crime makes us buy burglar alarm systems, lock our children up at night, seek permits to carry firearms, and arrange our employment to avoid travel during nighttime hours.

Violent crime is almost always committed by the poor, uneducated, or stupid. Crimes of passion are committed by everyone, of course, but a trial involving a middle-class man meticulously planning the murder of his wife, so he can collect the insurance and run off with his secretary, is sensational precisely because it is so rare. Traveling salesmen who spend their off-hours robbing all-night grocery stores, married schoolteachers who take nights off to rape sixteen-year-old girls, and prosperous farmers who routinely eliminate market competition in the neighborhood by setting fire to their neighbors' barns are real oddities. Consequently, the entire criminal law system most often boils down to the powerful state with all its weapons—police, prosecutors, courts, prisons, and probation officers—going after poor, uneducated, stupid folks. (That is not to say, however, that the poor, uneducated, stupid folks did not commit the crimes.) This lower class of criminal suspects is not exactly possessed of enormous political power which it can summon to protect its rights, particularly since when it is not on the receiving end of the whole system geared up to get it, it is the group in society crying most loudly for more law and order.

In the early 1960s, the average criminal defendant was treated like a piece of meat on its way to dressing and processing. A person was arrested, brought in for interrogation (seldom conducted in a gentlemanly manner), threatened with the many dire consequences which awaited him if he did not cooperate (such as a thirty-year sentence for simple burglary), and encouraged to plead guilty. Of course a lawyer could do wonders for him, but ordinarily there was not any lawyer and would not be any lawyer unless he came up with the money to hire one or was accused of a capital crime. For those who knew enough to make a scene and demand to have a court-appointed lawyer, a lawyer might be appointed, but it was frequently the case with overworked courts that the judge indicated either outright, in open court but off the record, or through hints delivered informally by third parties that things would go a lot easier for the defendant if he would plead quilty rather than make a lot of trouble asking for a lawyer and demanding a jury trial. If a person pleaded guilty, that was it—off he went to prison, having waived all grounds for appeal except the jurisdiction of the court, and he just sat in prison until the sentence expired or the parole board released him. Often this process ran an entirely innocent man through its machine, a man so frightened of the circumstantial evidence against him that he would agree to plead guilty to a lesser offense or to confess to a crime he did not commit in the hope of receiving more lenient treatment from a system which was going to get him anyway.

It usually happened that in any small town or city where this particular form of expedited due process occurred all the participants were friends, buddies, and colleagues. The sheriff, prosecutor, and judge were probably all members of the same political party who exchanged fishing stories together over lunch down in the jail, while the prisoners served them a subsidized meal, and since each one probably had some power over the others, they had long ago developed the live-and-let-live mentality sometimes known as "You've got to go along to get along." Almost everywhere prosecutors, sheriffs, and judges were elected and the staffs were not civil service, so that they presented no counterbalance to the alliances of party politics. Furthermore, criminal trials have always been both expensive and a lot of work for everyone concerned, and since neither judge, prosecutor, nor sheriff was paid by the case, real due process took money away from payrolls for relatives and a lot of time away from the farm and the trout stream.

Not only was the system a fiasco at the interrogation, pretrial confinement, and guilty plea stages of the process; it resembled some of the more unpleasant features of Nazi Germany or modern Russia in the investigative stages. Men were routinely picked up off the street without a warrant, brought down to the police station, left to sit on hard benches without access to water, food, or sometimes even a clean restroom for hours at a time before "questioning," which frequently involved humiliating insults and a good bit of slapping around. In many cases, the police had nothing more to direct them to their particular suspect than a prior criminal record, the "suspicious behavior" of the arrested person, or personal animosity. The entire "questioning" process went on without any regard for the person's need to be at his job, his school, his wife's side in the hospital, or anywhere else. The convenience of the authorities organized the lives of those without power who came to the authorities' attention. And who was available to give redress? The political process, where most aspirants for office run on a "crack down on crime" platform? The local judge, who would need to dress down the local sheriff or police chief in the morning before they all went out for lunch together? The executive authority, whose very henchmen all these rights violators were? Not very likely.

However, the parade of horrors did not end there, for there was the entire area of search and seizure to be abused. It often happened that when the police came to search a house in the 1960s, their routine procedure involved turning out dresser or desk drawers, making holes in the wall, ripping apart all the beds, tearing up the pillows, kicking down the doors of locked closets and cabinets, and rousting people from their night's slumber. Again, what recourse did a victim have? The political process? See above. A damage suit? Only if the victim had the money to afford a lawyer and could find one willing to take on the incumbent local political machine with which the lawyer was compelled to work every day. Furthermore, given the generally high regard which the middle class accords the police, the likelihood of a substantial jury award, which must be the unanimous judgment of *twelve* persons, being recovered against the police by a group of suspicious-looking and unsavory people involved in criminal activities was remote. Of four damage actions filed in Marion County, West Virginia, in 1970 against a group of Caligulaesque state troopers who routinely beat the patrons of local beer joints, none resulted in a damage award by a jury. Police officers routinely lie, particularly to save their own skins, and when they do, they make enormously credible witnesses.

The institutional abuses of the criminal justice system which I have just described created substantial unnecessary and unmerited suffering, seriously reduced the degree of personal liberty among people of particular socioeconomic and racial backgrounds, and generally got worse rather than better as society became more urbanized and people were increasingly without the financial, emotional, and political support of an extended family. The U.S. Supreme Court and other federal and state courts, consequently, began the widespread development of "constitutional" principles to correct these institutional abuses. The Supreme Court recognized that the traditional damage award against responsible officials, which for over a hundred years had been the primary myth system remedy for invasions of personal rights, simply did not work and that some other remedy was necessary which could be automatically applied by the courts without jury intervention to hurt the system enough to force it to change its ways.

Enter the "exclusionary rule"—a new, judge-made, constitutional remedy unknown to many state courts. According to this ingenious doctrine, if the police failed to comply with any of the new rules concerning procedure, any evidence gathered during a period when the rules were being violated was to be excluded from all court proceedings. For example, evidence could be excluded which the suspect himself gave the police if the police failed to warn him of his right to remain silent, his right to retain counsel of his choice before he was asked any questions, and his right to court-appointed counsel if he could not afford to hire a lawyer on his own. Usually the evidence excluded because the police failed to give the proper warnings or otherwise observe the suspect's rights made the difference between a conviction and an acquittal, and the defendant went free. The exclusionary rule also applied to questions of search and seizure, the aspect of the criminal process to which the Fourth Amendment refers. If the police suspected that there were fruits or tools of a crime in a particular house, such as stolen goods, drugs, or weapons, they were required to appear before a magistrate to make an oath that they had probable cause to believe the evidence they sought was in that particular house and to state in detail what the source of their belief was—for example, a reliable informer, personal observation of the goods being transported into the house, or a pattern of comings and goings leading a reasonable person to infer some illegal activity in progress within. But if the police entered a person's house without such proper warrant and discovered exactly what they thought would be there, none of the evidence could ever be used in court, because all the evidence was tainted by the violation of the suspect's constitutional rights. Again, the exclusion of the tainted evidence would probably lead to an acquittal.

The streets began to swarm with released criminals. All the agents of the criminal justice system concluded that the courts had finally gone stark, raving mad and envisaged a world of wall-to-wall felons. At first, police officers and prosecutors did not believe that the U.S. Supreme Court meant what it said, so they continued to do business as usual, and the Supreme Court itself was forced to reverse hundreds of convictions, release the accuseds, and over a span of ten years indicate that it was really serious about individual rights.

Meanwhile, what was going on back at the station house? The police and prosecutors were sitting around saying, "Son of a bitch!" (policemen are known to say this on occasion) and feeling very insecure about their jobs. Many criminals were on the streets because of criminal procedure violations, which was leading irate citizens to talk about "changes of administration" and "department reform." Oddly enough, jury damage suits, constitutional mandates, the elective political process, and general notions about unmerited suffering and consideration for one's fellowman could not clean up the system, but the fear of unemployment managed it very neatly. Suddenly police departments sponsored training programs to instruct their members where and when a warrant was necessary to make a lawful arrest or what extraordinary circumstances—such as a felony committed in the presence of an officer—justified an arrest without a warrant. Officers began carrying cards with the official warning (known as the "Miranda warning" from the *Miranda v. Arizona* case in 1966), so they would not make an error in informing defendants of their rights to remain silent and to have a lawyer appointed if they were indigent. At the same time, lower state courts instituted systems to appoint lawyers for criminals in all prosecutions, both felony and misdemeanor, where there was any possibility of a jail sentence, and state legislatures appropriated money to pay private lawyers to serve as court appointees or to pay for public defender systems. The courts not only required that those being prosecuted be represented by counsel, but also that they be represented by "competent" counsel, which meant that appointing some hack who, but for court appointments, was such a dud that he would not otherwise find work no longer passed muster on appellate review.

Since it was no longer permissible to obtain confessions by intimidating a suspect, keeping him all night without an opportunity to use the bathroom, depriving him of food for long periods of interrogation, or subjecting him to dire threats for failure to testify against himself (something quite explicitly forbidden by the Fifth Admendment), the police had to think of new ways of solving crimes. It dawned on them that investigation, regular patrols, and scientific laboratory analysis of clues à la Sherlock Holmes might substitute for some of their cruder techniques, so they inaugurated training programs in these areas as well. When they were unable to finance necessary new equipment, the federal government came to the rescue with cash grants and other help from the Law Enforcement Assistance Administration (LEAA).

As the U.S. Supreme Court ruled that there must be no substantial delay between an arrest and appearance before a magistrate for the setting of bond, along with formal court-administered instructions concerning appointment of counsel, states began reorganizing their judiciaries so that the tobacco-chewing, one-gallused, illiterate justice of the peace who refused to hold court during squirrel season, deer season, after 5 P.M., or on weekends became a thing of the past. In his place appeared a professional lay or lawyer magistrate with extensive state-sponsored training, who was part of a pool of minor judicial officials available at a moment's notice around the clock to set bond, issue warrants, and otherwise mete out justice according to a modern concept of individual rights.[1] Furthermore, since everyone feared that the nature and conditions of pretrial confinement would be raised in court, the more inhumane aspects of local incarceration facilities were eliminated, and a nationwide program of upgrading criminal detention facilities was promoted.

The actual level of improvement in any given area is a function of diverse factors; in the large cities where the volume of crime greatly exceeds the national average and the expense of constructing new facilities, given land acquisition and related costs, places a greater than normal strain on already overstrained budgets, there has been little alternative to renovation of existing medieval structures. Similarly, in small rural counties where both the crime rate and the local budget are very low, there has been little new construction. However, in between these two extremes there has generally been a significant improvement, not only in physical facilities, but also in other less obvious areas such as twenty-four-hour monitoring to prevent suicide and attacks by fellow inmates.

In summary, then, a quantum leap was made in the whole administration of the criminal justice system from 1960 to 1980 as a result of the development of constitutional standards through the creative imagination of the courts. None of this was mandated by the U.S. Constitution itself. Nowhere in the Constitution, or any of its state counterparts, is there a requirement that the remedy for a violation of a person's rights be the exclusion of the fruits of the rights violation from use in any way in the criminal process. In fact, just the opposite had been thought the law throughout almost all the history of this country; until recently, the citizen's only remedy was the private damage suit, and that is still the rule in England. Nothing in the Fifth Amendment requires a warning before the police can begin interrogating a suspect, and nothing in the Sixth Amendment guarantees the right to a lawyer appointed at government

1. While even today this latter improvement may not be the case everywhere, it is emphatically the case in West Virginia. One day I was so concerned that our Supreme Court's directives about magistrate availability were not being enforced that I took the entire staff of the administrator of state courts, all my court's writ clerks and per curiam clerks, and all my own staff and sent them out on a Sunday with sealed orders, so that they would arrive at the county seats unannounced at 3:00 A.M. to see how many people were in jail without commitment by a magistrate and how available a magistrate was at that ungodly hour. What we found was that in circuits where the chief circuit judge was philosophically committed to the proposition of immediate access, independent of the supreme court rules, the level of availability was comparatively high. However, where the circuit judges considered the rules unreasonable in light of manpower or were just plain cavalier about the problem of overnight jail sojourns, our rules were completely disregarded. There is nothing one can do short of a daily shoot-out against an active program of passive resistance.

expense. During most of our country's history, an indigent did not get a free lawyer except in capital cases.

If the success of the courts in the area of civil liberties can appropriately be judged by comparing the criminal process of 1960 with that of 1980, then the courts have been quite successful. The reason for their success was that they took institutions which were performing badly and made them perform better. The legitimacy, in a society dedicated to individual freedom, of reforms such as the right to court-appointed counsel, the right to an expeditious preliminary hearing, and the right to be free of police harassment during questioning are not seriously debated even by the die-hard advocates of law and order. What are debated, of course, are the appropriate remedies. Yet the political process did not provide these reforms, because those with political power were seldom on the receiving end of the old system. When a solid citizen got the typical home-cooking treatment in some small town over a speeding violation, it was almost always in a foreign state. What society paid for this improvement in governmental civility was a higher incidence of crime, since more felons were released to the streets. The cop shows on television never cease pointing out these costs. The difficulty, as I have pointed out earlier, is that the costs were not spread evenly throughout society; they disproportionately fell upon the poor, who are most frequently victimized by virtue of their geographical proximity to criminals.

If we use as our standard for evaluation of improvement some ideal, imaginary system of criminal law, rather than the twenty-year track record of actual reform, the courts' success rating fares less well. As I have already indicated, in the big cities and real boonies, the state of the jails where prisoners are held pending trial is still a serious problem. Even in medium-sized cities and in the suburbs, the problem is not completely solved; it is still possible to find filthy, overcrowded, and dangerous jails. To construct modern, safe jails is enormously expensive, and the level of humane treatment in any given locale is completely dependent on the willingness of the political authorities in both the state and federal systems to appropriate the necessary funds. To build a decent jail in even a small rural county costs over one million dollars; regional detention centers are not economical in the long run because of the manpower necessary to transport prisoners to and from court. Renovations of the existing jails, even in a small state like West Virginia, will cost over one hundred million dollars, which must be taken from somewhere, either existing programs or the taxpayers' pockets. Should the courts attempt to order that this money be spent? To the knee-jerk civil libertarian, the obvious answer to that last question is a resounding "yes," yet the same urgency can be argued for other social programs like schools, mental health hospitals, and housing for the aged. Here we return to the entire problem of rule by junta.

There is almost no end to society's thirst for worthy projects, and theoretically the courts could find some constitutional justification for ordering higher standards in all public facilities. No minority in society, whether it be prisoners, mental patients, or the dependent aged, is sufficiently well represented politically to get all the resources it or its advocates think it deserves. The reason that roads and schools are such a high priority for government at all levels is that everyone uses both. When we come to facilities which are used by a captive minority, I suppose the correct rule of thumb is that courts should apply pressure up to the point where the other branches begin large-scale guerrilla operations. What the courts are doing is splitting the difference; they are requiring certain minimum standards in jails, but they are indeed minimum.

From a purely practical perspective, much of the success of the courts in civil liberties reform came from the fact that they were upgrading institutions *without* diverting a great deal of money from other areas all at once. The cost of social change came, not in terms of money, but in terms of increased criminal activity. It was this fact, more than any other, which avoided adverse reaction from the other branches on a grand scale. The cost, for example, of providing all of the court-appointed lawyers in the West Virginia criminal system in any given year is substantially less than one quarter of the annual interest at the modest rate of 8 percent on the hundred million dollars necessary to upgrade the jails. It did not cost a great deal of money to train the police to get warrants, or to forbid the rousting of suspects and witnesses for questioning, or to require that the police not beat confessions out of suspects. There have been expenses, but the costs have risen gradually over twenty years, and budgets were able to adjust smoothly.

In the field of criminal procedure, the courts were responding to all the other branches' institutional rigidities in the operational system, which have already been catalogued in earlier chapters. In every state legislature, there had always been reformers dedicated to protecting civil liberties, but there was not enough interest in overall reform to overcome the inherent inertia. In the executive branch, in this case the police and prosecutors, everything was set up for the benefit of those working in the system, rather than those upon whom the system worked. Since confessions are the easiest way of solving a crime and a guilty plea is the simplest way of convicting a defendant, all procedures were designed to achieve both results. Even the trial judges looked like Russian bureaucrats, since any extensive "due process" inevitably cut into their long lunches and early golf games. What the United States Supreme Court achieved was a vast upgrading of an existing system of interlocking institutions with only an ancillary increase in expenditures, as opposed to the example of the school cases in the chapter to come, where the courts are primarily involved in allocating money with only an ancillary improvement in the functioning of existing institutions.

Once we conceptualize the entire criminal procedure revolution as an exercise in upgrading institutions to guarantee civil liberties, there may even be some hope for the die-hard law-and-order advocate. In fact, it is for this reason that I devote an entire chapter to dissecting criminal law reform, because once we begin to articulate our constitutional law in terms of real institutional relationships rather than history or linguistic interpretation, we become better equipped to accomplish desired goals without sacrificing other desired goals. This is the long way of saying that we can be more incisive and reduce the overall cost of social reform. No one in his right mind, for example, is interested in compensating any particular guilty felon for the violation of his constitutional rights by saying: "Here, although it is a fact that in the dead of night you crept up to the porch where the little girl was sleeping, cut through the screen, put your hand over her mouth and stealthily took her from her house to the construction site, raped and tortured her, and then strangled her and left her body underneath a pile of rubble; nevertheless, because the arresting officer did not advise you of your right to remain silent, we want you to have your liberty in compensation for that gross violation."

Everything must be considered in perspective; obviously, the intentional violation of constitutional rights on a grand scale by law enforcement agencies is very dangerous, but a society which cannot protect its citizens against criminal invasions is equally dangerous. While I cannot think of a practical way to avoid releasing defendants in a majority of cases where there has been a trespass upon their civil liberties, some of the more absurd results of the current rules of criminal procedure could be eliminated by focusing on what the purpose, in terms of institutional reform, of the new criminal procedure was and still is.

Many of the draconian sanctions conceived by the Supreme Court have been in response to the passive resistance of the state courts, which have taken a long time to get with the civil liberties program. Higher courts and lower courts are natural enemies; the lower courts always consider that they are "closer to the ground" and must respond to practical problems, such as lack of money, poor personnel, and inferior institutions, by bending the law in order to achieve a practical result in each case, while the higher courts believe that they are guardians of sacred principles and can *never* respond to practical problems without compromising their pristine principle-articulating function. I have seldom known a trial judge who thought well of the court above him; a majority of my own trial judges regard me as something between a fiend and a fool.

When the Supreme Court began its program of criminal law reform in the 1960s, it met with Maginot Line-type resistance from the state courts, which were being compelled to release dangerous felons in the face of universal public outrage. Many of the state judges of that era, particularly at the trial level, were elected for short terms and felt personally threatened politically by the rules they were called upon to enforce, since they would be accused of turning the criminals loose. Thus they did not do it and left the hard decisions for the courts above them. It took twenty years for a new generation of lawyers who had come to their maturity under the new procedures to ascend the bench before the protection of civil liberties became a reflex response in the state courts. It was, in fact, in recognition of the general improvement in state court performance that in 1976 the Supreme Court tightened the rules for federal district court review of state court criminal proceedings, giving greater weight to the state court judgments.

The Supreme Court and the highest courts of the states are notoriously impractical—they formulate rules which completely dislocate existing structures and cause temporary chaos. I have discussed earlier the West Virginia court decision in 1977 forbidding the incarceration of juvenile status offenders with criminal offenders. There was utter havoc for two years. The legislature did not appropriate any money for status offender facilities, and the result was that the children ran wild in the streets and schools for a couple of years, because they knew the authorities were powerless. By 1980, however, the legislature had given authority to the commissioner of welfare to maintain secure facilities for status offenders, and all over West Virginia local halfway houses and juvenile refuges were built. While it took some time, the ultimate result was a dramatic improvement in the state's treatment of children—again, an example of upgrading institutions through the court-ordered decimation of existing institutional arrangements.

If appellate courts always took seriously the admonition to "be practical," their rulings would be so bland that they would not have the desired effect of changing institutions. Only by the black or white ruling, such as "status offenders shall never be incarcerated in any secure, prison-like facility with criminal offenders in the State of West Virginia," can a court detonate the anarchist's bomb of appropriate size and intensity. In fact, courts often proceed on an implicitly anarchist premise, namely, that by utterly destroying existing structures, the new structures put in their place will be significantly better, because the decent and concerned members of the legislature will have a hand in the design of any new system which is forced upon their unwilling, Neanderthal colleagues.

The question is not, obviously, whether we want civil liberties *or* protection from criminals; the question is, how do we get both? One observed phenomenon on the part of experienced criminal defense lawyers is that federal agents make substantially fewer blunders than their state counterparts. According to the West Virginia federal public defender, it is infrequent indeed that a federal criminal prosecution is dismissed because of a procedural technicality. There are, of course, two explanations for this, only one of which helps our analysis here. First, federal crime is high-class crime—conspiracy, bank embezzlement, importation of narcotics, tax fraud, etc. Seldom is a federal agent in hot pursuit of a stick-up man at 4:00 A.M. or the casual discoverer of serious criminal activity in the course of a routine traffic stop or investigation of a wife beating. Nonetheless, there is enough federal concurrent criminal jurisdiction over run-of-the-mine, low-class crime, like interstate shipment of stolen motor vehicles, that the differing success rates of federal and state officials is not exclusively attributable to their differing clienteles.

Federal agents are extremely well paid, which means that federal service can attract smart people; federal agents tend to make federal service a career; and federal agents are remarkably well trained. The result is that they make very few mistakes in the application of existing law. Furthermore, they have sufficient resources that they need not sweat a defendant to give a confession, since they can usually build their case by other means. Consequently, it is *possible* through good training and adequate resources to achieve convictions under the new rules, while at the same time protecting civil liberties. At the state level, however, adequate resources and training are the rub. Training and investigative resources cost money, and at the state level money is scarce, partially because state government, unlike the feds, cannot print it.

Probably the bottom line of criminal law reform is that once the mind-set of local law enforcement agencies is changed and self-perpetuating institutions dedicated to the protection of civil liberties are created, the courts can become more flexible in their exclusionary rules, because it will then be possible to "be practical." I suppose that what I am talking about is a tradition of civility on the part of government, which is as much a part of culture as it is of anything else. Certainly there is a pervasive lack of civility out there now. Every police department has its bully boys who cannot be controlled absent constant drilling and draconian sanctions. Yet the world of the street is likely to make the most committed civil libertarian have second thoughts about the daily value of a lot of due process.

When the level of institutional change finally begins to satisfy us and it becomes time to rethink the design of the criminal law civil liberties structure, the point of entry should probably be the difference between an intentional invasion of rights and a negligent invasion. The Supreme Court has never said that denying the state a conviction, either through the suppression of a confession or the exclusion of evidence, is a constitutionally required *remedy;* all the Supreme Court has said is that there are certain constitutional *rights* which will be enforced through release of defendants until some better, practical remedy is developed.

Criminal law enforcement is administered for the most part by state and local police officers who have had only rudimentary legal training. It is possible to give police officers a working knowledge of criminal law essentials during a three-month police academy course, but no amount of training can insure that a policeman will make the right on-the-spot decision every time. The problems he confronts on the beat are sometimes so complex that when they eventually reach a five-man appellate court having ample time for research and reflection, they are decided by a 3–2 margin. If the question of whether a particular warrantless search was within the narrow exceptions to the warrant requirement is so close that five trained judges divide 3–2, how can the average policeman operating in an environment where decisions must be made in less than ten seconds be expected to make the right decision every time?

That question returns us then to the difference between the intentional and the unintentional rights violation. Unfortunately, to say that "unintentional" rights violations will be forgiven would be to beg the basic civil liberties question because, if country boys are routinely hired off the streets to do police work without any training, most violations will be "unintentional." Ignorance cannot be a complete defense if what we are attempting to do is to upgrade institutions. Consequently, within the category of "intentional" violations must be subsumed the entire class of invasions which are the direct result of inadequate commitment to training and to following the rules. Among the appropriate questions, therefore, are: What are the duration and quality of training? What are the standard operating procedures of the enforcement agency? What is the agency's commitment to the recruitment of quality personnel and the exclusion of bullies? Once all of these questions can be answered in favor of the prosecuting authority, the next question is obviously whether the specific rights violation under consideration was intended or merely negligent. While the standards may be difficult to work out, this approach may in the long run achieve a cultural breakthrough which the mechanical application of procedural rules will never achieve. A standard which looks to institutions focuses everyone's attention upon the doughnut rather than the hole.

It would appear that state and local law enforcement has reached a plateau; everyone has learned to live with the exclusionary rules, and no one is any longer shocked by the release of a felon for a procedural defect. A direct emphasis upon institutional structure rather than the results of that structure could inspire greater attention to a dramatic cultural change. The rewards to the affected institutions would come in the form of relaxed sanctions for purely technical, unintentional enforcement errors. In its simplest form, this amounts to saying that where an appellate court splits 3–2 over a procedural point, if the officer was properly trained and there was no intent to profit from a rights violation, the conviction should stand. That, by the way, would cause the courts to stand in far higher esteem among the citizenry than they currently do. In conjunction with this approach, the courts could be empowered to grant a monetary award to the defendant from a specially created legislative fund to compensate him for the violation of his rights. While the payment of a thousand dollars might seem paltry in comparison to release in a felony case, the cumulative cost of rights violations can become quite punishing, and there will be an incentive to do things correctly, since failure to do so may impair local budgets.

Sketching the grand design of the law is the social equivalent of architecture. This is a significant function of the appellate courts, but unfortunately not all the members of these courts are architects—many are simple craftsmen. Unlike the architect, who is always searching for the better material, more functional design, and more energy-efficient construction, the craftsman is concerned with executing the old designs. Craftsmen, in fact, are threatened by architects, because new approaches always imply new learning and unmastered problems. The craftsmen judges who perceive the science of "law" as an independent body of knowledge with a closed set of internal principles now apply the new criminal procedure as mindlessly as their craftsmen predecessors applied the old. The danger is a self-satisfied, smug belief that when individuals' civil liberties are protected, the entire job is done, losing sight of the fact that a society which cannot protect itself from crime is in grave danger.[2]

One of the reasons that nothing better has come along is that state court judges have been content to be craftsmen. I have served with judges who are ideologically disposed both in favor of and against the enforcement agencies. In both cases, the judges tended to manipulate the existing rules to achieve preconceived ends. The proprosecution judges always found the *facts* in favor of the police officers, while the antiprosecution judges would not believe a cop on a stack of bibles. Both groups became fascinated with achieving either law-and-order results or civil liberty results through the manipulation of the existing rules, rather than through formulating new rules which would achieve both results simultaneously. Yet there is little justification for releasing the guilty except to achieve institutional ends. The most absurd, though craftsmanlike, manipulations come out of crimes like possession of marijuana or moonshining, where the courts are frequently unenthusiastic about prosecution anyway. The judges do not want to convict, so they manipulate procedural principles which then come back to haunt them in cases where conviction is required by good sense. After nine hundred years of our law, we still have not learned that achieving equitable ends in individual cases through the creation of new technicalities only causes the technicalities to get piled on top of each other until the system is all technicality and no equity. Then there is procedural reform, and the whole process starts over again.

Obviously a focus upon the overall quality of an enforcement institution implies spending more money on law enforcement. Since courts are not in the budget-making business, and by a long constitutional tradition are forbidden financial powers, why is civil liberties with its attendant costs an appropriate focus for court supervision, while school finance is not? The answer, in the most practical terms, is that in proportion to the

2. I cannot help but remark a persistent phenomenon in the area of both poverty and civil liberties advocacy, namely, that a new generation of craftsmen carry out the design of geniuses and believe themselves to be the geniuses. Children emerging from law school take jobs as poverty lawyers or civil rights lawyers at salaries around $20,000 a year (thus a married professional couple makes $40,000) and believe that they are as great heroes as those who went south in 1958, living on cheese sandwiches and riding on bald tires, waiting to be beaten, murdered, or at best jailed in some filthy southern dungeon. The observer of human nature must be amused at strutting technicians basking in the heroism of a generation almost old enough to be their fathers.

entire task, the money alone is insignificant. Furthermore, there is a consensus about the myth/operational disparity, because everyone agrees upon what is and is not appropriate behavior for a law enforcement agency. While the guys down at the barber shop may laugh over scenes from old *Kojac* flicks where the cops rough up the bad guy, even the good ol' boys do not seriously approve of two officers placing a suspect in the back of a car and informing him that while he may beat the rap he'll never beat the ride.

In the United States, there is general admiration for the English police, who do not carry weapons and who have a cultural pattern of consummate civility in their dealings with the average felon. Even the law-and-order enthusiasts do not gainsay the ideal of civil liberties; they merely question the intelligence of using felon release as the universal sanction against prosecutorial misconduct. Consequently, there is some general agreement about what the institutions we are molding should ultimately look like, yet there is not sufficient practical political pressure to force the executive and legislative branches to initiate reforms. Money in the state budget is allocated in direct response to pressure, and aside from the courts, there just is not any pressure. Court pressure, which substitutes for political pressure, in this instance is legitimate, because civil liberties are an area traditionally entrusted to the courts for protection.

In summary, it is possible to say that criminal law reform gets close to a ten on the imaginary scale of appropriateness for court involvement for the following reasons: (1) There was a significant disparity between what society thought it could expect in the area of civil liberties and what the operational structure actually delivered. (2) The victims of the failure of the operational system were predominantly a minority which had no access to the political process. (3) Significant change could be accomplished merely by upgrading existing institutions and was predicated only incidentally upon the relationship between additional money and improved quality. (4) There was no practical alternative within the existing political structure for achieving a satisfactory result. (5) There was general consensus about the goals which society should be achieving, that is, what the institutions should look like at the end of the reform. This is the long way of saying that the whole problem was susceptible to judicial management. The standards were clear, and while the means are certainly controversial, they were exclusively within the courts' control and did not place an impossible administrative burden on the judicial system.

As we shall see, however, in the next chapter, there are instances of myth/operational disparity which are not susceptible to judicial management; I have alluded to one in this chapter and earlier in mentioning the problem of the jails. What happens if the courts order a new jail and the county commission refuses to appropriate the money? Does the court take the county treasury into receivership, and if so, who allocates the money left over from jail construction? If the county commission or other governing body resigns, does the court appoint a new one? Criminal law reform was easy, because the courts did not need to go outside their own system. The sanction of felon release was peculiarly within their power and required only the exercise of judicial responsibility, and not administrative responsibility, which would necessarily encompass other aspects of the governing process.

7

COURTS AND THE INSTITUTIONAL DIALOGUE

PART II: THE SCHOOL FINANCE CASES

When there is a problem, throwing money and people at it will usually solve it. It is a cliché that money does not bring happiness, but it is a common household experience that money makes unhappiness a lot more bearable. Similarly, money and people will usually solve most of government's mundane problems; even creative research which depends upon some unknown combination of art and science can be organized and expedited by an infusion of money, as both the development of the atomic bomb and the conquest of space prove. Notwithstanding the conservative criticism that "money and people are not enough," there are remarkably few areas of concern at the state and local level which more money will not turn around.

While the democratic process may have certain limitations, one of the few areas where it is superbly responsive is taxation; there is almost a perfect statistical correlation between rising taxes and legislative unemployment. In fact, the English Parliament developed as a forceful political institution primarily during times of rancor over property rights and taxation. When the king was living on his own, Parliament tended to atrophy, while during times of fiscal strain, when the king was seeking new sources of revenue, Parliament tended to become obstreperous. An interesting side effect of the universal public loathing for higher taxes is the tendency to hide taxes by imposing them on business (since business receives little public sympathy) in full recognition by tax professionals that the consumer will pay them. One input into the inflation equation of the 1980s, in fact, is the cost of state and local government, which is not paid for on April 15th by an income tax or at the grocery store by a sales tax, but rather by producers who raise the prices of their products. Every time we buy a car or a loaf of bread, we involuntarily buy a road, hospital, welfare benefit, or schoolteacher.

Most of what courts do does not cause great budget dislocation. Even integration, with its mandate of all deliberate speed, did not immediately involve the construction of new schools or the purchase of new school buses. The increased appropriations for schools came as a natural result of forces other than integration; if white parents had been willing to let their children go to the previously black schools, no increased capital outlay would have been required. Similarly, the one-man, one-vote case required no money, nor did the new rules about abortion.

In the area of administrative law, the courts are more likely to forbid government action, which means reduced expenditures, than they are to do anything else. Increasingly, however, government by court order has become so popular that the courts have been invited to appropriate money for every worthwhile cause. The difficulty is that when courts order other branches of government to meet certain standards, which obviously implies redirection of existing funds, they have no responsibility for increasing taxes, an unpleasant task which devolves upon *elected* officials, who are as likely as not to join the welfare ranks involuntarily as a result.

If I could say that courts should never redirect money or force tax increases, I could give an absolute rule which would be easy to apply. The problem, however, cannot be distilled that far; in the final analysis, general rules do not work very well. Judges have power, and that power includes the right to make up the rules. While a general rule about appropriating money may make sense in the abstract, when it comes time to apply the rule each judge will carve his own exceptions for entirely subjective reasons according to his personal evaluation of the urgency of the need for court participation. Nevertheless, the appropriation of money is one critical factor which should be considered before courts accept an invitation to intrude themselves into the political process. Furthermore, I would offer the following correlation: the greater the extent to which money *alone* is the relief sought rather than institutional reform, the less legitimate is court intervention into the matter.

In those cases where I have voted to enter orders which implied some reallocation of state money, the money was always ancillary to overall institutional reform. The mental health and juvenile institution cases are prominent examples. In the mental health cases the court did not require the construction of community mental health centers, but we did forbid the warehousing of disruptive people in the state asylums unless they were more than annoying; they had to be dangerous. Furthermore, we mandated fairly elaborate hearings with court-appointed counsel, a transcript, and an automatic appeal from commitment proceedings, which made the whole process of involuntary hospitalization much more difficult. The result, ultimately, was the development of community centers which attracted voluntary patients, along with a significant upgrading of the state hospitals. The entire process was aided by increasing enlightenment in the executive branch in the late 1970s. The courts' intervention was justified on a number of grounds. First, mental patients are peculiarly an insular minority without meaningful access to the political process. Second, involuntary commitment is an area involving civil liberties, almost akin to the criminal law, which is traditionally under court supervision. Third, the courts did not directly order the appropriation of money, but merely ordered that the executive branch could no longer take the easy way out by warehousing disruptive people. Finally, the courts did not frustrate the legislative will, since there was no positive commitment to any other method of handling the mentally ill; the courts actually aided concerned legislators who wanted to upgrade public hospitals, because we gave them a lever to move their colleagues off dead center.

In the juvenile institution cases we ordered that wayward children, that is, truants, runaways, sexually promiscuous girls, and the ungovernable, had a constitutional right not to be confined in secure, prison-like facilities with criminal offenders. Again, while a system of control for the wayward which met our mandate necessarily involved spending more money, the legislature was left free to do nothing, which, in fact, is what it did for almost two years. While the money involved in upgrading facilities was not exactly pocket change, the real change came in the attitude and work habits of personnel already in the system and being paid. Suddenly probation officers and trial court judges were expected to make an investigation of all alternatives short of incarceration, many of which were funded by charities like the Boys Town Foundation or the Junior League of Fairmont, and not the state. The Department of Welfare began publishing guides to all facilities available for juveniles, and the administrative director of courts started holding seminars for the trial judges to discuss the use of halfway houses, residential group centers, and community-based counseling services. Consequently, the dog of institutional reform wagged the money tail, which distinguishes the juvenile cases from the school finance case, which we are about to investigate, where the relief sought is for the money tail to wag the institutional dog.

I pick the school finance case as the quintessential object lesson in improper court intervention into the political process with mixed feelings, since I agonized over the decision for several months. Except for the mad egotist or the consummate cynic, most people who enter public life do so at least initially to improve the social order. Judges are no exception, particularly those who became judges as a consolation prize for not making it in big-time politics. At times my subjective inclination to help the children of Lincoln County overwhelmed my analytical faculties, which told me that in the long run the precedent of courts' tinkering with school finance would make for very bad government. I have always disliked the "Pandora's box" argument[1] and have taken quite seriously the incisive remark of J. M. Keynes that "in the *long run* we are all dead." We all live in the short run. Nonetheless, in the end I finally concluded that the political role of the courts is institutional balance and not determining how much money and people should be thrown at what; thus I reluctantly dissented from the majority opinion. It is, nevertheless, difficult to criticize a majority which is trying to make life better for the most deprived children in their jurisdiction.

The West Virginia school finance case decided in 1979 is styled *Pauley v. Kelly* and was brought by public interest lawyers on behalf of the parents of five children attending the public schools in Lincoln County, one of the poorest counties in the state. The plaintiffs sought a declaration that the West Virginia system of public school finance violated the state constitution. The plaintiffs argued that the existing system did not provide a "thorough and efficient" education as required by the state constitution and failed to afford equal protection to children living in poor areas whose education was retarded because of a low tax base.

Our court agreed with the plaintiffs and found education a fundamental state constitutional right in West Virginia, although the U.S. Supreme Court in 1973 had *not* found education to be a fundamental federal constitutional right. Having found education to be a fundamental right, the court applied a strict scrutiny standard to see if the state could demonstrate some compelling state interest to justify inherently unequal local funding, and the court concluded that there was no such compelling interest. Furthermore, the court determined that the "thorough and efficient" clause contained in the state constitution required the legislature to develop high-quality, statewide educational standards.

The majority opinion, however, did not do anything but remand the case for detailed factual development in the lower court. While the majority opinion scared the hell out of both the executive and legislative

1. One of my roommates in law school was fond of pointing out that whenever he read about "Pandora's box" in a judicial opinion he knew that a big shellacking was coming for the little old lady in tennis shoes, along with a big judgment for some rapacious corporation.

branches, it was more a speech about good education than a court mandate. Unsatisfying though a speech was to the plaintiffs, the majority recognized that lack of money alone may not be the cause of a poor school system, and I infer that the court's threat to intervene ultimately in education after years of lengthy development of the case in the lower court was an attempt to incite activity in the other institutions of state government without taking education immediately into the courts for management. As I noted earlier, while there may be no published opinions discussing this judicial technique, it certainly makes a great deal of sense and is employed more frequently than anyone will admit. My concern, however, is about what will happen when the case returns.

West Virginia education is financed from four basic sources: (1) an amount raised from local levies on real and personal property; (2) state foundation aid, or money the state pays out of general revenue funds to the counties based on a formula composed of seven components; (3) state supplemental benefits; and (4) amounts raised locally by special levy through vote of the people of the county. The court noted that the amounts raised from local levies pursuant to popular referendum had already been challenged unsuccessfully and the U.S. Supreme Court had upheld a state constitutional requirement of 60 percent for passage and appropriation of special levy money.

For the purpose of developing an appropriate factual record, our Supreme Court directed the lower court's attention to possible inequities in the seven-factor formula by which foundation aid is computed. The court also directed the lower court to develop a record on the distribution of supplemental aid to needy counties. Finally, while the court acknowledged that amounts raised through property taxes in the various counties were disparate due to differences in property wealth, the court directed that evidence he developed to show whether Lincoln County's low property tax revenue resulted from illegally low appraisals based on political influence. The majority recognized the matrix of interlocking political problems in reforming education by recommending that the Speaker of the House of Delegates and the president of the state Senate be joined as parties defendant upon remand and stated that other essential parties were the state tax commissioner, the Lincoln County superintendent of schools, the Lincoln County School Board, the Lincoln County tax assessor, and the Lincoln County Commission. This fact, in and of itself, should lead to the conclusion that the problem is beyond judicial management.

The school systems in West Virginia are dependent upon local property taxes for approximately 30 percent of their funds. About 60 percent of the funds are provided by the state government, which makes West Virginia sixth in the nation in percentage of state funds provided for local education. West Virginia, however, ranked forty-fourth nationally in terms of dollars spent per pupil at the time the *Pauley* case came before the court. The record amply demonstrated that Lincoln County students were provided an education which was markedly inferior to the education provided in wealthier counties. The lower court had initially concluded that the physical plant, counseling, medical and library services, and vocational training programs failed to meet minimum educational standards.

The factor which was most strenuously urged upon the court was the dilapidated physical plant for the entire school system in Lincoln County. While the state provided a far higher percentage of the *total* funds for education in property-poor counties, state subsidies had developed over a forty-year period and were keyed in large part to supplementing the pay for professional teachers. This phenomenon, obviously, was in direct response to the lobbying power of the teachers' professional association. Consequently, while there was state money to finance current expenses, a county which started out with poor physical plants had to build new ones itself with special levy money, which required a 60 percent favorable vote in a referendum. Even with the best possible commitment from the voters in approving special levies, without additional state funds the necessary plants cannot be constructed. The court accepted the plaintiffs' assertions that most of the state foundation aid was based upon the number of professional teachers and that where the number of teachers was limited by lack of classrooms, the state foundation grant was necessarily reduced. Out of fifty-five counties, according to a chart included in the majority opinion, six counties had per pupil expenditures lower than Lincoln County, and many were almost exactly equal. Lincoln County's per pupil expenditure was $900, while the state average was $1,036. The high for the entire state was $1,428 and the low $832 per pupil. Eleven counties had not passed any local excess levy to support the schools.

Obviously what is implied if the case finds its way back to the West Virginia Supreme Court after further factual development, in the absence of dramatic policy change by the legislature, is that the court will mandate expenditure of large sums of money on the schools, but as I pointed out in a dissent, I cannot imagine how this is to be done. Preeminent among the problems is the West Virginia constitutional requirement that 60 percent of the electorate must ratify by referendum any issue of general obligation bonds. Since the case indicated that the most serious deficiencies were in the area of plant facilities, it would appear impossible to raise the necessary money without a statewide bond issue, which would require an election. If, indeed, there is to be an election, I cannot conceive of the more populous, wealthy counties voting for a bond issue, the proceeds from which would already be dedicated exclusively to the rural and underfinanced counties. Even assuming there were a practical way around this particular problem, such as ordering the legislature to build plants out of current revenues and to tax in sufficient amount to accomplish this, we would still be at only the beginning of the problem. In New Jersey, in fact, in a series of six cases styled *Robinson v. Cahill,* the New Jersey Supreme Court enjoined the opening of the schools in 1976 until the legislature provided a method of eliminating wealth discrimination. The result was that New Jersey passed an income tax to support the schools. West Virginia already has an income tax, but I suppose that if the court closes all the schools until the legislature raises taxes, the same result can be achieved. The legislators then have three options: they can leave the schools closed; they can impeach the court; or they can raise taxes and lose their jobs. Quite frankly, my initial choice were I in the legislature would be impeachment of the court.

When the average bright law student first encounters the doctrine that courts will not decide "political questions," it usually appears that such deference is either cowardice on the part of the courts or the validation of a status quo which the judges wish to maintain. Nevertheless, Justice Brennan's classic definition of a "political question" from *Baker v. Carr* occasionally does make some sense, particularly his recognition that a question is beyond court competence if it lacks "judicially discoverable and manageable standards for resolving it." Few issues fall more within this ambit than school finance, particularly since it is not money alone which makes a public education system "thorough and efficient." Certainly there is no objection from the state Board of Education, the superintendent of schools, the local county administrators, or the teachers and support personnel to the court's forcing more money out of the legislature. In fact, the education lobby, which is led by the West Virginia Education Association, spends its year-round efforts performing exactly that function. However, if the courts can take control of education to direct money, can the courts also make other educational policy? If the answer to that last question is "yes," the professional educators will certainly become outraged over the whole undertaking.

The preeminent difference between the school finance cases and integration, mental health, criminal procedure, and standards for juvenile detention is that in the area of schools there is no political indifference.[2] While in all the other areas listed above, the legislative process was characterized by inertia, in the school cases it is characterized by frenetic activity. Each house of the legislature has a full-time committee concerned with nothing but education, and in every session of the legislature no less than ten bills on education pass both houses and are signed into law. Failure on the part of the legislature to pass an acceptable raise for teachers in 1980 led to the defeat of both the president of the state Senate and the Senate Finance Committee chairman, plus a host of other prominent incumbent legislators.

While this is certainly not a book about education, there is little choice but reluctantly to enter the puzzle palace of educational policy. My reflections on education are intended only to suggest problems; they must not be taken as suggestions for solutions. College teaching, in which I am experienced, is not public school teaching, in which I am not experienced, and my own theories of education are about as useful as a whistle on a plow.

Only the most naive believe that the schools are run for the benefit of the pupils; education is big business everywhere. It takes up 32.9 percent of the total West Virginia revenues at all levels. That amounts to $692,839,778, which are earnestly sought after by textbook publishers, educational consultants, school bus manufacturers, teachers, support personnel, administrators, and purveyors of everything from new school construction to paint and toilet paper. The rural counties like Lincoln are not the only ones scrambling for a bigger share of the educational buck—everyone everywhere wants to put both paws in the trough. In

2. As I mentioned in chapter 3, Yale's Guido Calabresi and other legal scholars have been working toward a theory of "structural due process," a theory which explicitly recognizes the inherent inertia of the legislative branch. Under this constitutional rubric, courts could strike down statutes for no reason other than a need for legislative reconsideration of their subjects. It is assumed that if the courts create a void, the legislature will be forced to reconsider its former policy choices without the reinforcement of the status quo which the legislative structure imposes. I know of no reported case which raises this theory to a conscious level chez the judges themselves, but it is definitely an unarticulated consideration in many of the reported cases. Explicit recognition of this court function avoids one current evil, namely, the discovery of some *constitutional* infirmity in the existing statute above and beyond the simple need for reconsideration. Opponents of conscious acceptance of this principle argue that it is theoretically unmanageable for courts to be able to *demand* legislative reconsideration of certain issues and thereby set legislative agendas. However, I find this more manageable in practice than the current alternative, namely, performing a "structural due process" role while at the same time finding it necessary to go further in order to sustain a theoretically correct facade which requires for its maintenance the dictation of substantive reasons for the striking down of a given statute.

most places education is the most robust, healthy, controversial, and thoroughly considered political issue around.

There are hundreds of pages of statutes in the *West Virginia Code* relating to education, a substantial part of which concerns teacher tenure, certification requirements, rates of pay, sick leave and personal days, voluntary and involuntary transfer, and procedural requirements for discharge. Next to judges, teachers have the most protected employment in state government. Since teachers in West Virginia are not "unionized" (the professional association abjures vulgar labor tactics), labor-management relations are carried on in the legislature, a body, by the way, to which teachers are regularly returned in large numbers. Any good labor organization, regardless of what it calls itself, is even more concerned with job security than it is with wage rates, and that fact is reflected in the statutory scheme which makes it almost impossible to fire a teacher for incompetence.

Furthermore, there is an interesting symbiotic relationship between the working teachers and the education departments at the state colleges. The teachers, obviously, wish to avoid excessive competition in the job market and have successfully influenced the state Board of Education to establish "certification requirements," which revolve around the education curriculum offered at the state colleges. The certification requirement demands that a prospective teacher have had eight or more education courses, so most high-school teachers have majored in education. While this certification requirement keeps education professors employed, it turns out high-school teachers who know a lot more about how to teach than about what to teach. Nationwide, in fact, few science teachers know calculus, many social science teachers have no solid grounding in history, and many language teachers have only a bare reading knowledge of the language they "teach." Once a teacher is hired, his or her promotion is predicated upon completion of further "education courses" in the summer. There is, in this regard, a tacit agreement among teachers and their summer professors: the professors will demand nothing but attendance at glorified bull sessions, and in turn the "students" will patronize that college's summer program and provide work for the professors. Lots of "A's" and "B's" are given, and everyone goes home having achieved personal goals which have nothing to do with teaching children. This is one small piece of the education system's trading for its own account.

I suppose that many of my opinions about the inner workings of the educational system come from having been on the receiving end of the high-school educational product as a college teacher for so many years.

Many of the better students at the University of Charleston where I lecture in economics are my advisees, either because they are economics majors or plan to go on to law school. Uniformly these good students were utterly bored in high school, because the teachers were almost completely uninspiring. Usually each student can remember one extraordinary teacher who motivated him or her, but otherwise their high-school teachers are regarded as pedestrian at best. Aside from a few students who are interested in the sciences and complain that their local high schools did not have facilities for chemistry and physics, my students do not complain about the physical plants, but rather about the paucity of both competence and enthusiasm on the part of their teachers.[3] If, as a judge, I am entitled to appropriate money for the schools by cudgeling the legislature in the New Jersey fashion, am I also entitled to strike down the teacher certification requirements and tenure statutes? The same "thorough and efficient" or "equal protection" reasoning which applies to money would apply to quality of personnel; certainly, if I am responsible for higher teachers' salaries, I should also be responsible for requiring teachers to know calculus, Latin, and history. Is that task judicially manageable?

The robust politics surrounding education does not stop, however, at the state level, since every country has its own local board of education. Many of the critical decisions about curriculum, consolidation of schools, and educational priorities are entrusted to the locally elected board, which then selects the county superintendent of schools. Local teachers are hired by the county superintendent with the consent of the local board, which obviously means that there is a lot of politics about who teaches school. My suspicion is that knowing a member of the Lincoln County Board of Education will get a prospective teacher a lot farther along than holding a Masters of Arts in Teaching from Yale. If I give Lincoln County money, can I also hire its teachers?

What type of a curriculum does a "thorough and efficient system of free schools" envisage? Is it a course of study heavy in mathematics,

3. In general, West Virginia grade-school teachers are better than high-school teachers. In teaching the primary grades, the "child-centered" skills taught by the college education departments are far more relevant than they are to high-school teaching. Furthermore, I apologize to the competent, dedicated teachers who teach because they love it and work far harder than they are paid for. Unfortunately, the good teachers are often concentrated in the "good schools." When teachers are uninspiring or lazy, they are frequently transferred to the poorer schools, which means that all the bad teachers and unmotivated students interact with one another. While there is no alternative but to dwell on teacher incompetence, the real tragedy of the structure I am discussing is that there is almost no monetary reward for the competent and hard working nor sanction against the incompetent and lazy. Real teaching is real work and should receive real pay.

science, history, English, and foreign languages, or should the curriculum center around life adjustment courses? Should we have an option of two curricula, one for the college-bound which is heavy on the former and another for the non-college-bound which is heavy on the latter? Should we start tracking in the first grade, so that all the motivated, middle-class students are in one group and all the unmotivated and deprived in another? Or should we offer one unified curriculum to everyone, the classic bed of Procrustes? If there are only four students who want to take chemistry or physics, are we required to build a lab and hire a teacher? Usually the answer to these questions is supplied at the local level in response to both a professional and political input. If the preeminently middle-class members of any court force money to be given to Lincoln County, are they also entitled to force its high school to look like a duplicate of St. Grottlesex?

Few issues have stirred such local controversy around the United States as the question of school consolidation. Where few people are spread over a large area, there are often as many as four tiny high schools in a county. The result is that each part of the county has a community school which is a comparatively short distance from everyone's home; however, the small student body makes it prohibitively expensive to provide laboratory facilities, specialized language teachers, and the spectrum of courses which a larger high school can offer. The local residents usually value their local teams, cheerleaders, and bands, along with all the local color which the high school brings to the community. The professional administrators and parents of children going on to good colleges, however, usually favor consolidation, which provides one central high school with a varied curriculum and greatly superior facilities. The ordinary students complain about the loss of their teams, the long hours spent each day on a bus, and the greater competition for places much sought after in athletics, student government, and other extracurricular activities. This, in fact, is the situation in Lincoln County, which has four high schools. I asked the plaintiffs' lawyer from the bench the day the Lincoln County case was argued whether we could order the consolidation of the schools to ensure that our court-appropriated money was used efficiently. As I recall, counsel ducked the question and attempted to focus our attention on the money issue alone. In fact, for a moment plaintiffs' counsel looked like the mask of tragedy when he thought that the court might go beyond the simple appropriation of money and begin tampering with the delicate political accommodations which have developed through the years around the schools.

Anyone who has even a passing acquaintance with school affairs probably realizes that the correlation between money and quality education, while always positive, is certainly not perfect. In the 1950s, many of the country's most expensive and best private schools were operated on old New England estates where the classes were conducted in quarters which would have been unacceptable in almost any public school district. In addition, the teachers were paid less than the wage prevailing in the public schools. The quality of those schools was attributable primarily to the motivation of the students and the quality of the faculty, who had voluntarily chosen to forgo salaries and benefits to teach pleasant, motivated, upper-middle-class students.

Where education is poor, lack of money is usually one factor, but bad teachers and bad students are out there in abundance. In fact, one of the reasons that we focus on money is the hope that money can compensate for bad students and bad teachers; we very much *wish* that proposition to be true, since money is the easiest factor in the educational equation to control. There is no reason to disregard the beneficial effect of money; the equivalent of combat bonuses can attract high-quality teachers to unpleasant schools. The practical flaw in this theory, however, is that political interests have made it almost impossible to get rid of the old, bad teachers so that their places can be taken by the ones which our money recruits. The statutory scheme of almost all states makes sure that we will be forced to pay the old, lousy teachers the new higher salaries—ergo, no improvement.

The relationship between a teacher and his or her employer, a local board of education, may at first appear to be one of simple contract similar to the one between an employee and any good corporation, like Eastman Kodak. But here, as in many areas of government, there is far more involved than first meets the eye. The relationship is covered in minute detail by statute and case law, both of which make getting rid of the incompetent almost impossible.[4]

The complex legal and political structures surrounding teaching in the public schools vary from state to state, but they are sufficiently similar that I can take the West Virginia model in full confidence that it will

4. My wife once taught third grade in a Mercer County grade school alongside an elderly male teacher who literally slept at his desk a substantial part of the day while the children did busy work. His system involved giving all the kiddies abnormally high grades, thus quieting any parental complaint, and adopting a live and let live relationship with his fourth graders. Since he was approaching retirement, the administrators were reluctant to discharge him; however, during his last four years he did substantial damage to large numbers of students.

instruct our understanding of the process everywhere. The process starts when the superintendent of a local school board recommends employment of a teacher. This is no formality. If a school board should take it upon itself to hire someone whom the superintendent has not recommended, the contract is invalid. A starting teacher will be given a probationary contract, and the teacher must successfully complete a three-year probation before acquiring tenured status. Theoretically, the school board has probationary contracts to afford itself an opportunity to evaluate teachers before giving them permanent employment. Logically it might be thought that during probation the board can terminate the probationer's contract with little procedural impediment. That, however, is not the case. The dismissed teacher is always entitled to a hearing, even when the contract is conditional. Since both the federal and state courts have created constitutional, due process obstacles to discharging even a probationary teacher, the local boards often consider discharge more trouble than it is worth for all but the most incompetent even at this stage.

Once a teacher has completed three years of service, dismissing him may be like pulling nails with your teeth. To begin with, the teacher cannot be dismissed for lack of motivation, poor performance, or uninspired teaching; the only grounds for dismissal are set forth in the statutes. They are immorality, incompetence, cruelty, insubordination, intemperance, and willful neglect of duty. Since it would appear that you could get almost anyone under one or another of these grounds if you really wanted him, the courts have defined each in the narrowest possible manner.

The complex process of dismissal is governed by treacherous statutory and decisional law. It boils down to requiring that the teacher whose dismissal is contemplated be afforded most of the due process rights of a defendant in a criminal case. The burden of effecting a dismissal is upon the superintendent, who is the leading actor in the entire play, but he can hardly do his assigned duties without running headlong into one due process requirement or another. The process is purposefully designed to protect the teacher and to give the superintendent every possible opportunity to fall into a hole. The superintendent begins as an investigator when possible teacher misconduct comes to his attention. It is his responsibility to gather evidence about a teacher's conduct and then play prosecutor to decide whether the evidence warrants a dismissal action. Here he faces considerable uncertainties, since the grounds for dismissal are not clearly defined. A court may later disagree about whether the conduct is immoral or intemperate, etc., and order the teacher reinstated with back pay. Since these proceedings often take three or four years, the back pay can amount to as much as $40,000, which is a significant gamble with taxpayers' money.

Once the initial decision to seek dismissal is made, the superintendent's problems have only just begun, and several factors conspire to make his life difficult. He must first send a notice to the teacher telling him why dismissal is sought and informing him that he has a right to a hearing within a specified time before the school board. By this time the board will have probably gotten wind of what is going on, and this frequently puts the superintendent in a touchy position. The board will come to him and ask about the case, but he cannot tell them much because they will be hearing the teacher's argument against dismissal, and due process requires an impartial panel.

The hearing itself is similar to a full-blown trial, with the board sitting as a jury. The teacher has the full range of procedural rights: the right to assistance of counsel; the right to be confronted by witnesses and documentary evidence; the right to argue his case; and the right to a decision on the merits by an impartial panel. If the superintendent or the board (neither of which has extensive legal training as a rule) should fail, for whatever reason, to follow any part of this procedure, the teacher may subsequently be reinstated by court order. At the hearing, the superintendent will find himself confronted by a situation other prosecutors only have nightmares about: he is also the chief prosecution witness and must take the stand to testify.

After all the evidence is presented and a decision made by the board, the case may still be far from over. If the vote to dismiss the teacher is not unanimous, the teacher has a right to appeal to the state superintendent of schools, and if the state superintendent's determination is adverse, the teacher may appeal to the courts. If the vote is unanimous, the teacher may still appeal the decision to the courts. If an appeal is taken, both the grounds of dismissal and the procedure used will be subjected to judicial scrutiny, and any flaw may be the grounds on which the court orders reinstatement with back pay. From 1976 to 1980, frequently over my vigorous dissent, my own court reinstated almost every teacher who appealed to us. As Sir Henry Maine, the nineteenth-century legal historian and author of *Ancient Law* once noted, substantive law is "gradually secreted in the interstices of procedure." With all the levels of administrative tribunals and state and federal courts reviewing teacher discharge, we have in effect said that teachers cannot be fired. As if all this were not enough, the teacher can bring a damage suit against the superintendent and members of the school board in federal court in an ancillary civil rights action.

This whole process may appear absurd at first; however, it is not too terribly different from labor's view of a good employment security clause in a labor–management contract. All industrial labor unions are concerned first with the job security of their members, and capricious firing is one of the first evils which a good union leadership will eliminate. Since in most American jurisdictions teachers are not unionized, and where unionized are denied the right to strike, their only remedy is through the political process in the first instance, and through the courts' sense of equity in the second instance. Certainly, local school board politics is vicious, and it is as likely that a creative, imaginative, and enthusiastic teacher will be fired because he or she aggravates the existing social order as it is that only incompetents will be fired. Since the discharge cases are brought by the teachers, the focus is always upon the discharged employee and his sympathetic circumstances rather than upon the children. His students do not intervene and demand a hearing; thus the natural sympathy of judges is given unbridled play, because the real issue of teacher versus student is seldom appropriately developed. It is upon the law articulated in these cases that everyone in the system predicates expectations and actions. Thus when it appears that no procedure, no matter how fair, will satisfy the reviewing authorities, both state and federal, superintendents give up bringing even the strongest cases—it simply is not worth the trouble and expense. After all, school administrators work 9:00 to 5:00 just like everyone else.

The one thing which this scheme absolutely guarantees is that the mere appropriation of money will not assure us better teachers. It must be remembered that the superintendent of schools is elected by the board of education, which in turn is elected by the voters. How then does a teacher get recommended for employment? Well, by political influence, of course. A friend of a board member suggests a candidate to that board member, who in turn suggests him or her to the superintendent, who if he knows what is good for him recommends the candidate to the board. If the courts appropriate money, will that fact alone alter the politics of employment? Certainly not. In fact, the higher combat-pay salaries will become choice political plums capable of making active, machine politics an attractive way of doing school board business.

While the ardent proponent of the "public interest" can make a case that the schools should be run exclusively for the students, a good case can be made that the teachers have their lives invested in the schools as well. Teachers pursue studies in education in college and are constantly attending classes either at night or in the summer to upgrade their credentials. While I have already discussed my reservations about these classes, nonetheless they do require both attendance and money. By the time a person has gone through college and graduate training and has taught for four or five years, he or she has a substantial investment in a career which is entitled to some respect and protection. Some accommodation of all these competing interests is achieved by the political process, and while no one is wholly satisfied, most people can live with the result. Politically, fooling around with teachers is like fooling around with fire. The teachers in most places put all other labor unions to shame in terms of political power. Teachers are part of that solid middle-class community which votes to a man in both primary and general elections; teachers are articulate and experienced in group activities; and teachers talk with a lot of other solid citizens who also vote.

The political forces which bring us poor-quality teachers notwithstanding money are only the beginning, however, since we still have the entire problem of poor-quality students to address. Education is inherently a middle-class phenomenon: the teachers are middle-class; the administrators are middle-class; and the goals of upward mobility and social improvement are middle-class goals. Many students from school districts which are not middle-class find the entire school structure alien, but more to the point, their alienation is actively reflected in the political process. This returns us for a moment to the question of consolidation of high schools, the choice of curriculum, and the goals of education. Simply put, the educational system, being primarily middle-class, has a tendency to institutionalize certain rites of passage and provide an elaborate system for certifying the passage, ending with the high-school diploma. Yet those who fear that their children will not successfully complete rigorous requirements work actively through the political process to lower the standards to provide universal successful passage. This is not irrational; it is no more unreasonable for the disadvantaged to oppose meritocracy than it is for landless peasants to oppose aristocracy.

Possibly, if it could be said that the courts know what curriculum is best for educating children, there might be some justification for court intervention in the school question; however, not only is there active political disagreement among the recipients of educational services, but there is active disagreement among the providers as well. Educators cannot reconcile the competing goals of integration, affirmative action, high academic standards, upward mobility, and American scientific technical superiority. Consequently, there is no consensus about the relevance of any "scientific principles" to the field of education in the same way that there would be in physics. If there are poor students in the schools who have a deleterious effect upon education, they are there for a good and valid political reason.

This leads us then to the reason why intervention in the schools by the courts is entirely different from intervention in the areas of mental health facilities, juvenile institutions, or even civil liberties for criminal suspects. No one is interested in these latter areas, and the political process is characterized by inertia. Court mandates are not in opposition to legislative compromises, because there is no viable legislative intent. With the schools, however, the legislative process is working full speed ahead every moment of the day and night. When I was a member of the legislature, I used to take the service entrance of the Daniel Boone Hotel through all the garbage pails to get up to my room in order to avoid education lobbyists still working the legislature at 10:00 P.M. in the hotel corridors. In education, the political process is working; we may not like the result, but there is no lack of democracy in its most robust, free-wheeling form.

When the West Virginia school finance case came to decision conference in my court the first time, I voted *in favor* of the plaintiffs. It took us over six months to decide that case, and we had numerous conferences—it was hardly a routine case to be decided in one conference. I vacillated about my position because, notwithstanding all the good theoretical reasons for opposing court intrusion into a political area like schools, there was no question that the children in Lincoln County were suffering from a lack of money. While I have never visited a Lincoln County school, I assume that they were also suffering from poor teachers and poor students; nonetheless, throwing some money at them would upgrade the physical plants and, if nothing else, enhance the self-image of the students. As the English often say, first men shape buildings and then buildings shape men—a phenomenon which has been proven time and again at Oxford, Cambridge, Yale, and Harvard.

In my hypothetical scale of one to ten, certainly the school finance case gets much higher than a one because while the political process was actively working to reconcile all the competing forces of teachers, parents, and budget makers, the problems of the five or six rural counties like Lincoln, with low tax bases and very poor physical plants, fell between the cracks. Conceivably, if those counties allied themselves in the legislature and traded everything they could trade for a one-shot appropriation of state money to upgrade their schools they might have gotten it, but the fact of the matter is that their legislators have other agendas as well. Who then is going to help the children? More to the point, if one has power, what is it for except to do good things? In all fairness to the courts, the history of the United States is of a legal and constitutional structure accommodating itself to men of vision doing good things.

Ultimately I dissented in the school case, because for once in my life I found the Pandora's box argument persuasive. As I studied the problem, I became increasingly convinced that in the area of education, the courts would not serve a balancing function, but rather would be enlisted on the side of one of the best-organized and most tenacious special interest groups in the state, namely, the professional educators. While the seduction of the courts would be effected by showing the distressing conditions in a few counties like Lincoln, ultimately the courts would find themselves ranged on the side of a special interest group, the exact result which any sound analysis of the proper role of courts finds most discreditable.

Certainly if the courts got into the business of ordering the legislature to appropriate money for the schools, requiring a round of tax increases, in order to make the schools "thorough and efficient," the next step would necessarily be a law suit by some interested group either to require consolidation of schools in a county, or to find the cumbersome system of teacher tenure with its security for incompetents unconstitutional, or to reorder the curriculum and upgrade the certification requirements. As long as the court undertook to work in tandem with the education lobby, using its power to exact more money from the public coffers, everything would be comparatively peaceful; however, as soon as the court carried through to its logical conclusion the constitutional requirement of a "thorough and efficient" system of education, there would be widespread political repercussions.

If the teacher lobby can defeat the leadership of the legislature any time it really puts its mind to it, it takes little imagination to figure out what it could do to *elected* state judges, who hold the least visible and least understood positions in state government. As soon as a powerful interest group concludes that the election of five men and women to an appellate court can give it the same political advantages that the election of one hundred thirty-four men to the state legislature can give it, the whole nature of the judiciary changes. It is only by a long tradition of consistent refusals to ally with powerful, active political interest groups that the judiciary prevents itself from becoming an adversary force and retains its position of either neutral arbiter or balancing force.

The proposition should immediately leap to mind that appointed judges with life tenure would not need to assume an adversary role. However, as I pointed out in the last chapter, there are sanctions short of ejection from office which can be brought to bear by the legislative branch on a politically active judiciary. Returning for a moment to the school finance case itself, while I decry the shoddy treatment accorded the rural county of Lincoln, the courts are not the only progressive force at work trying to upgrade facilities. For example, the state superintendent of schools is charged with scrutinizing problems like poor physical plants in selected counties, and each year he proposes legislation based on the objective needs of the total school system. Historically, the governor pressures the legislature to correct obvious injustices in the allocation of state resources, and even the legislature itself frequently passes remedial legislation. Although this book has tended to focus on disparities between the myth and operational systems, emphasizing everyone's inclination to trade for his own account, it is quite unrealistic to be *totally* cynical. Most people in government genuinely want to help their fellowcitizens, and that motivation is manifested in public policy far more often than is generally recognized.

In summary, it is possible to catalogue the reasons why the school finance case should receive a grade on the low end of our scale of suitability for court intervention. (1) The schools are the subject of intense, active political management which has resulted in a matrix of interlocking political compromises. Interference by the courts with one part of the compromise will cause immediate adjustments to other parts which were thought long settled. (2) In the school case, the primary relief sought was the allocation of money, traditionally the most jealously guarded prerogative of the legislative branch. The courts were not asked to overcome inertia in the legislative branch or eliminate trading for one's own account in the executive branch; the relief envisaged involved no institutional improvement, but merely more money to feed an existing institutional structure. (3) Any attempt to take seriously the proposition argued by the plaintiffs that the courts should enforce the constitutional guarantee of a "thorough and efficient" system of education would ultimately involve the courts in the active management of the schools, a function to which they are remarkably unsuited. The power to force the appropriation of money also implies the power to review teacher certification requirements, curricula, consolidation, and teacher employment, all of which are hot political issues. (4) If the courts limit themselves to the appropriation of money, they become nothing more than the ally of a powerful political interest group, which changes courts from a neutral, balancing force to an adversarial one, with untoward political consequences for the court system in general. If they approach the regulation of the schools evenhandedly, they will incur the active hostility of *every* vested interest in education and will become a super board of education with little time left to do anything else. (5) Even if the courts decide to commit themselves to the reform of education, there is no consensus in society nor in the courts regarding what appropriate reform should be. Unlike the area of civil liberties, where only the means and not the ends are seriously debated, in education both means and ends are up for grabs. (6) Education is not an area traditionally entrusted to the courts for supervision, and the courts have absolutely no expertise in the area; consequently, there is no reason to believe that in total they will do a better job than the existing institutions.

While this list is not entirely exhaustive of all the reasons for nonintervention, it does give some depth to Justice Brennan's definition of a "political question" when he speaks of lack of manageable standards. If nothing else, the reasons assigned above for deciding that the courts cannot run the schools should show that if they attempted it they would have time to do nothing else. Once they undertake even a little piece of school management, their staffs will mushroom, and since there is not sufficient legal manpower to present every educational issue which they would be forced to decide in an adversarial manner, they would become administrators deciding issues on their own internally generated information rather than judicial officers determining issues on the basis of material presented by opposing sides. While the institution might stand one deviation from the standard judicial model, ours is a system of precedent—both good and bad. If the school cases are used as bad precedent for doing good things, we will then dramatically change the nature of the judicial institution, which currently is working in a more or less satisfactory manner.

8
THE COURTS AS AN INSTITUTION

In elected politics, the legislature and executive take idealistic, energetic, ambitious young men and turn them into whores in five years; the judiciary takes good, old, tired, experienced whores and turns them into virgins in five years. The men are not the source of either transformation—they are of the same type, particularly since judges are either graduates or rejects of politics. The decisive factor is the institution—whether the exact same creatures are quartered in the local house of ill fame or in the Temple of the Vestal Virgins.

Just as the legislative and executive branches, all bureaucracies, and political machines have lives of their own apart from the individuals who man them, courts as institutions have certain qualities which are completely independent of the judges sitting on the bench. Courts are absolutely unlike any other structure in government, and because of their structural features, courts are the institution of government least likely to be manipulated for a selfish purpose by individuals in them or by the institution as a whole. Since it has been implicitly recognized that officials will be either whores or virgins in response to their surroundings, the emphasis in the judiciary has not been on the selection of personnel but rather on the molding of the institution.[1] For more than nine hundred years, each century has contributed institutional improvements. In the beginning of the seventeenth century, the famous Sir Francis Bacon lost his position as lord chancellor of England because he accepted gifts from litigants, thus establishing a fairly obvious principle which had, nonetheless, previously been disregarded. Only within the last generation have we eliminated fees paid directly to judicial officers based on the volume

1. The fight over whether judges should be appointed or elected will never be settled. Since people will always disagree with court opinions, it will always be thought that where judges are appointed things would be better if they were elected, and where judges are elected that things would be better if they were appointed. In fact, in my experience, it makes no difference.

or outcome of litigation—another simple principle which was difficult to establish because of fiscal conservatism.

For those who did not find my comparison to virgins compelling, there is another simile: judges bear a striking resemblance to eunuchs; their emasculation entitles them to free access to life's temptations. This emasculation is the product of both historical accident and conscious molding of the institution. Historical accident provided an institution characterized by decentralized decision making with few *administrative* hierarchical features, thus minimizing the rewards to bureaucratic empire building. Conscious molding has given us an institution more circumscribed by formal procedures, codes of conduct, and constant public scrutiny than any other power force in government. There is even a lower incidence of outright graft in the judiciary than in other branches though graft does occur. We can dismiss vulgar corruption in the judiciary in the same way that we have dismissed it in the other branches. While a relative absence of graft helps the judiciary, its distinguishing feature is the absence of the sophisticated political and institutional trading which so permeates the legislative and executive branches.

No individual judge has very much power through the judicial lawmaking function. There is a hierarchy of courts, with appellate courts supervising trial courts, federal courts supervising state courts, and the Supreme Court supervising everyone. All of these independent courts interact with one another slowly to grind out a body of law. The major courts (excluding magistrates' courts, traffic courts, domestic relations courts, etc.) are (1) trial courts of general jurisdiction, which in the federal system are called United States district courts and in state systems are most commonly called circuit courts, district courts, or common pleas courts; (2) intermediate appellate courts, which in the federal system are called United States courts of appeals for the twelve federal circuits and in state systems are most commonly called state appellate divisions or courts of appeals; and (3) courts of last resort, which in the federal system is the United States Supreme Court and in state systems are state supreme courts.[2] This system is counterbalanced, with each level of courts reviewing the level below. Since the appellate procedure is expensive and time-consuming, it probably works injustice in individual cases as often as it works justice, yet the very process of review has a chilling effect on the

2. In New York, because of an accident of history, this title is reserved for the lowest general jurisdiction trial court, while the highest court is called the Court of Appeals. Maryland has the same title for its highest court, while some of the trial courts are referred to as the Supreme Bench. What I have given is the structural outline, although, as in these examples, the names may occasionally differ.

natural human tendency to be arbitrary and capricious. Like all other courts, appellate courts are successful because of the cases they do not decide.[3] As we shall see directly, the appellate court hierarchy controls the decision-making process through reversing lower courts; it does not, however, exercise any administrative control the way higher authorities in the executive branch exert administrative control over lower-echelon decision makers.

Appellate and trial judges rarely see one another and quite often live in different parts of the state or district in which they serve. They are acquaintances rather than friends. One senior federal court of appeals judge who had also been a trial judge once referred humorously to his former colleagues on the trial bench as appellate judges' "natural enemies." Except in a few states with unified court structures, the budgets, personnel allocations, and physical accommodations of the courts are entirely separate, and each judge and court is individually funded. Lower courts are brought into compliance with developing case law by appellate opinions reversing lower court decisions. Written opinions are widely circulated among lawyers and trial judges, all but the most recalcitrant of whom fall in line with the higher court mandates. However, any higher court is always dependent upon the good will of the lower courts for the effective execution of the policy which it makes. In the judiciary, there is absolutely no penalty for making wrong decisions and no sanction against creativity. You cannot punish a judge for a wrong decision by taking away his office budget or his travel allowance. Since an innovative trial judge has nothing to fear in the form of "administrative" retribution, he can compel appellate courts to address difficult issues by refusing to follow precedent and "anticipating" developing law. When this occurs, the higher courts must not only reverse; generally the appellate judges must think out exactly why they are reversing and explain themselves. Frequently this places a naturally conservative appellate court in the position of trying to force an opinion which "won't write," which usually leads to a reconsideration of the subject matter. No similar process exists in the legislative branch, since the force of inertia makes it easy to avoid the reconsideration of settled issues when the settlement is comfortable, notwithstanding that it is also irrational.

The conscious molding of the institution and the historically inherited structure interact with one another to produce the branch of government

3. It is through the appellate process that statutes are interpreted and new law is generated. The U.S. Supreme Court selects an average of one hundred and fifty cases a year for full opinions, and those cases are chosen from thousands of applications because of the importance of the points they raise to the overall fabric of the law.

which appears to be the most neutral and objective of the three. In the practice of law, there is an absolute prohibition against a lawyer talking about a case with a judge without the other side's lawyer being present. This is not an idle requirement; it forms the very heart of the judicial process. While there are lawyers and judges who do engage in private communication (almost always oral) such people are the scum of the bar and bench and are generally regarded as such by every responsible practicing lawyer. Everything which a court does is public, and in most cases there is a verbatim transcript of all proceedings.[4]

While the ordinary due process rules concerning all judicial proceedings, with their emphasis on open, two-sided hearings, are an important structural pillar of the institution, simple procedural rules governing the formal part of judicial proceedings are not enough. There is, in addition, a code of ethics for judges which governs their private lives outside the courtroom and which is vigorously enforced by either formal sanctions or heavy peer pressure.[5] It is the code of ethics which completely emascu-

4. There are, however, certain exceptions, both formal and informal, to this general rule. Formal procedural rules frequently allow applications for temporary injunctions, writs of error, and rules to show cause to be made by one side alone. Rulings on these applications, however, are temporary and become final only after a full hearing is given to both sides. A lawyer can call a judge to request advice about the proper method of bringing a case before the court, since practice frequently differs dramatically among courts. Simple advice about procedure is informally accepted most places as a proper type of ex parte communication. A lawyer cannot, however, go further and discuss the merits of his case with the judge.

5. Under a typical state judicial code of ethics a judge must: uphold the integrity and independence of the judiciary; avoid impropriety and the appearance of impropriety in all of his activities; regulate his extra-judicial activities so as to minimize the risk of conflict with his judicial duties; regulate and file reports of any compensation received for quasi-judicial and extra-judicial activities; manage his investments and other financial interests so as to minimize the number of cases in which he is disqualified; and make a reasonable effort to inform himself of the personal financial interests of his spouse and minor children residing in his household. A judge should *not:* serve in a civic or charitable position if it is likely that the organization will be engaged in proceedings that would ordinarily come before him; solicit funds for any educational, religious, charitable, fraternal, or civic organization; engage in any financial and business dealings that might reflect adversely on his impartiality, interfere with the proper performance of his judicial duties, exploit his judicial position, or involve him in frequent transactions with lawyers or persons likely to come before the court on which he serves; accept gifts, bequests, favors, or loans except under specified circumstances; serve as executor, administrator, trustee, guardian, or other fiduciary except for the estate, trust, or person of a member of his family and then only if such service will not interfere with the proper performance of his judicial duties; or engage in political activity inappropriate to his judicial office, which includes not publicly endorsing a candidate for public office and not acting as a leader or holding any office in a political organization. The rules applicable to a political campaign for judicial office indicate that the judge is expected to maintain a nonpolitical role throughout the election, since he is not allowed to solicit funds directly, is not allowed to make any promises, is not allowed to have any people working for him make promises for him, and is allowed to obtain funds only through committees. During his campaign, a judge is allowed to attend political gatherings, but he cannot speak on political issues and may discuss only activities to improve the law, the legal system, and the administration of justice.

lates judges, because it prohibits all the activities which make active politics fun and interesting. First, judges are absolutely forbidden to talk about pending cases and should not discuss their decisions even after they have made them. When the press asks a *good* judge about a controversial case, he usually tells them that a court speaks through its orders and that they should read the order in the clerk's office. When the press is merely seeking illumination concerning the law, most judges refer them to practicing lawyers to explain the court's actions, because courts are not in the business of giving advisory opinions about what yesterday's case means for tomorrow's law. Thus a judge who helps to make a dramatic ruling cannot crow about it; he is forbidden to bask in the media glow as labor's hero, the schoolchildren's hero, the blacks' hero, or even the B & O Railroad's hero. Although the judges make the law, the lawyers take the credit. Judges cannot speak out on controversial issues, and this applies even where the judges are elected on a partisan ballot. While an elected judge can identify himself as a member of a political party, he is prohibited from taking any part in the affairs of that party, and he cannot support the positions of that party publicly. Furthermore, he cannot be active even in community affairs.

All financial dealings by both judges *and* their families are severely scrutinized. While a judge can own real estate and manage his own investments, he cannot accept a position as a corporate board member (except, in some places, on a board in a family business or on a board on which he served before becoming a judge, and then only if the company is noncontroversial), nor can he accept consulting fees or practice law in any way. While he can write and teach, he is not allowed to moonlight in an ordinary job. There is no prohibition against legitimate honoraria for actual services rendered, like giving a speech or contributing to a book, but foundation payments which are unrelated to actual work are basically graft.

Well-regarded judges do not socialize extensively, and judges are prohibited from accepting anything but ordinary hospitality. My family owns a house near Palm Beach which I visit in the winter, and one of my better friends at the bar frequently flys his private plane to Boca Raton, where he keeps a winter apartment. While I am flying with my wife on a commercial airliner, he is flying with four empty seats, yet he would neither offer me a ride nor would I accept one merely because it would *look* improper. While in politics lack of *actual* impropriety is an absolute defense to everything but the raging of the press, in the judiciary the *appearance* of impropriety is as reprehensible as the real thing. If a judge in my court system accepted more than ordinary hospitality from a member of the bar, notwithstanding that he could prove that he had held against that particular lawyer's clients consistently for the past twelve years, I would vote to impose sanctions under the judicial discipline procedure.

Since the most important commodity which the judiciary has to sell is no self-dealing, the molding of the institution through the centuries has centered around that single desideratum. It is perfectly proper for a pro-labor politician to accept plane rides and speaking honoraria from labor unions, since they are his constituency and his friends. Unless favors are extended as an explicit quid pro quo for legislative votes, that type of activity is considered part of the political process. In fact, at all levels elected politics is basically *about* the making of deals—presidents, governors, and legislators routinely meet for long sessions in private with the representatives of vested interests without a breath of criticism. For a governor to agree to support public employee collective bargaining in return for labor support in the next election or to agree to oppose strip-mine regulations in return for campaign favors is business as usual; political action committees are actually created by *law* to exchange campaign money for promises of favorable votes.

My experience in West Virginia, where we have traditionally had an honest judiciary, may cause me to paint a naively rosy picture of the judicial structure. As mentioned in the preface, I do not believe that courts work very well in their day-to-day conflict resolution functions; however, I do believe that they work fairly well in their political functions. It cannot be emphasized enough to most readers who are not lawyers that the man on the street's experience with the judiciary occurs in the lowest levels of courts, namely, magistrate courts, justice of the peace courts, or small claims courts, depending on the name in the locale. I am not talking about these courts, which notoriously are the most incompetent and corrupt parts of the judicial system. I am talking about general jurisdiction trial courts, either federal or state. Furthermore, I do recognize that even where there is no outright bribery, judges often base their routine, day-to-day decisions on personal relationships which they enjoyed before they became judges or on political alliances which sustain their judicial careers. The amazing thing, however, is not how much of this goes on, but rather how little, given the normal human tendency toward self-dealing. I am not unmindful that in the urban areas there exists what the Eastern Europeans refer to as "protectziah," or the development of interlocking social alliances designed to ease one's way with the governmental authorities. Engaging in these practices is done and done often, but the judicial institution fights harder against these abuses than any other in government.

Self-dealing in the completely vulgar, abjectly self-serving sense, is perhaps the easiest problem to cure. What about neurotic personalities who love authority, intrigue, or rabble rousing for their own sake? Judges are as likely as anyone else to build political machines or to be unacceptably "activist" for the sheer hell of it—a phenomenon completely unrelated to any personal gain or political advancement. Robert E. Lee pointed out at the battle of Fredericksburg that it was a good thing war was so horrible; otherwise men would grow too fond of it. Since politics is a form of low-intensity warfare, many people enjoy all types of political battle just for its own sake—very much like Tom Sawyer's romantic compulsion to effect slave Jim's escape through a tunnel rather than the open smokehouse door. The judiciary attempts to handle this type of problem (with differing degrees of success) through education, leadership, and heavy peer pressure. The more intelligent the offending judge and the more dedicated he is to becoming an acceptable part of the institution, the greater the success of these techniques. When all else fails, many states have formal disciplinary procedures, and the judge can be fined or suspended for improper conduct. This is not true, however, in the federal system.

The force which permits the judiciary to survive popular reproach for unpopular decisions is its incomparable prestige. Unless a judge is remarkably cavalier about the ethics, traditions, and responsibilities of his profession, he knows that judicial prestige—acquired through a reputation for decisions made without regard to personalities or anything but the merits of the case itself—may be perpetuated only by his, and his colleagues', good behavior. It would be absurd to allege that every judge behaves perfectly in this respect, but judges who do not make a good faith effort to conform their behavior to the ideal are remarkably rare. Every other branch or agency of government can trade for favors: a U.S. senator can trade jobs in major agencies to a congressman for additional appointments to West Point; a president can trade dams in a senator's home state for votes on his pet issues; the FBI can trade information with the CIA; Social Security executives can trade favors with executives at the U.S. Department of State Passport Office, and so on. However, the only trading currency a judge has are decisions, and everyone knows that. Consequently, any private contact between a judge and members of other branches of government is immediately suspect, and while a bell does not begin clanging outside the judge's chambers or a red flag ascend over his courthouse roof when private contact does occur, a judge nevertheless comes to understand that extensive private intercourse with the officers of other branches of government calls his integrity into question. This sometimes places a state judge with administrative responsibilities in a bind. As chief justice I frequently need to meet with the Department of Welfare, Department of Health, and Department of Corrections in order to develop programs. Since these agency heads are frequently sued, I am very conscious that my private meetings with them about state facilities and programs might raise questions about my impartiality. In highly controversial cases, I point this out to the lawyers and invite a motion to disqualify if the lawyers or their clients are worried. Furthermore, as I indicated earlier, I must maintain friendly contact with members of the state legislature in order to move legislation which affects the courts and the administration of justice.

The judiciary is a diverse group ranging from big-time federal judges to two-bit municipal judges. For the most part, the higher the judicial position, the older the person selected. There is, therefore, a spectrum of age and elegance which starts with the young city police judge of a small town and extends to the aging justices of the U.S. Supreme Court. The federal bench, with its life tenure, high salaries, and authority superior to any state court, is usually considered the highest calling in the legal profession, and therefore the average caliber of men and women recruited to its ranks is usually superior to the average caliber in state courts. Since state trial judges are likely to be appointed or elected in their late thirties or early forties, there is a significant danger, without the code of ethics, that young and ambitious state judges will use their judicial position as a stepping-stone to higher office. I know because I have been there! As I indicated in the first chapter of this book, I became a judge originally to put myself in a political holding pattern to run for the U.S. Senate.

While it would appear that the judiciary should be as good a stepping-stone to higher office as any other important government position, it infrequently works out that way. I suspect that many young politicians accept judgeships under the impression that they will lead them elsewhere, but the nature of the institution forecloses lateral transfer. Any ambitious young politician who continues to act like an ambitious young politician soon discovers that the antics which brought him accolades and attention from the press when he was in partisan politics bring nothing but scorn and condemnation after he becomes a judge. That is not to say that there are not clowns in the state judiciaries; there are, and every state has its fair share, who will jump immediately to mind. However, the state judges who do move laterally to high elected office in the other branches, like former U.S. Senator Sam Ervin of North Carolina and U.S. Senator Howell Heflin of Alabama, were outstanding judges before they moved. Furthermore, there is not even much room for vertical advancement within the judiciary. Most state senior appellate judges were never trial judges, and while many federal district court judges are appointed from the state bench, it is certainly not the usual pattern. Fortunately for the judiciary, vertical movement is always dependent upon judicial competence—a fact which chills any incentive to clowning. Unlike executives and legislators, who must maintain visibility to survive each election, judges are either lifetime appointees or, if elected, have terms so long that they must run for reelection only once or twice in their entire careers,and then usually against nominal or no opposition. Consequently, even when a strong political personality achieves judicial office, his or her political skills tend to atrophy.

As the judiciary in general and the state judiciaries in particular have expanded their role in government, the strict enforcement of the code of ethics has correspondingly increased. In 1973, when I first went on the bench, the code of ethics was merely suggested by the state Supreme Court in West Virginia. By constitutional amendment in 1974, however, the code was made mandatory and the state Supreme Court set up elaborate enforcement procedures. The same movement toward stricter enforcement of codes of ethics exists in most other states. As a result of all these forces, big-time judges are comparatively anonymous and try to give the impression of being machines made out of meat which mechanically apply neutral principles. That is as it should be. All of this protective coloration is easy to achieve, because big-time judges are old, and, as Cicero once said in his essay on old age, the joy of old age is release from bondage to our passions.

Very few judges go anywhere from the judiciary, since being appointed or elected either a federal judge or a state appellate judge is usually a terminal condition. Therefore, unless one is a show-off by nature (and I have been there too!), there is no advantage to annoying one's peers by assuming a high profile. While trial judges are frequently in their forties, most policymaking appellate judges are in their fifties. As a group they are generally mature, but they are also tired. They have entered life's final act and are no longer playing to whatever audience originally inspired them, since by the time they become judges most of that audience is either dead or dying. There are no longer women to admire them, classmates to be impressed by them, or old high-school coaches to be taught a lesson. They have come to the point where they have more memories than dreams, and they have probably reached the pinnacle of their careers from which they cannot expect, or no longer desire, advancement. Consequently, there is no incentive to be anything but honest, since at that stage of life one of the prime considerations becomes the reputation which will be inherited by the next generation. They are old and recognize that mankind worships the rising, not the setting, sun and are content to make a worthwhile contribution to their country.

It might be argued that power is one thing a judge has to gain. Individual power, in the judiciary, is an illusion—the only real power is the power of the institution. A trial judge has the most individual "power," because he alone controls his courtroom, makes lawyers argue their cases or present briefs on certain days, and can decide motions and cases like a tyrant. Although the trial judge can make the lives of the people actually in his court miserable, he has no policymaking power, because all his decisions must follow the policy pattern dictated by higher courts. If he seeks to innovate, he must be prepared to be reversed by the court above him, although he may have had the dubious pleasure of putting the litigants in the cases which are reversed to the expense and inconvenience of an appeal. If a trial judge has power, it is a petty, personal, vain power exercised according to personal caprice by only the most insecure, small-minded, and dim-witted judges. Most of a trial judge's day is spent not in ego-enhancing activity, but in the highly tedious and mundane chores of listening to testimony, hearing motions, or reading briefs—in short, working.

In appellate courts, which do have more or less broad policymaking authority, the higher the court on which an individual serves, the less individual power he has. The average state trooper driving along a public highway in his patrol car has more power over the life of an ordinary citizen than does the chief justice of the United States. If one were to encounter the chief justice in an airport, or on the street, or in an antique shop, and revile him with a series of vulgar insults, there is not only nothing he would do; there is nothing he *could* do. In this respect an appellate court is different from any other agency of government. A United States senator, insulted by a citizen on the street, could without fear of impeachment call his political friends and make sure the appropriate IRS agent, health inspector, road crew, or licensing board made its routine call; a mayor could cause no end of trouble, since he controls the local police department; and a policeman could just arrest the offending citizen for "obstructing justice" and then for "resisting arrest." An appellate judge, however, has none of these spiteful recourses available to him, because as soon as he makes a threatening gesture he will be disciplined by the appropriate authority or reviled to such an extent in the press that there will be pressure for his resignation.

While not universal, there is even a tendency for trial judges to go beyond the code of ethics and divorce themselves from normal society because they have one-man power over ordinary, nonconstitutional matters such as criminal trials. If they are trying criminal cases, friends of the accused, employers, and relatives seek to "advise" them in restaurants, on the street, or by phone in the evening, and their political colleagues who helped them get elected or appointed feel a certain good-old-boy license to advise them of the "political angle" of certain cases. Since conversations of this type are unethical—even when the judge is merely being polite—trial judges soon stop going to social functions or frequenting places of public resort. Many retreat into their families and close personal friends.

Appellate judges can suffer from the same supplications, although their removal from the day-to-day strife of local communities permits them slightly more expanded social horizons. I suspect that members of the Supreme Court of the United States routinely attend social gatherings in Washington with members of Congress, the Senate, and the executive branch. However, at the state level the issues are more personal and the society much smaller, so that some appellate judges even find themselves foreclosed from normal social intercourse. Many state judges, for example, never attend a social gathering in the state capital unless it is an official function and socialize with absolutely no lawyers outside their own staffs, because they want to avoid all *appearance* of impropriety. The appearance of integrity is difficult to achieve if a judge fraternizes with members of the bar. Some judges do it; but then some people eat peas with a knife. Both groups rarely include people of influence.

As a result of age, maturity, and lack of opportunity or desire for advancement combined with largely self-imposed formal rules, the judiciary has the problem of trading for one's own personal political account about licked. This is probably the biggest single difference between courts and military juntas of banana republics, institutions which in other regards have striking similarities. Personal self-dealing, however, is only part of the problem, and the judiciary is not unique in formulating rules to avoid this evil. Both Congress and the state legislatures have recently begun to scrutinize the whole self-dealing problem, and Congress has promulgated its own code of ethics. What the other branches have not done, however, is attack the far more sinister type of self-dealing, namely, self-dealing for the institution as a whole. This returns us to the historically inherited structure, which is not conducive to the building of empires. Again, the set of highly formal procedures precludes delegation of most judicial work to others and discourages a pyramid-like structure which continuously expands at the base.

The judiciary is the only branch of government which absolutely requires that the person making a decision do his own work: the decision-maker must personally sit on the bench, hear oral arguments, listen to the testimony of witnesses, make his own findings of fact and law, and ultimately sign his own name to the order rendering a decision. To the extent that age, maturity, and experience have been important in the selection of the judge, this single fact alone adds a legitimacy, in terms of quality, which cannot be duplicated elsewhere, where senior officers mindlessly sign what their juniors place in front of them. While judges have clerks and occasionally individuals known as "masters" or "commissioners" to take testimony, analyze documents, and do wood hewing and water carrying in complex cases, most of the time (and always in jury trials) judges actually hear and (unless they are particularly lazy) read everything of any importance themselves. In the executive branch decisions are made by entire independent divisions, and in the legislative branch most of the voluminous technical work is, out of necessity, done by the professional staffs of legislative committees.

Courts may be foolish on occasion, their members may be consummate egotists, and taken together all courts may be cavalier about the suffering which the complexity and expense of their procedures impose—but at least they are institutionally neutral. Judging is work, and judges do not like to decide cases any more than post-hole diggers enjoy digging post-holes or elevator operators enjoy operating elevators. When a judge has lifetime tenure or a sixteen-year term, the novelty of judicial work quickly wears off. Judging is not amenable to bureaucratization, because the judge himself gives the process its legitimacy, so the temptation to amass an enormous staff to seek out new lines of endeavor is limited; in fact, judges find administrative duties the most oppressive of their chores.

Unlike government bureaucracies, there is never any need to justify a court's budget, since the position is constitutional. While there are legislatively funded bureaucracies, such as the Justice Department, which spring up around the courts, the judges' salaries are completely immune to fiscal attack. There is no incentive to expand the role of any given court, since everything must pass through the bottleneck of the judge himself, which means that expansion per se is merely garnering more work for the same pay. A judge is a judge; his power, salary, and prestige depend upon his office alone and not upon how many people he supervises. Since Congress and the state legislatures just plain do not like courts or judges, they are not going to raise their salaries even if they supervise an army the size of Alexander's. Furthermore, courts have been around for nine hundred years, during which their work has always increased and never decreased. Unlike the bureaucracies of the executive branch, courts wish to avoid work—to get rid of jurisdiction and throw routine cases back on administrative agencies or other courts.[6]

The statistics bear out that there is an increasing resort to the courts to solve problems which twenty years ago would never have been thought amenable to judicial decision. Consequently, the judicial wiring is overloaded, which causes delay. If the courts were an ordinary bureaucracy, like the Department of Energy, they would respond by enlarging their staffs, building new buildings, and creating new layers of lower court judges and administrators to serve as funnels. However, the very success of the courts is dependent upon their high prestige—what earlier I called their priest-like function—and the creation of new courts or judges depreciates the currency. While new judges would really help in automobile accident cases, the judges created to try fender benders will also be judges for all other purposes,[7] which is what the other branches of government do not want.

6. The federal judiciary for years has sought to eliminate diversity jurisdiction, which permits a citizen of one state to sue a citizen of another state in federal court on causes of action arising under state law. Most of these cases involve automobile accidents, and they are a crashing bore. If you have seen one car wreck, you have seen them all. While the federal courts have been unsuccessful in eliminating this pain in the neck, in other cases where they are routinely invited to act as super state appellate courts they have conceived sophisticated work-avoidance doctrines such as exhaustion of state appeals and exhaustion of administrative remedies. Federal courts hope and pray the routine litigation will be satisfactorily completed somewhere besides federal court. It is interesting to compare this mentality to that of the Veterans Administration, which is a bureaucracy in search of a portfolio now that the veteran population is dying off.

7. In the federal judiciary, there has been some interest in the creation of "Article I" judges, who would not have the same judicial powers as life-tenured "Article III" judges under the United States Constitution. In the regular judicial system (excluding tax, custom, military, and patent courts), the powers of the federal magistrates and bankruptcy judges have recently been expanded. This, however, has been in response to absolute and dire necessity. There appears little interest in continuing this pattern; both the magistrate and the bankruptcy judge have been delegated very tedious and mundane tasks in criminal and commercial cases, respectively. The position of bankruptcy judge evolved naturally from that time-honored functionary, the master in chancery, and therefore is not any great innovation or departure from the normal resistance to currency depreciation.

In my capacity as a justice of a state's highest court (although not as chief justice, because in that capacity I had an administrative staff), I have two secretaries and one law clerk. That is it; that is my entire staff. I am authorized as many law clerks as I can effectively use, but I cannot use more than one effectively. Assigning a twenty-six-year-old kid to read a complicated set of briefs and summarize them for me is like kissing a girl through a screen door. If the case is important, I must read the briefs myself, and if it is not, I will understand the case from other sources. The judge who is assigned the case will analyze it; I will hear it argued orally; and I will have a chance to approve the final opinion before it goes out. The office of the state administrator of courts is a separate bureaucracy which is concerned primarily with logistical support for the courts. That office, which I supervise as chief justice, has numerous employees, but it does no *judicial* work. While it trains judges, advises me about assigning judges to equalize the work load, and does research and development, it has nothing to do with deciding cases. All the judicial work for my one-fifth of the court is done by me, one young lawyer, and two secretaries, and that is for an entire state. Even the U.S. Supreme Court justices can wedge their entire personal staffs into a phone booth.

The long historical tradition of judges doing their own work does not alone explain the uniquely powerful role which courts are allowed to enjoy. Personal integrity, lack of institutional self-dealing, and high-quality personnel also explain only part of the phenomenon. The remainder is explained by the historical accident of a decentralized institution inherited from the Middle Ages which has never been "modernized." The uniqueness of the American court system in this regard is almost exclusively accidental. The original English judges, "justices in eyre," as they were called, were surrogate sovereigns. Their original function was as much administrative as it was judicial; in effect, they were sent into the woods to ride herd on the powerful feudal nobles, collect the taxes, and enforce the king's peace in his place and stead. Thus, from the outset, English judges were clothed with enormous power because they were the king's henchmen—they were his own upwardly mobile, lower-middle-class kids, groomed and promoted exclusively to cudgel the feudal magnates.[8]

8. There is a lot of good stuff in the Magna Carta designed to undermine the power of royal judges. Contrary to popular notion, as I mentioned before, the Magna Carta was reactionary as hell; it was the medieval manifesto of an ad hoc John Birch Society yelling and screaming about big government. Only in the seventeenth century did it ever dawn on anyone that judges were to be *independent*. Tenure for judges during their "good behavior" *(quamdiu se bene gesserint)* was a

In the same year that the American colonists revolted and Adam Smith published the *Wealth of Nations,* the largest commercial or industrial enterprise in England, to say nothing of the colonies, probably employed no more than fifty people. Obviously there were farms which had more, but most farming on large estates was done by tenants who worked as individuals and not as a team. Consequently, as the world entered the age of big industry and, perforce, big government, the only organizational model available was from the military, which had been managing thousands of men plus their logistical support for untold centuries. Even today the jargon of management is full of military terms, since frequently the only formal management training which many men have ever had came from their national service days. Throughout all bureaucracies, terms like "line," "staff," "chain of command," "span of control," "officer personnel," "tactical," and "strategic" appear with tiresome regularity. In fact, the only secular institutions in the United States which did not copy a military model are the universities and the courts, because they both predate the Industrial Revolution.

Since courts were originally designed to provide a "sovereign presence" in the far-flung shires of England, the entire original scheme was predicated on the exact opposite of the military model, namely, decentralized decision making. Although modern communications would now allow alternative models, we have deliberately chosen to retain the decentralized decision-making structure. Both federal and state trial judges are clothed with the power of either the president of the United States or the governor *and* the Congress or state legislature, although there is always an appeal to a higher court, which may reverse them. Strange, but that is how it comes down. Any trial court can order any member of the executive branch within its jurisdiction to do anything—under pain of fine and imprisonment—until a higher court reverses or grants a stay. This is basically the same power which an energetic president or governor would have if he personally oversaw all the workings of the bureaucracies. Furthermore, any trial judge can interpret statutory or common law or declare a law unconstitutional (although in the federal system it some-

towering achievement of the Act of Settlement at the ascension of William III in 1689. It was not until even later that judgeships ceased to become vacant upon the demise of the crown. The medieval judge was in all regards a royal officer, and while the king had an interest in the fair settlement of disputes between citizens and his bureaucrats, like tax collectors, in matters of importance, the theory that judges were to do something other than the sovereign's bidding was a long time in coming. The notion of an independent judiciary became *thoroughly* accepted only about the reign of George III, and that theory was incorporated into the United States Constitution.

times takes a three-judge panel to do the latter)—exactly the same thing which Congress or a state legislature could do either by changing a law or refusing to enact it in the first place. In every backwoods county seat and in every federal district courthouse, there is a man or woman who can give you as complete relief against incompetent bureaucracy as a governor or even the president him very self. Thus we still have the judge as surrogate sovereign.

This surrogate sovereign, unlike the real one, is available to everyone who cares to drop by the clerk's office and make an appointment by filing a complaint, and the judge will listen almost as long as an aggrieved citizen or his lawyer wishes to talk. That is an institutional advantage completely unrelated to the men and women in the institution—it provides institutionalized, decentralized decision making as a counterbalance to the *Washington, D.C. v. Smalltown, U.S.A.*, bureaucratic deadlock—again, measured straining in opposite directions. While the decisions of trial courts may have to pass appellate review, once they have been made the burden is on the government agency, if it has lost, to sustain its position on appeal. Frequently no appeal is taken, and the lower court decision decides the issue.

Judges as a *class* are probably the best-educated group in government. There are, of course, a lot of dumb judges and a lot of naturally smart ones who went through school shooting pool and chasing women; but all judges except magistrates must be lawyers, which means four years of college and three years of graduate legal training in law school. Judges' staffs, except for personal secretaries, are law clerks who have had the same college and law school training. When a master or commissioner is appointed on an ad hoc basis to sift through the technical material in a case, he or she is either an expert (for example, an engineer or an architect) or a lawyer, and the cases that a judge hears are presented and argued by other lawyers with similarly broad backgrounds and extensive training. Consequently, the judicial branch, relative to its size, has greater access to personnel familiar with advanced concepts in science, economics, sociology, philosophy, and history than do other policymaking agencies of government.[9]

9. Lawyers as a group have diversified backgrounds. Their undergraduate fields of study include political science, engineering, journalism, teachers' training, mathematics, physics, economics, sociology, and history. Interest in these subjects often carries over to later life, so that as a group the judges hearing a case, the law clerks helping them to organize the material and research the law, and the lawyers arguing probably share familiarity with an enormous body of knowledge which can be brought to bear on any given problem. The more important the matter under consideration, the higher

It is the ability of a local judge to give complete relief and his broad access to expertise which makes the courts so attractive as a political agency. Yet there are structural defects in the judiciary which make government by judges less than perfect. Just as the legislative process was not originally designed to initiate good legislation, but to kill bad legislation, the litigation process was not originally designed to decide broad political questions, delicate balances in the allocation of scarce public money, or questions regarding rights and liabilities of interests not represented before the court. The traditional lawsuit is between two parties, one of which is frequently the government—as when it seeks to collect taxes, condemn land, or send you to jail. In this traditional context, the government is just an adverse party presenting its side of a narrow issue. When the litigation is between two parties, each with an adverse interest in a narrow issue, all of the relevant facts which could bear on the judge's decision are brought before the court by the parties, which zealously present their sides of the case. In public law litigation, however, the adverse party is frequently a straw man, like the superintendent of schools or state director of public institutions. In this type of case, there is no sincere effort to bring before the court the interests of every other group in

---

the court to which it has progressed, and the more eminent the counsel retained or appointed to argue it, the more the real world conforms to this ideal. Even in situations where education alone is not particularly helpful, participants in the litigation share a logical way of organizing issues and proceeding systematically from one problem to the next and can lay the entire matter bare through a method which is the product of years of training and practice.

I must confess, however, that I submit this analysis with certain reservations. Everyone has seen remarkably incompetent lawyers and judges, and the professional reader will be aware of the ways in which traditional legal processes can be abused to frustrate the decision-making function or to hide or avoid the real issue in a case. Nonetheless, when the orderly process of the courts is compared with the hit-or-miss procedures used in administrative agencies or the Chinese fire drill which usually occurs during the last week of any legislative session, the comparative superiority of the judicial process becomes apparent. To say, of course, that judicial procedures are superior to other procedures is not saying very much!

As a science, the law offers a coherent body of precedent which is available to any lawyer who has access to a good law library. Unlike other areas of knowledge, such as economics or sociology, in which access to source material is greatly circumscribed, the law is fortunate in having spawned a whole industry which does nothing but organize precedent, so that it can be quickly retrieved and used to good advantage. Consequently, judges are more aware than any other group in government of what has happened before and of the beneficial or unpleasant consequences of previous actions. While a young legislator might think it a wonderful idea to build public works by issuing bonds without raising taxes, the judges will remember cases from as long ago as fifty years, where a similar scheme nearly resulted in bankruptcy and produced this or that provision in the state constitution designed to prevent a similar mistake in the future. More important, not only will judges know of the existence of the constitutional provision; they will also know the reasons for its being there and the reasons why it should not be emasculated by interpretation.

society which could be adversely affected by a decision. Ironically, the reason for resort to the courts to settle complex public policy matters, like school finance, makes a mockery of legal science: resort to the court in those instances is to *avoid* the representation of the classes in society likely to be adversely affected by the decision should it be left to the legislature. In public law litigation where the nominally adverse parties have the same interests (in the same way that the state superintendent of schools was on the side of the students in the school finance case in West Virginia), the object is to give the illusion of an adversary proceeding, while enlisting the court's military junta powers. It is a neat trick, and frequently it gives very good results. We tolerate it because the alternatives are at least as unattractive, as I have discussed in chapter 3 concerning the legislature. Nonetheless, it is important to recognize the sham for what it is and to point it out in some intelligent manner when the friendly neighborhood federal court begins to look more like Pancho Villa than Oliver Wendell Homes. I understood this drill, so in the school finance case we required the legislative leadership to be made parties—since, as the taxing authority whose jobs depended on reasonable fiscal policies, they were the real adverse parties.

Although the capacity to intervene in the political process is part of courts' legitimate function, they, like everyone else, can be very, very wrong. Their preeminent shortcoming is looking at one small part of a total social problem—the aspect brought to them by the litigants—and arriving at a solution for that piece of the problem out of the context of the total social system in which the problem exists. Unless all classes who could be adversely affected have their advocates in court, there is a good chance that their interests will not be brought to the court's attention. It is for this reason that an effort to make public law cases truly adversarial is of such importance. Outside the courts' private conflict-resolving function, they are probably wrong about as often as the other two branches of government, but fortunately wrong in a different direction. While the legislative branch is usually wrong because of lack of activity, courts often err because they are too eager to correct one abuse without consideration of new abuses which their decision will create. While the executive is usually wrong because of an excess of zeal, courts are usually wrong because their cumbersome procedure impedes necessary action. It would appear paradoxical that courts can be wrong in opposite directions at the same time. But courts have always been interested in balance, and they have, therefore, designed different techniques for handling the problems posed by the institutional infirmities of the legislative and executive branches, respectively. Public law litigation, with its sloppy representation, is slow—far slower than executive action, but nonetheless it is much faster than the legislature. Judicial proceedings impede precipitate executive action, but they are delaying tactics and not final prohibitions like statutory amendment by the legislature. While the courts move at about the same pace in all cases, their effect is either to delay or expedite depending upon the pace of the branch they are balancing. As all the mistakes are not in the same direction, the system usually works within tolerable limits.

Throughout the country, there are some ominous effects of pervasive government by judges. A great point is made among the federal judges at their annual meetings, like the Fourth Circuit Judicial Conference, that the judges are being asked to govern the United States and that the judicial machinery cannot stand the load. Yet at the same time there is a universal fear that the expansion of the judiciary would undermine its effectiveness and destroy the prestige of the institution. If the courts of appeals which generate the law were so large that they looked like the typical state senate, it is easy to see how even the courts would become paralyzed. The result, therefore, of work-load expansion, combined with both the judiciary's and the other branches' reluctance—for different reasons—to create more surrogate sovereigns, is delay and more delay for litigants.

Obviously the press of routine litigation has a direct bearing on the delay problem. In the federal system, criminal trials take precedence over other work, and they are very time-consuming. The federal courts still try automobile accident, products liability, and medical malpractice cases which clog their dockets to a fare-thee-well. In today's court system, delay itself has a decisive effect upon the nature of litigation; the very existence of more judges would change the nature of litigation. Some plaintiffs who want affirmative relief do not bother to go to court, but rather settle for minor concessions, because they know that the delay will defeat their goal, while other plaintiffs go immediately to court, relying on the delay alone to give them relief. Unfortunately, building the judiciary is like building roads. Years ago an interstate highway from Charleston to Huntington was designed, predicated on the volume of traffic going between those two cities before the interstate was constructed. What appears to have been forgotten was that the very existence of a good highway *created* more traffic. Lawyers, merchants, students, and everyone else who previously confined his activities to his own local area began regularly to go to the other city. There has always been a tendency for the judicial system to be loaded beyond its capacity; if, therefore, we increase its size, we will generate more litigation by that fact alone.

Since judicial work will naturally expand to the point where it strains whatever machinery has been created, no matter how large, there is no across-the-board remedy for delay. However, delay in some cases is more destructive than delay in other cases; open-ended litigation is impeding the revitalization of the American economy. Any proponent of a sizable project, whether it be state or federal government, a local utility, or a market firm in the private sector, must budget for years of litigation-related delay in any financing plan. Environmentalists, conservationists, ecologists, competing businesses, outraged local residents, unsuccessful bidders on government contracts, and anyone else with a real or imagined grievance goes immediately to court, where everything stops. Economic devastation inevitably and unintentionally accompanies the grinding of the engines of justice.

The whole due process panoply of procedures—hearing, confrontation, appeal, review, remand, rehearing, reappeal, etc.—sounds wondrously fair, but the price of theoretically perfect fairness is the most rank practical unfairness: length, expense, and complexity are luxuries exclusively for the rich. By "rich" in this regard, I do not mean the run-of-the-mine company, which will quickly be bankrupted by the law's delay, but rather the huge, organized, collective intelligences like Exxon, Kodak, and IBM, which have staffs and budgets rivaling those of half the member states of the United Nations. When it comes to a major rethinking of their own procedures, judges are as conservative as Robert Taft. They fear, along with law professors and bar committees, that any rethinking of routine procedure will undermine the fairness achieved in the current system. Since I think the level of fairness of the current system mediocre, I do not share those fears.

There is a great difference between commercial litigation and criminal litigation. Commercial litigation is always about money, property rights, or the environment—all things which have a price tag. When litigation per se bankrupts everyone, both winners and losers as a class, then it is time to rethink the problem. The defenders of the environment or those advocating zero growth will automatically oppose any streamlining of the litigation process, because the delay of the law per se is their primary remedy, desirable in and of itself. While we can live with a rule which says that nuclear plants will *never* be built or government lands will *never* be taken for timbering, business and government cannot live with the uncertainty and caprice of current judicial process. At least with blanket prohibitions we can get back to building coal-powered generators or constructing windmills and solar receptors—we could probably even find substitutes for lumber. Everyone is adversely affected as employees, consumers, and taxpayers by pervasive delay. For example, vast sums of money are budgeted to pay interest charges on half-completed construction which has been halted by litigation—money that would otherwise be available for capital investment, the creation of jobs (particularly since construction provides entry-level jobs to the unskilled), and the reduction of prices or taxes. If the annual inflation rate is 10 percent, then a two-year delay results in a 20 percent increase in costs, which someone—taxpayer or consumer—must pay.[10]

I have seen countless administrative appeals where the records amounted to twenty thousand pages, yet I know of no judge who ever read such a record in its entirety. Occasionally, when some particular point is in dispute on appeal, a law clerk will be assigned to read part of the record, but the things I look for are those discussed in chapter 4 concerning self-dealing, encroachment upon the legitimate private sector, immature policy judgments made by junior bureaucratic staff, and, in rate regulation cases, inadequate or excessive rates of return. When you are dealing with an armed robbery prosecution or an automobile accident case, reliable eye witness testimony can decide the case, because the only issue is one of fact. In administrative appeals, however, the factual issues are secondary to the social and political perspective from which those facts are viewed. If that is the case, then we can do the world a great favor by admitting it. The developer who is told "no" in a summary proceeding can keep his money in his pocket and go elsewhere. There is no point continuing the sham that administrative decisions are based on the same type of careful factual development as in a criminal case. The nuclear power controversy, *Vermont Yankee Power,* boiled down to the Court of Appeals for the District of Columbia being against nukes and the Supreme Court being for them. If that is what it is all about, let us approach it that way and save time and money. On rare occasions, of course, there are

10. Antitrust cases are the worst example of unduly long court procedures. While the government's antitrust case against IBM, which was filed on the last day of President Johnson's administration and is hardly half-completed twelve years later, is the notorius Methuselah of the antitrust cases, it is not an oddity. For private antitrust cases reaching the trial stage in 1977, the medium length of time from initial filing to final disposition was nearly four years. An action under § 2 of the Sherman Act, which requires proof of monopoly power and intent to acquire that power, generally takes about eight years before a final judgment is rendered. Some cases never actually end, because attorneys for the defendant corporation have perfected the art of "snowing" the government—that is, burying the government in a blizzard of supporting documents.

administrative decisions where the major input is factual, but oddly enough these are not the cases which lead to protracted litigation. What, for example, is adequate proof of "convenience and necessity" for the chartering of a new bank? For the administrator who believes in rough-and-tumble free enterprise, no factual record will demonstrate saturation of the market, and for the proponent of government-regulated, orderly markets, any competition is excessive. Consequently, bank charters are basically allocated according to some theory of economics which emerges in the interaction of administrative agency personnel with one another and with the courts. That has nothing to do with facts, and while certain facts are essential to the decision, concentration on factual determinations just creates a sleight-of-hand effect.

In the field of government regulation, court delay is only part of the problem; as I indicated in chapter 4, it is often necessary to go to court to force administrative agencies to render a decision. Consequently, what is called for is an entire recodification of administrative procedures, beginning with a requirement that government agencies act upon applications for agency approval within a specific time and upon denying approval, give a detailed blueprint of what must be done to secure approval. Furthermore, the agencies should pay damages from their budgets when they fail to act within the time period allowed. The courts then should organize themselves to hear these matters on an expedited basis and articulate the substantive reasons for their decisions rather than hiding behind the shield of procedure, requiring as it sometimes does millions of dollars to go through duplicative hearings, hire experts, prepare reports, etc., all to provide the backdrop for the ultimate sleight-of-hand trick when the court says "no" because it does not like the substance of the agency action but reverses for some alleged procedural irregularity.

While in other areas of the law the courts can grind along in their lethargic way, confident that their greatest achievement will concern the cases which they do *not* decide, in the area of administrative law, issues like whether to build a power plant or construct a dam cannot be compromised. Any attempt to settle a contest over a nuclear power plant, new dam, or even a bank charter is utterly unavailing, since the opponents are usually ad hoc committees of outraged citizens or competing businesses, and once they have been satisfied, there will be another *ad hoc* committee or competing business which will bring legal proceedings. I single out the delay involved in administrative law for special attention because it *is* a special case. My analogy to the road and traffic flows accurately depicts what would happen to the system if the problem of delay were attacked on all fronts—there would be more litigation but very little reduction in delay. However, if we discretely attack one element of delay in the one area of overwhelming public concern, we can have a decisive impact on that one area.[11] All litigants feel their agendas are urgent, but reform of administrative review is a special case, since administrative cases transcend the agendas of individual litigants and go to the heart of American life. As it stands now, many small companies are foreclosed from markets or pushed into unwanted mergers solely because they are not equipped to handle the unknown and unknowable open-ended financial risk of litigation.

I do not believe that there are any easy answers to improving the overall performance of the judiciary. Of course, when a commentator begins with the old "there are not any easy answers" gambit he usually recites all the problems and gives no solutions. I do have an answer or two, but they are not the stock answers about changing the method of judge selection or expanding the number of judges. The solution of creating many more judges does not usually get to the heart of the problem. In some of the state systems, like South Carolina, where a powerful legislature has deliberately kept the judiciary small for conscious, political reasons, the creation of more judges would help—and that may even be true other places where judicial personnel have not kept up with the natural increase in workload. My reservations about expansion are more precisely limited to the federal system. The object of the other frequently suggested reform, changing the process by which judges are selected, is to get judges with philosophies conducive to the new selectors. While this may be an "improvement" from the point of view of the new selectors, it is not an improvement from any neutral point of view—if there is a neutral point of view, which there probably is not.

Oddly enough, a judge's background does not appear to make much of

11. This is not just an idle suggestion. For years in West Virginia, we had appeals in rate regulation cases from the Public Service Commission which were completely unstructured. The lawyers brought up records so voluminous they had to be rolled around in carts, and they argued everything from accounting conventions to the mechanics of setting up a depreciation schedule. The result was that our court, which disposes of about thirteen hundred cases a year with five judges, could not possibly understand what was going on. Finally, in a case I wrote, we said that there was only one issue on appeal of a rate regulation case, that is, whether the utility was making a fair rate of return. Since that *is* the crucial issue in any rate case, the whole process suddenly became much more structured. We have had fewer appeals; the Public Service Commission has been much more attentive to that fundamental issue; and the time that the consumer has had to pay high rates under bond pending appeal has been shortened, because judicial stays of commission orders are less frequent.

a difference.[12] In this instance, at least, the old truism that men rise to the institution is accurate. The finest federal judge in recent memory in West Virginia was the biggest machine politician in the southern part of the state during John Kennedy's presidential primary campaign in 1960. Because of his former machine activities, there was widespread outrage when he was appointed, but after he had been on the bench three years there was not a lawyer practicing before him who did not hold him in highest esteem. This judge, to help the bar, wrote publishable opinions when they were not required, traveled regularly to small towns to hold court, dictated opinions and orders while driving from one place to another so that he could begin hearings early the next day, and finally, developed a reputation among government lawyers for having the quickest grasp of social security law of any federal judge in five states. He was humane and considerate to all litigants, particularly those seeking government benefits, and was understanding as a criminal judge. He was always the perfect gentleman. He knew about life—its travail, injustice, sorrow, and tragedy—and he did what he could do to make things better for those who came before his court. There was absolutely nothing inconsistent in these qualities and in his capacity before he became a judge to set up precincts, distribute patronage, or raise and spend large sums of money to influence votes. He became as conscientious a judge as he had been a conscientious machine boss. Sidney Cristie died a few years ago, after all too brief a career, leaving West Virginia considerably the worse for his absence.

On the other hand, I have known judges who have been colorless, odorless, and tasteless all their lives; who have progressed from undistinguished, but equally uncontentious, careers as agency commissioners; who were well regarded by the local law school and who otherwise seemed ideal candidates. Occasionally they too make fine judges, but I

12. During the publication process for this book, Yale University Press sent the manuscript to Professor David Danelski of Stanford University for his comments. He made one comment with regard to men rising to the institution that I think worth quoting in its entirety.

> I don't agree that putting on the judicial robe has the impact on a judge that Neely asserts. And I am not sure that judges in practically any other part of the world would play the active role in government that judges in the United States do. My guess is that we have an activist judiciary because of the way we recruit judges—that is, politically from the bar—and do not have a career judiciary like France, Germany, and Japan. Our great judges—I have in mind Marshall, Taney, Hughes, and Warren—were politicians before they came to the bench and remained politicians on the bench in the best sense of the word. That is touched on in the manuscript, yet Neely could have gone further.

have as often found that they are lazy, arrogant in a taciturn way, and prone to indulge personal whims by being utterly inconsiderate of the litigants. I have seen these men, as appellate judges, refuse to write opinions in cases submitted eight hundred days before, while abject political hacks on the same court routinely turned out adequate, if not brilliant, opinions in a reasonable time. Consequently, the ideal judicial candidate does not necessarily make the ideal judge, but then the truly poor judicial candidate frequently does not either.

While it is probably valuable to have representatives of minority groups in the judiciary because of the *appearance* of justice,[13] beyond that concession to reformers, proposals to change the method of selecting judges are beside the point, because it is the institution, and not the men, which make a court. What is a "better quality" appointee? If federal judges are no longer appointed through the political patronage system (which has substantial checks against gross incompetence, such as a required Justice Department investigation, bar association evaluation and recommendation, and Senate confirmation), how are they to be appointed? If state bar associations are to do it, they will obviously suggest lawyers who have been active in the bar. Bar associations, like other committees and clubs, are run by small groups of active members. Usually these lawyers come from big firms with big clients who subsidize participation in bar activities. Are these people necessarily better candidates than the rough-and-tumble lawyers who are involved in politics?

If any group outside the political process is required to make nominations to the bench, the likely result will be compromise, which selects persons who have made the fewest enemies, are the most bland, and have had the most generally acceptable if undistinguished careers. Except for candidates who are downright slow-witted (and there are many of them on the bench), it is difficult to predict how any given man or woman will respond to judicial office. I have not noticed any significant variation in quality between elected and appointed state judges. I have further observed that on the federal bench, where all judges are appointed, those

13. I say this with reservation, because I have always thought that the only workable rule of law in the long run is that race is no criterion for anything. Nonetheless, to understand my exception in this regard it is necessary for WASPs to imagine themselves in a courtroom in Kenya attempting to defend their property rights in a suit brought by black plaintiffs before an all-black appellate court. Would we not all have a warmer sense of confidence if there were one white man or woman on the court who would adjourn to the decision conference, if for no reason other than to keep us from being referred to as the "honkys" rather than the "defendants"? The first step in depriving people of their rights is to dehumanize them and deprive them of their "personhood."

who come from day-to-day politics maintain a higher level of civility, consideration, and gentlemanly conduct in their courts than those who come from United States senator bosom-buddyhood or suggestion by anonymous committees. The correlation between good judging and extensive political background is strong: witness Earl Warren, Hugo Black, and William Brennan. As long as there is a requirement that judges be lawyers who have evidenced some technical competence in their former lives, there is no way of eliminating the inherent middle-class bias of the judicial institution for those who are bothered by that fact.

It is possible to have enormous regard for the judiciary as an institution while being quite spare in one's praise for individual judges or for the pace of reform in the judicial system. Most trial judges and many appellate judges, however good they may be in their own courtrooms, lack a sense of their position in the overall political structure. Fortunately, that usually makes little difference, because the system is set up to accommodate the judge of limited learning. For example, this book has pointed out that two centuries of American law developed a body of doctrine to protect the American economy from the encroachment of both hungry bureaucrats and greedy private entrepreneurs. Miraculously, it is possible for a judge without the slightest knowledge of economics to apply this body of law merely by reviewing precedent. Without ever having heard of Adam Smith or John Maynard Keynes, a judge can consult accepted economic wisdom by following the rules in previous cases—even those cases where the economic reasoning either was not explicit or was written in such a way as to emerge as utter nonsense. When a judge looks at five cases with similar facts, all decided the same way, he need not understand the reasoning behind them in order to decide the sixth case the same way. It is, therefore, unnecessary for everyone in the system to understand the total structure. The system yields good results because in this respect it is set up like the army: an organization designed by geniuses which can, when necessary, be executed by idiots.

Almost everyone has seen really bad judges; many have even seen corrupt judges who, if they do not sell decisions, have at least been co-opted by their social friends at the bar and routinely favor one set of lawyers or interests. In addition, almost everyone has been on the losing side of a court encounter he thinks he should have won. So we all know that judges are not supermen and that the judiciary does its job no better than the executive or the legislative branches. Courts perform, as I have said before, about as well as hospitals, automobile mechanics, plumbers, and architects. Judges do not make their impact on the governmental process in the United States because of any inherent personal superiority, since for the most part they are not only interchangeable with the people in other branches of government, but often have actually been interchanged. It is certainly no disgrace for the other branches of government to be overruled by the courts, either by having administrative action reversed or a statute struck down as unconsitutional. The other branches are responding to pressures and imperatives that demand action which may not pass court review, but it is the job of these branches to respond. Judges are peculiarly immune from pressure of any type, which makes their lives easy and secure beyond the wildest dreams of any robust politician.

The key to improving the performance of courts is an understanding of their function. Once we are willing to admit that courts have political roles which are dictated by the nature of other institutions, we can begin to speak to those roles directly and not in the slave language of constitutional interpretations, statutory construction, or result-oriented standards of review dressed up as neutral principles. The recognition that public law litigation is vastly different from private law litigation and that the procedures should be altered accordingly will help a little. Finally, it should be recognized that we cannot really attack judicial delay across the board, but that we can incisively attack it in certain critical areas, which will go a long way toward furthering the "reindustrialization" of this country.

The American constitutional convention of 1787 was strongly influenced by the ancient publicists, particularly Polybius, a Greek historian of the Roman world who wrote a reliable history of Rome from 262 B.C. to 120 B.C. It was Polybius who pointed out that any "pure" governmental form eventually degenerates into something else—pure democracy into class tyranny or anarchy, pure aristocracy into a selfish oligarchy, pure monarchy into absolutism. This analysis informed the judgment of the founding fathers when they conceived the doctrine of balance of powers. Many of the framers dimly perceived that the judiciary would serve some type of balancing function, but of course they could never have envisaged the functions which are currently undertaken by courts. The proper role of courts is still evolving. Dean Rusk once told me that after Earl Warren's retirement from the court, he went to speak at the University of Georgia, where Secretary Rusk was teaching, and met with a small group of law professors. At that meeting the former chief justice said that the primary political function of the courts was to break the impasses which are inherent in any structure of balanced powers—a function which I doubt even John Adams anticipated. If the courts are going to break impasses, only the courts can define "impasse." So the limits on court power in government are not set by either constitutional theory or discoverable law, but rather by the tolerance of the countervailing powers. What happens when Plato's millennium of the philosopher kings actually arrives, I am not sure. Polybius never told us what pure rule by judiciary would eventually degenerate into.

9 NEXT TO THE LAST CHAPTER

This is the next to the last chapter, but as the reader will discover, there is no last chapter. The last chapter of a book is usually the one in which an author feels obligated to set forth his remedies for the ills which he catalogued in the rest of the book. There are many books of brilliant social analysis where the author, having explained how the social system works, concludes his tome with some ill-conceived suggestions about how things could be improved. Such suggestions are usually impractical at best and madness at worst. Apparently it is thought by many that if an author does not at some point in his book pay obeisance to the notions of "more democratic control," "returning the power to the electorate," or the need to reduce the "power of corporations," he cannot expect regular invitations to highbrow cocktail parties, where the upper echelons of academic or literary society air their dissatisfaction with the existing system. Unfortunately, most of the suggestions for improvement, which pit the ideas of one man against the latent wisdom of evolved institutions, are like the thirteenth chime of some ridiculous clock. The thirteenth chime is not only absurd in itself, but it casts doubt as well on the reliability of the other twelve.

In this book I have catalogued many infirmities in various government institutions, but I do not now intend to turn upon these institutions in rage and offer proposals for sweeping reform. The infirmities have existed in relatively the same form for three hundred years and they are known to almost everyone actively engaged in government. We are not the first reform-minded generation, nor will we be the last. The system which has evolved, characterized by what I call the "measured straining in opposite directions," has evolved in much the same way an oyster makes a pearl. An oyster finds a piece of sand inside its shell which it cannot dislodge, but its inability to dislodge it is a function of the physiology of its shell and the laws of physics, not of its own lack of effort or motivation.

Finding itself thus constrained by natural laws, the oyster proceeds to coat the sand with a substance to make it less abrasive, whereupon oyster and intruder proceed to coexist comfortably.

It would appear to me that unless some dramatic improvement occurs in the nature of man which will reduce lust, avarice, egotism, and indifference to suffering, no remedies to the system's ills can be found that are not worse than the ills themselves. In a system characterized by measured straining in opposite directions, drastic reform might destroy the equilibrium of the whole structure by elevating one force over all the others. Evolution's equilibrium is certainly worth protecting, because in the modern world evolutionary systems have done a better job than revolutionary systems in giving their citizens a life worth living. Our system's implicit distrust of ideologies—even the ideology of democracy when carried too far—demonstrates that most of the time ideology, like all the institutions of government I have described, is enlisted in the service of selfish interests. History suggests that ultimately any new system based on a revolutionary ideology will look, taste, and smell exactly like the system it is coming to replace.

I began this book with Thomas Macaulay's observation about politics in the middle of the nineteenth century, and now I think it worth citing Lionel Trilling's observations on politics in the middle of the twentieth, a century which has seen us do battle three times in as many generations with grim realities often clothed in attractive ideological garb.

> A politics which is presumed to be available to everyone is a relatively new thing in the world. We do not yet know very much about it. Nor have most of us been especially eager to learn. In a politics presumed to be available to everyone, ideas and ideals play a great part. And those of us who set store by ideas and ideals have never been quite able to learn that just because they do have power nowadays, there is a direct connection between their power and another kind of power, the old, unabashed, cynical power of force. We are always being surprised by this. Communism's record of the use of unregenerate force was perfectly clear years ago, but many of us found it impossible to admit this because Communism spoke boldly to our love of ideals. We tried as hard as we could to believe that politics might be an idyll, only to discover that what we took to be a political pastoral was really a grim military campaign—or that what we insisted on calling agrarianism was in actuality a new imperialism. And in the personal life what was undertaken by many good people as a moral commitment of the most disinterested kind turned out to be an engagement to an ultimate immorality.[1]

1. This quotation comes from his introduction to the republication of George Orwell's *Homage to Catalonia* (New York: Harcourt Brace, 1952).

It is a sad fact that America's newfound self-doubts about the value of American world leadership are predicated not only on our Vietnam experience, but as well on our incapacity to explain our economic and political system either to our own people or to the rest of the world. To use Trilling's conceptual framework, we fail to speak boldly to mankind's love of ideas and ideals, except in terms of the most simple, unmarketable, one-man, one-vote ideology, which is no match for our cynical opponents, who maintain that the freedom to vote is no antidote to the freedom to starve.

But must this always be so? Despite all its apparent defects, is not the system described in this book a monumental achievement in balance, fair representation, straining for social justice, and protection of individual liberty? Is government's often cumbersome, delayed response to social ills too great a price to pay for freedom from the caprice and whimsy of every two-bit administrator who decides he will undertake a program of puritanical reform? These are the questions we must ask ourselves before anyone undertakes to write the last chapter of this book.

There have been very few successful experiments in democracy other than in the United States, English colonies with European populations, and Western Europe primarily because the crucial role of traditional institutions was not adequately understood. Not every successful democracy has a structure like an American court—in fact, none but our own has a truly powerful judiciary—but all have traditional structures such as monarchies, bureaucracies, or extra-governmental institutions which provide balance. The nonjudicial balancing structures may be well-suited to the other democratic countries where they are found, but there is no conclusive or even persuasive evidence that they could adequately perform the functions of our powerful judiciary in the United States. No other democracy has our diversity of race, religion, ethnic background, geography, or economic and social skills. In this respect we look like many of the developing nations of the Third World. In the United States, the courts have been responsible for pacing the rate of redistribution of wealth, determining the rate and extent of social, economic, and racial integration, and protecting people from abuses of the government. These are the tasks which some institutions must ultimately assume in such diverse countries as the Republic of South Africa, Chile, and Nigeria if peace, economic development, and social justice are ever to prevail there.

In the Russian Empire the non-European population is dominated by the same outside racial and cultural group that oppressed them during the time of the czars, and the governmental bureaucracy in Russia has become as entrenched as any hereditary oligarchy. The Russians are paralyzed by their cumbersome bureaucratic machinery, the lack of motivation of all employees, and the suppression of any creative thought which would threaten the existing order. Yet Russian communism speaks boldly to the whole world's love of ideas and ideals in a way which I cannot duplicate in a book devoted to the greatest social, economic, and political triumph in the history of governments. It is ironic that even the young of this country resist being inspired by the totality of our evolved system and instead are attracted by the easy abstractions of both the left and the right. Consequently, there is no last chapter because I refuse to compete. Justice or equity in any social structure is inherently a function of complexity, and complexity usually involves paradoxes. Neither complexity nor paradox lends itself to successful propaganda.

At this point in the book, I have a Hobson's choice: either I must make some effort at an outline of grandiose reform to assure the reader that I am not a cheerful cynic, or I must end the book on a thoroughly trite and pedestrian note. It is not possible to suggest sweeping reforms without looking stupid, naive, or both, since this society never implements sweeping reforms. Furthermore, sweeping reforms which solve one problem are very likely to create other, even more intractable, problems somewhere else. Consequently, all that I can suggest is careful tinkering with the machinery. As I have emphasized throughout the book, the greatest contribution to improving the system at the moment is a general understanding of how it works. Consequently, I shall conclude with only a few specific suggestions in the area of law, where I at least have some pretense to expertise, which are representative of the type of tinkering with the machinery which understanding of the system will permit.

The most important innovation would be to remove from the system the time-consuming, cumbersome procedures shown, through rigorous application of cost/benefit analysis, to lack utility. Whenever in a discussion with other judges or court administrators I mention the application of cost/benefit analysis to the judicial enterprise, I am asked, "How do you measure justice?" The answer is that you do not measure justice, just as you do not see the wind. But when the roof goes flying off your house you know very well that some powerful wind is out there. When courts take four years to arrive at final decisions, when cases involving simple matters cost tens of thousands of dollars in legal fees, and when litigants are put to enormous inconvenience, it is possible to say the process does not work. To say that courts perform vital government functions better than the institutions of almost every other country in the world is to say only that we have a Model-T Ford while the rest of the world is driving oxcarts. Often, as I have pointed out, procedures are grafted onto the entire legal process because some big-time court, in some complex case, was too lazy to explain its reasoning and chose instead to turn the decision on a procedural point, around which develops a ceremony which exacts a command performance from every lawyer and litigant in any similar case forever afterward.

We should begin to laugh at judges who write stupid procedural traps into the law instead of taking them seriously. It is time for both bar and bench to come to terms with the fact that lawsuits are not games of forfeits. While lawyers must use every procedural point they can find to their client's advantage, courts should be in the business both at the trial and appellate stages of making sure that procedural traps are not permitted to insinuate themselves into the process at all. How stupid it is for a trial judge to stand by and watch a lawyer commit a procedural error which will eventually impale his client. Judges are experts in trial procedure, while lawyers are required to be experts in everything—a little help now and again is never amiss, although some lawyers are too stubborn to take a hint and some judges are too stupid to hint correctly.

The legal profession is an important part of the governmental process whether it wants to be or not. In fact, all lawyers admitted to practice become, at the time of their admission, officers of the court. In that capacity they are expected to accept court appointments with inadequate compensation; to be honest in the presentation of their cases to the court; to decline to countenance illegal acts contemplated by their clients; and to advise clients concerning their good faith interpretation of the law even if it conflicts with a client's desires. While many of these ethical requirements, as a matter of practical course, are honored by some only in the breach, there are enough honorable lawyers around to justify the privileged position in which the bar has always found itself.

Although some law school graduates never do more than return to the family hardware business, most lawyers engage in practices even the most routine of which eventually involve them in cases with substantial public policy implications. Furthermore, the most unlikely candidates in any law school class are liable to become federal and state appellate judges. Because a law student claims when he is young that all he wants to do is write wills and deeds, work on his rural farm, and bring up his family in a modest manner does not mean that he will actually so limit his endeavors later in life. What if his college or law school roommate becomes a United States senator and remembers that all through school when he was poor as a churchmouse his good buddy bought all the beer and always insisted that he share it? That, gentle reader, in and of itself, is the making of a United States Court of Appeals judge, for better or for worse.

What courts do is legitimate, but what courts do is not always right. Courts obviously are frequently wrong, and in my own particular compartment of the machine, the whole apparatus would work better if we took seriously the high governmental calling which will ultimately be thrust upon almost all lawyers. The vogue today in professional education is to insist on "competence," "relevance," and extensive "technical training." Many law students and professors view law as a technical exercise requiring the mastery of a body of exclusively legal knowledge. It is axiomatic that technical knowledge is necessary in the day-to-day practice of law; statutory, administrative, and common law rules must be mastered before a lawyer can serve his client in routine litigation. But a good grasp of legal technicalities does not begin to solve the major institutional infirmity of the judiciary—the severe lack of imagination and creative thinking. Lawyers and the court system need to know more about fields other than law; they need the capacity to integrate legal and nonlegal reasoning, to be able to think in terms of calculus as well as English and in terms of sociology and economics as well as law. In their quest for relevance, modern law students reject everything not "modern," decline to master the common language which educated men of only one generation earlier still speak, and decline to cultivate the ability to reduce complex ideas to simple statements or to draw analogies between legal subjects and classical literature. While there is absolutely no substitute for technical competence in the law, technical competence alone is insufficient for the adequate discharge of a lawyer's and a judge's responsibilities.

A lawyer who practices estate law needs to know the latest tax decisions, but he will serve his client adequately only if he also knows *King Lear*. When a lawyer advises a client to give part of his property to his children, he needs to temper his knowledge of the tax advantages with knowledge of how children behave toward parents from whom they have nothing more to expect materially. A reading of Dickens' *Bleak House* will teach a lawyer more about the pitfalls of complicated trusts than an advanced seminar on equity, because *Bleak House* is not just a sterile analysis of the law, but illuminates people's interaction with the law.

We learn about how society is organized from fields other than law; the law is merely a mechanism for translating knowledge into action. Consequently, when the court system makes policy, it is not making legal policy; rather it is making social policy, which must come from an understanding of history, literature, economics, sociology, philosophy, and often science. How are we to make the new rules concerning what is or is not permissible experimentation in the area of biological science? Obviously the legislative branch will draw the broad outline, but courts must fill in that outline. Expecting law as a discipline to answer questions involving a complex intertwining of science, philosophy, and morality is like expecting the fecund union of two mules.

In order for men and women to help each other think, they must share a common language of images and ideas. Science's inductive logic long ago rejected the English language, or any other spoken language, as a primary scientific tool and replaced it with mathematics. In the social sciences, mere words cannot be the exclusive vehicle for communicating complex ideas. The purpose of the liberal arts is to refine a lawyer's spontaneous reactions, which are essential to the decision-making process. By "spontaneous reaction" I do not mean untutored "feeling," but a general theory of life grounded in wide reading in all the various fields I have mentioned. It is that wide reading with its attendant images and distilled conceptualizations which forms the common language of the educated. The majority of the problems confronting a practicing lawyer or policymaker are not unique to the twentieth century. The great beauty, for example, of Greek and Latin classics and of European and American literary works written between 1550 and 1900 is how few there really are. By mastering most of this limited body of literature, one gains a common language for communication in a well-educated community. One is capable, for example, of explaining a highly complicated interpersonal relationship simply by saying, "It is like the relationship between Swann and Odette." In a society where as a matter of course everyone is expected to have read *Swann's Way,* the statement is both descriptive and concise.

How are the courts and the bar to integrate economics into sociological patterns if they have never heard of Max Weber or Talcott Parsons? How are they to understand the inherent nature of man if they have not read, among others, Shakespeare, Jane Austen, Theodore Dreiser, or John Fowles? These are questions which law schools and colleges are not seriously asking themselves. The average law school still runs its admissions policy along lines established twenty years ago, when the entrance exam consisted of the dean's taking the applicant's pulse. While by 1960 there may have been keen competition for entrance to the top ten law schools, almost all state universities and many other fine law schools took everyone who applied with a passing undergraduate record. A lot of students flunked out of law school, but almost everyone, regardless of undergraduate training, was admitted. Today there are few really poor law schools in the United States, and many of the previously mediocre institutions are a match for the Yale, Harvard, or Columbia of twenty years ago. Furthermore, there are many more applicants for places in even the least distinguished, nonaccredited law school than can be admitted. State universities and prestigious private institutions can pick and choose, and they do, but upon criteria almost entirely unrelated to how potential law graduates will help govern America. They choose based upon the applicant's performance on a "game-type" test called the Law Boards, which tests skill in spatial relations, so-called legal reasoning, and the English language. While scores may reveal something about relative competence at the extremes, for the most part the test measures an applicant's ability to take the test.

Furthermore, law schools actually penalize anyone who attempts to get a real education. The only academic criterion is grade point average, which means that an applicant with an "A" average in government or sociology—notoriously unstructured subjects where evaluation of performance can be very subjective—will have preference over the person with a "B" average in physics, a very objective subject at the undergraduate level. In addition, the serious government student who wants to go to law school but who also feels a need to know something about physics, mathematics, and economics, dares not take a course in any one of these subjects lest his reduced natural aptitude cause him to lower his overall grade point average. Consequently, he opts for another government course with its sure "A," because his undergraduate college and prospective law school do not encourage him to do otherwise. Law school is too late to begin to teach people liberal arts; there is too much technical material to be mastered, although an entering class knowledgeable in economics, sociology, physics, and so on will be able to do a great deal more with the technical material than will a class of functional illiterates. Most so-called policy discussions in such law schools as Yale (which is famous for them) are reduced to unstructured, psychodrama sessions, because the students come without the background to build a coherent structure. All these ignorant students, however, can do the *New York Times* crossword puzzle—they have been tested for that skill and encouraged to develop it.

Law schools can and should begin to formulate admissions standards for the future which will force their student candidates for admission to approach an undergraduate education the way a hungry student approaches the local Chinese restaurant. Everybody needs a course from Group A, a course from Group B, and a course from Group C. Obviously, some first-rate law candidates will not be able to do well in mathematics, but that does not mean that they cannot learn a foreign language, which will expand their horizons and help them analyze English and write concisely. Some will have a block in foreign languages but be capable of doing mathematics and physics. There must be checks built into the system to prevent a student from finding a major easy for him, taking all his courses in it, accumulating a tremendous grade point average, and then beating out a candidate who has actually tried to realize the Renaissance ideal, only to find that society did not want him to have an education, but merely a high grade point average.

To assume the leadership position which a community often demands of him, a lawyer must master the skills of his profession and have good judgment in addition. Judgment takes into account, under the heading "nature of man," all the factors discussed in this book. Except for limited personal experience, judgment can be learned only by studying the liberal arts. The most famous lawyers and jurists, including Clarence Darrow, Oliver Wendell Holmes, and Earl Warren, have been men noted more for their humane reactions and common sense than for their technical legal craftsmanship.

The purpose of this book has been to explain the complexity and paradoxes of our evolved governmental system, so that by better understanding it we can eliminate its imperfections; it has never been my intention to offer a new design for the entire system. Most men are both heroes and whores, brave and cowardly, selfish and generous. Almost every living person in the institutions I have described would like to be more of a hero, braver, and more generous. Frequently, however, he behaves contrary to his aspirations because he does not completely understand what he is doing or where his actions fit into the entire system. In this respect, understanding is the key. For those out there in Readerland who are disappointed that there is no last chapter, and who have the inclination to write one, please feel free to do so. I would like to read the last chapter myself, and if you send it along, we will be glad to include it in the second printing, the paperback edition, or even the movie version of the book.

INDEX

Abortion, 5, 8, 13, 44–45, 75, 145, 171
Adams, John, 216
Administrative law, 4, 5, 82*n*, 84, 92, 93, 102–03, 111, 171, 211–12
Administrative review, 81–114, 138, 210–11
Affirmative action, 75–76
AFL-CIO, 48, 51, 52
Africa, 139–40, 141
Agency for International Development, 129
American Jurisprudence, 59
American Law Institute, 25
Amin, Idi, 139
Antitrust cases, 210*n*
Appellate courts, 148, 166, 191, 199–200
Appellate procedure, 191–92, 205
Average citizen, 12, 25, 27, 28, 77, 109–10, 144, 150, 151, 152; lack of interest in politics, 23, 24, 29

Bacon, Sir Francis, 190
Bacon, Sir Nicholas, 130
Baker v. Carr, 4*n,* 14, 149, 176
Bakke v. Cal. Board of Regents, 75–76
Balance of powers, 113–14, 146, 147, 148, 208, 216
Barron, W. W., 118
Bickel, Alexander, 2
Bill of Rights, 17–18. *See also* U.S. Constitution
Black, Hugo, 215
Brennan, William, 4*n,* 176, 189, 215
Bribery, 13, 59, 130
Bureaucracy, 79–114
Burger, Warren Earl, 45
Burr, Aaron, 42
Business, 92–93, 94–95, 131–36, 212
Byrd, Robert C., 63

Calabresi, Guido, 74, 177*n*
Campaigns, 14, 32–33, 34–35, 36–37, 118
Candidates, 29–30, 31, 116. *See also* Challengers; Incumbency
Carter, Jimmy, 26, 80
Challengers, 31*n,* 36, 37, 60, 117, 118
Chile, 127, 220
Circuit Court of Appeals for the District of Columbia, 82, 111, 210
Circuit courts, 191
Civil law, 4, 5
Civil liberties, 149–69, 172
Civil rights, 3, 54
Civil servants, 25, 80, 103–09, 111
Civil service, 80, 107, 117, 123; in England, 139
Civil Service Reform Act of *1978,* 90
Cohen, Morris R., 144
Coke, Sir Edward, 42
Commerce clause, 2, 6, 57
Common law, 41, 43
Common pleas courts, 191
Communism, 219, 221
Conservatism, 51, 56–57, 62–63, 209
Conservatives, 18, 98, 99
Constituencies, 30–31, 32, 37, 60, 64, 67, 87–88
Constitutional conventions, 13, 75, 216
Constitutional law, 2–22, 43, 100–01, 127, 162; irreversibility of, 73–74, 75
Constitutional revision, 5, 7, 145
Constitutional rights, 151, 165–66

Constitutionalism, 141
Constitutions, 17; state, 6, 11, 136, 139. *See also* U.S. Constitution
Contract clause, 57, 100-01
Corruption, 13, 33, 83, 135, 136, 138-39
Cost/benefit analysis, 95, 96, 102, 221-22
Costs, 100*n*, 103, 157, 160, 161, 162
Court activism, 57, 76-78, 137-38
Court agendas, 49-50, 71
Courts, 50, 81, 91, 145, 147, 191, 201, 213*n*; anarchist function of, 73-74, 78; of appeal, 208; balance legislatures, 57-58; in business/government deals, 136-37; can be wrong, 112, 207, 223; competence of, 113; conflict-resolution function, 195, 207; criticism of, 5, 39, 40, 41, 81, 113, 114, 138, 151-52; and grievances, 36, 37; hierarchy of, 191; higher, 59-60, 71, 162-63, 192; as institution, 137, 190-217; lack institutional bias, 112-13; and institutional dialogue, 145-89; issue-avoidance techniques of, 49-50; and issue-oriented politics, 36, 37, 38-40; as juntas, 144, 145, 161, 200, 207; limits on, 145, 147-48, 149-50, 217; lower, 71, 162-63, 192; political function of, 195, 216; power of, 1-22, 217; prestige of, 147, 166, 196, 202; role of, 57, 113, 216-17. *See also* Administrative review; Economic policy; Judicial lawmaking; Public policymaking
Crime, 153-54, 162, 167
Criminal justice system, 154-56
Criminal law, 4-5, 150; reform of, 145-69
Cristie, Sidney, 213

Damage suits/awards, 156, 159, 184, 211
Danelski, David, 213*n*
Darrow, Clarence, 226
Delay, court-initiated, 103, 138, 202, 208-09, 211-12, 216
Democracy, 8, 25, 28-29, 50, 81, 135, 136, 138-39, 140-41, 144, 216, 219, 220; participatory, 13, 14, 21-22, 37, 149
Democratic control, 80, 87, 104, 148
Developing nations, 43-44, 130, 138-44, 220
Dewey, Thomas, 125
Didcott, Justice, 143*n*
Discrimination, 8, 149
Disenfranchisement, 127, 129
District courts, 191
Douglas, William Orville, 45
Due process of law, 2, 15, 17-18, 57, 70, 82*n*, 100-01, 151, 165, 193, 209. *See also* Procedural due process; Structural due process

Economic policy, 9, 20-21, 70-72, 97-98, 102, 113, 209-10, 215
Economic system, 3, 97-102, 137-38
Economy, 68, 129-31, 137
Education, 8, 149, 173-74, 176, 177-86, 189. *See also* West Virginia, school finance case
Elected officials, 26, 50-51, 80, 87
Election reform, 13, 36-37, 119
Elections, 26, 115, 124; primary, 37, 88, 115, 116, 117, 121, 122
Election-stealing techniques, 119-27
Elizabeth I (queen of England), 42, 130
Eminent domain, 133, 136
Employment, 20, 38, 70, 85, 96, 97, 100
Employment Act of *1946*, 70, 71
Energy and Water Development Appropriations Act, 91
England, 59, 96, 159, 168, 203-04; Bill of Rights of *1689*, 17; judiciary, 40-41, 42, 130, 139; Parliament, 40, 42, 52*n*, 59, 139, 170
Environmental Protection Agency, 111
Equal protection, 9-10, 11, 17-18
Ervin, Sam, 198
Escobedo v. Illinois, 151
Exclusionary rule, 156-57, 165, 166
Executive branch, 12, 21, 70, 79-114, 145, 201, 207-08; and criminal law reform, 161-62; employees of, 105-09
Export-Import Bank, 95
Extortion, 36-37

Farm Credit Administration, 95
Farmers Home Administration, 95
Federal court system, 60*n*, 191, 202*nn*, 204–05, 208, 212, 215
Federal Election Campaign Act of *1971*, 36
Federal employees, 90
Federal Home Loan Bank Board, 95
Federal Housing Administration, 95
Federal judges, 99, 124, 208
Federal Power Commission, 5
Federal Reserve Board, 80, 85, 137
Federal Reserve System, 84–86
Federal Trade Commission, 5, 80, 84, 86–87, 89
Fiscal policy, 69, 85
France, 96, 213*n*
Frankfurter, Felix, 2–3
Freedom, personal, 97–98
Friedman, Milton, 85

Galbraith, John K., 68; *Economics and the Public Purpose*, 102
Garrity, Arthur, Jr., 146
Germany, 96, 213*n*
Goals, 76; of education, 185–86
Goldwater, Barry, 25
Government, American system of, 14, 25, 29, 92–93, 95, 102, 103*n*, 115, 218–26; access to, 66–67, 71, 77–78; is evolutionary, 41–42; myth/operational systems disparity in, 12–13, 14, 23, 37, 80, 113–14, 148–49, 168, 188; protection from, 111, 220; is technical, 23–25, 32
Government agencies, independent, 5, 80–81, 103, 211; courts' review power over, 81–114
Government contracts, 118
Government expenditures, 70, 71, 85
Graft, 87, 90, 131, 136, 191, 194
Grievances, 36, 37, 80, 209

Harris v. Calendine, 74–75
Harvard Law Review, 144
Harvard University, 45, 225
Heflin, Howell, 198
Henry I (king of England), 41
Holmes, Oliver Wendell, 226
Hoover, Herbert, 37
Housing, 39, 45
Hughes, Charles Evans, 213*n*

Ideology, 9, 25–26, 32, 64, 114, 219, 221
Impeachment, 6, 10, 71, 145, 176
Incumbency, 23–46, 60, 116, 117, 118
India, 29, 139
Inertia, 15–16, 23–46, 50, 55, 58, 65, 67, 68–71, 161, 177, 186, 192
Inflation, 20, 73, 84, 85, 97, 170, 210
Institutions: courts as, 190–217; political, 17, 20–22, 92, 114, 144, 218–19; social, 10–11, 14, 19; traditional, 220
Integration, 13, 171, 220
International Harvester case, 111
Issue consensus, 67–68, 69–70, 72, 73, 77
Issues, 9–10, 23, 86–87, 116; economic, 26, 28, 29
Italy, 37, 42

Japan, 96, 213*n*
Jay, Peter, 27–28
Johnson, Frank M., Jr., 146
Judges, 11, 14, 22, 59–60, 112, 146, 162, 166–67, 190–91, 192; age of, 110, 197, 198–99; appellate, 99, 222–23; appointed, 190*n*, 198, 214–15; bankruptcy, 202*n*; code of ethics, 193–95, 196, 197, 198–200; do own work, 201, 203; education of, 205; elected, 49, 187, 198, 214; government by, 206, 208; ideological convictions of, 148; independence of, 203*n*; and legislative branch, 145–47; and myth/operational disparity, 13, 15–16; numbers of, 212; personal relationships of, 194, 195, 196–97, 200; as politicians, 110–11, 198, 213*n*, 215; power of, 191, 199–200, 203–05; quality of, 197, 201, 215; salaries of, 201–02; selection of, 212–16; state, 167, 197–98; as surrogate sovereigns, 203, 205; trial, 204–05

Judicial activism, 14, 16, 42, 47, 213*n;* scale for ranking, 14, 15, 16, 17, 149, 168, 186, 188. *See also* Court activism
Judicial control, principled, 143–44
Judicial lawmaking, 7, 39–40, 98–99, 204–05, 206, 208; forces institutional reform, 164, 168, 171, 172–73, 174; legitimacy of, 7–9, 42–46, 49, 67–68, 72–73, 160, 168, 171–73, 188–89. *See also* Public policymaking
"Judicial restraint, doctrine of," 2–3, 9, 57, 98
Judicial staffs, 145, 147, 201, 203
Judiciary, 195–96, 220, 223; advancement in, 197–98; balancing function of, 216–17; expansion of, 202, 208–09; improving performance of, 212–17; minority representation on, 214; nature of, 187–88, 189; overloaded, 202, 208–09; sanctions in, 188, 195; structural defects in, 206–07; unique structure of, 203–05
Justice, William Wayne, 146
"Justiciability," 19

Kenya, 139
Keynes, J. M., 173
King(s), 40–41, 51, 203, 204

Laissez-faire, 20*n,* 130
Landlord-tenant law, 39, 45
Law, 4–5, 11, 17, 192*n;* general and special interest, 49, 50, 67; implications of U.S. system of, 138–44; reform in, 221–26; science of, 45–46, 206*n,* 207
Law schools, 224–26
Lawyers, 18, 20, 25,194, 222–23, 226
"Least intrusive remedy, doctrine of," 73*n*
Legal aid societies, 92
Legal education, 223–26
Legal principles, 4, 9, 11–12, 17, 216
Legislation, 52–54, 56, 60–61, 65–66, 113; special interest, 47, 49, 51, 71–72, 75–78
Legislative agenda, 49, 51, 53; access to, 66–67, 71, 77–78
Legislative branch, 5, 12, 21, 33, 42, 47–78, 64–65, 95, 113, 161, 201, 207–08; designed to strike balance, 48–49; implementation of policy, 84, 86; inertia of, 177; negative role of, 47–48, 51–52, 55, 56–57, 60–62; power of, 62–63, 145–47; structural weakness of, 69; trading for power in, 59–60, 60–61, 64, 66, 67
Legislators, 50, 58, 62–66
Lex Edwardi Confessoris, 41
Liberals, 98, 99, 102, 140
Litigation, 72, 128–29, 137, 206–07, 208–10, 212, 216
Lobby: education, 176, 187; good government, 87, 88
Lobbyists, professional, 34–35, 36, 51, 65–66, 67, 71
Local government, 26, 27, 31, 81, 90, 96, 115, 117

Macaulay, Thomas, 219
McGovern, George, 25
Magna Carta, 18–19, 203*n*
Maine, Sir Henry: *Ancient Law,* 183
Majority rule, 14, 139–40, 144
Mansfield, Mike, 61
Marcos, Ferdinand, 135*n*
Marshall, Alfred, 68
Marshall, Thurgood, 45, 213*n*
Massachusetts, 127, 146
Means, Gardiner, 68, 92
Media, 24, 30, 34, 36, 67, 91, 116, 123, 127–28
Meek v. Pittenger, 32*n*
Miller, Peggy and Steve, 79, 80, 81, 103–04
Mills, Wilbur, 58, 59
Minority rights, 139–40, 141
Miranda v. Arizona, 158
"Modernizing elite," 43–44, 45
Monetary policy, 68, 69, 84, 85, 97, 137
Money, 23–46; court appropriation of, 168–69, 171, 175–76, 187, 189; and education, 174, 176, 181, 184; in politics, 115, 117, 118–19, 124, 131

Monopoly, 68, 92, 101, 137
Montana, 61
Montford, Simon de, 52
Moore, Arch A., 119
Moorhead, William, 69

National Association of Manufacturers, 48, 49
National Labor Relations Board, 84
Natural law, 42; crime, 153–54
Neely, John Champ, 108, 109
Neely, Matthew Mansfield, 1, 35, 62, 98, 117, 124, 125
New Deal, 3, 9, 20, 45, 57
New Jersey, 84, 176, 179
Newspapers, 24, 88, 124
New York (city), 21, 45, 96, 115
New York (state), 33, 56, 115, 126*n*, 191*n*
Nigeria, 220
Nixon, Richard, 37, 49, 131
Nondelegation of powers doctrine, 84
Norway, 59
Nuclear power, 81–82, 86–87, 210
Nuclear Regulatory Commission, 80, 86–87, 89

Oates, Titus, 17
Occupational Safety and Health Administration, 106
Oligopoly, 68, 92
One-man, one-vote concept, 126, 127, 139–40, 144, 171, 220
Ours, Larkin, 63–64

Parliaments, medieval, 51–52
Patronage, 115, 117, 122, 123–24, 214
Pauley, Harry, 130
Pauley v. Kelly, 16–17, 173–75
Philippines, 127, 135
Police, 152, 153, 156, 157–58, 164, 165
Political activism, 27, 33, 35–36, 129, 131
Political agenda, 36, 48
Political control, 62, 80–81, 87, 89–90
Political machines, 21, 98, 115–44, 156
Political participation, 26, 28, 29. *See also* Voters, turnout of
Political process, 36, 46, 136–37, 144, 160, 186; courts' intervention in, 2–4, 14, 78, 207. *See also* Judicial lawmaking; Public policymaking
Political question doctrine, 4*n,* 50, 145, 176, 189
Politicians, 11–12, 14, 25, 55, 83, 87, 106, 111; as judges, 110–11, 198, 213*n,* 215
Politics, 17, 21, 98, 115, 116, 149, 195, 219; British, 27–28; in education, 178, 179, 184–85, 187; inertia, money and incumbency in, 23–46; intrusion of courts into, 145–48; issue-oriented, 26, 31–32, 35–36, 37
Polybius, 216, 217
Power, 6, 44, 53–54, 58, 59, 62–63, 68, 69; of courts, 1–22
Precedent, 99, 101–02, 173, 189, 206*n,* 215
Predation, 47, 49–51, 56–57, 72, 75–77
Private sector, 96–97, 99–103, 113, 123
Procedural due process, 82–83
Procedure, 112, 183, 193, 201, 206*n,* 209, 221–22; appellate, 191–92, 205; in criminal law, 150–51, 156–57, 165–66
Product liability, 39–40, 42–43
Public interest, 47–48, 50, 76, 91, 131, 184–85
Public policymaking, 7–8, 11, 44–45, 57, 70, 71–72, 147, 176–77, 179, 185, 186, 207, 222, 224. *See also* Judicial lawmaking
"Public purpose," 96–97, 99, 136

Randolph, Jennings, 35, 119
Reagan administration, 69, 70, 71–72, 85
Reapportionment, 4*n,* 5, 13, 14, 17, 149
Reform, 54–55, 92, 212, 216; election, 13, 36–37, 119
Regulation, 21, 70, 72, 83, 84, 85, 100, 106, 111, 211; and political machines, 132–36; trade, 86–87, 101
Rehabilitation Act of *1973,* 68
Reich, Charles A.: *The Greening of America,* 102

Religious activism, 26, 32*n*
Robinson v. Cahill, 176
Roe v. Wade, 44–45
Roosevelt, Franklin D., 9, 20, 27, 57, 70, 87, 100, 101
Rusk, Dean, 216
Russia, 220–21

Sartre, Jean-Paul, 86
School finance cases. *See* West Virginia, school finance case
Segregation, 5, 8, 77, 98
Self-dealing, 89, 136, 195–96, 200–01; institutional, 83, 89–92, 93, 100, 103, 113, 201. *See also* Trading for one's own account
Simon, William E., 95
Smith, Adam, 68, 100, 101, 103; *Wealth of Nations,* 57, 96, 102, 130, 204
Smith Act, 129
Social change, 157, 160, 161, 162
Social policy, 10, 11, 20, 85, 97–98, 161
Social Security Administration, 92, 108–09
Social welfare legislation, 54, 66, 72
South Africa, 140, 141, 142–43, 220; Terrorism Act, 143
South Carolina, 212
Special interest groups, 47–48, 71, 131, 187. *See also* Predation
State: boards and agencies, 81; court systems, 162–63, 167, 191; employees, 90; governments, 80, 96, 115; judges, 99, 200; legislatures, 53, 59, 83, 85; supreme courts, 191
Status quo, 28, 73, 74, 107
Steelworkers v. Weber, 75–76
Stockbridge, Mass., 80, 149
Stone, Harlan F., 57
Structural due process, 74, 75, 103*n,* 177*n*

Taft, Robert, 98, 209
Taxation, 10, 11, 21, 48, 50, 170
Tax Reform Act of *1976,* 25, 58–59
Teachers, 51, 112, 178, 179, 181–84, 185
Technology, 101–02
Television, 24, 124
Tellico Dam, 91
Tennessee Valley Authority, 83, 91, 95, 114
Tocqueville, Alexis de, 143
Trading for one's own account, 83, 87–88, 89, 178, 188, 191, 196–97, 200–01; in legislature, 59–60, 60–61, 64, 66–67
Trial courts, 191, 195, 204–05
Tribalism, 141, 142–43
Trilling, Lionel, 219
Truman, Harry S, 100, 125
Tydings, Joseph, 35, 36

U.S. Congress, 14, 56, 57, 59, 62, 80, 83; code of ethics, 201; committee system, 52–55, 58, 60; House, 55; Senate, 26*n,* 55; shifts responsibility to agencies, 84–87, 89
U.S. Constitution, 8, 10, 11, 41, 57, 71, 100–01, 137, 204*n;* Amendments: First, 20, 98, 128–29; Fourth, 70, 151, 157; Fifth, 2, 6, 17, 21, 70, 82*n,* 136, 151, 158, 159; Sixth, 151, 159–60; Eighth, 17; Fourteenth, 6, 17, 70, 82*n,* 136, 151; and criminal law reform, 159–60; interpretation of, 6, 9–10, 13, 14, 17–19, 44; natural law in, 42
U.S. Department of Justice, 123, 124, 201
U.S. Department of the Treasury, 137
U.S. Supreme Court, 3, 5, 10, 13, 18, 37, 57, 68, 70, 71, 73, 101, 123, 128, 173, 191; cases, 4*n,* 14, 32*n,* 44–45, 117, 151, 192*n,* 210; and criminal law reform, 156–58, 162, 163, 164, 165; and economic policy, 9, 20; and issue consensus, 72; justices, 197, 200; Nixon appointees to, 49; judicial power of review, 81–82; special/general interest law, 75–76; staff, 203
Uganda, 127, 139, 140
United States, 6, 96, 97–98, 138–44, 220; courts of appeals, 191; district courts, 191; electoral system, 127. *See also* Government, American system of
Urban renewal, 96, 97, 136

Values, 43–45, 97–98, 114, 144
Vermont Yankee Power, 81–82, 210
Veterans Administration, 62, 95, 202*n*
Vietnam, 26*n,* 104–05, 107–08, 129–30, 220
Virginia, 127
Vote fraud, 123. *See also* Election-stealing techniques
Voters, 36, 116, 122, 126–127, 129; turnout of, 26, 37, 115, 116, 117, 118–20, 125–26
Voting, 8, 24–25
Voting Rights Act, 70

Wall Street Journal, 93
War of all against all, 139
Warren, Earl, 14, 18, 146, 213*n,* 215, 216, 226; court, 127, 153
Watergate scandal, 49, 131
Wealth, 29; redistribution of, 21, 27–28, 76, 139–40, 220
Westminster constitution, 139
West Virginia, 27, 32–33, 38, 56, 88–89, 118, 159*n,* 160, 213; House of Delegates, 64; judiciary, 60*n,* 195; juvenile offender law, 15, 17, 74–75, 163, 171, 172; Kanawha County, 147; legal clinics, 90–91; legislature, 52–53, 87, 88; Lincoln County, 17, 76, 173, 174, 175, 177, 180, 186, 188; Marion County, 87–88, 99, 125, 156; Public Service Commission, 212*n;* school finance case, 16–17, 19–20, 173–76, 177, 186–87, 188, 207; teachers, 178–79, 181–84, 187; voting in, 117, 119–20
West Virginia Board of Regents, 89
West Virginia Education Association, 51, 176
West Virginia Human Rights Commission, 38, 45, 83–84
West Virginia Supreme Court, 15, 72*n,* 174, 175, 198
West Virginia University, 88–89
Whitehouse, Charles S., 104–05, 108

Yale University, 2, 45, 89, 225
Yale University Press, 30, 213*n*